CHARLIE'S APPRENTICE

CHARLIE'S APPRENTICE

Brian Freemantle

G.K. Hall & Co. • **Chivers Press**
Thorndike, Maine USA   **Bath, Avon, England**

This Large Print edition is published by G.K. Hall & Co., USA
and by Chivers Press, England.

Published in 1994 in the U.S. by arrangement
with St. Martin's Press, Inc.

Published in 1994 in the U.K. by arrangement with the author.

U.S.   Hardcover 0-8161-7489-X (Mystery Collection Edition)
U.K.   Hardcover 0-7451-7765-4 (Windsor Large Print)

The text of this Large Print edition is unabridged.
Other aspects of the book may vary from the original edition.

Set in 16 pt. News Plantin by Rick Gundberg.

Printed in the United States on acid-free paper.

British Library Cataloguing in Publication Data available

Library of Congress Cataloging in Publication Data

Freemantle, Brian.
    Charlie's apprentice / Brian Freemantle.
    p.   cm.
    ISBN 0-8161-7489-X (alk. paper : lg. print)
    1. Large type books. 2. Muffin, Charlie (Fictitious character)
— Fiction.   3. Intelligence service — Great Britain — Fiction.
I. Title.
[PR6056.R43C43   1994b]
823'.914—dc20   94-5394

Oh, laugh or mourn with me the rueful jest,
A cassock'd huntsman with a fiddling priest!
William Cowper,
'The Progress of Error'

One

This title was more pompous than most — today's Foreign Office offering was 'The New Reality of the Future' — but the contents were the same, just reconstituted and served up differently: mincemeat from previously left-over scraps.

Charlie Muffin preferred his own title. Bullshit. Which was how he'd judged every other analysis and thesis interpreting the dissolution of the Soviet Union into its uncertain Commonwealth of suspicious republics which was supposed to lead to a New World Order. All bullshit. He'd said it, too, although in language more acceptable to civil servants in the response arguments he'd had to make, to every woolly-minded exposition. He'd say it again, of course, about this effort. And be ignored, as he appeared permanently to be ignored these days.

Charlie sat in his favourite launch position, chair tilted back, legs splayed over withdrawn bottom drawers to support awkward feet, the waste basket propped in the far corner of his rabbit hutch office. He sighted, minutely adjusted the trajectory, and fired the dart carefully crafted from the last page of what he'd just read. Lift-off looked good, all systems go, but then abruptly the missile dipped, early impetus gone, to crash among the other failures already littering the heel-chipped floor largely uncovered by the minimal square of frayed, Ministry grade III carpet. It put the final score at three in, seven out. Bad. Or was it? On the recognized scale for intelligence operations three out of ten was a bloody good success rate: remarkable even, considering the cock-ups that inevitably occurred along the way and usually, and more importantly, to him. But then he wasn't assessing an intelligence operation. Just the hit rate of a paper dart made from yet another document circulated throughout Britain's clandestine agencies, setting out guidelines for intelligence gathering after the momentous political adjustments and realignments in Europe and what once had been, but was no longer, the Soviet Union.

Charlie sighed, lifting his feet to bring his chair more upright. Charlie realized that on a scale of ten he'd so far awarded zero to every assessment he'd been called upon to review. Which would upset people, particularly those whose assessments he'd dismissed as a load of crap. But then he often seemed to upset people, even when it wasn't intentional. Which it wasn't here: he was just being honest.

Charlie rose and scuffed around the desk, the spread-apart Hush Puppies even more spread apart by his having loosened the laces for additional comfort: launch directors don't need tight shoes. Charlie carried the waste basket to the shredder first, before collecting the darts which had run out of impetus.

What about his own impetus? What was the New Reality for the Future for Charlie Muffin? He wished he knew: was almost desperate to know.

The personal upheavals and uncertainties exceeded all those international changes he'd been professionally commenting upon, for all these months. And been a bloody sight more difficult to assess. Impossible, in fact. Some still remained so: always would, he supposed. The familiar — almost daily — recriminations came and he accepted them, the remorse still sharp.

Where was she? Alive? Dead? Happy? Sad? Hating him? He stopped the run of questions at the one he thought he could answer, the one he always answered. Natalia had to hate him, if she'd survived. She had every reason. He'd been insane to let her go. However dangerous it had appeared — however dangerous it had undoubtedly been — he should have kept her with him. Found a way. Instead of like this, in a permanent vacuum.

He didn't have any doubt — there couldn't *be* any doubt — that she'd been allowed out of Moscow under those now long-ago emerging freedoms to be the bait, personally to trap him. But she hadn't been part of it: not known the purpose or the direction of whatever had been set up against him. He was sure of that, after so much mental examination. More convinced than he'd ever been of anything he couldn't positively prove in a professional life where so much had lacked proof. She couldn't have been part because she *wouldn't* have been part. Because she loved him. Or had done, then. What about pressure upon Eduard? The freedoms had only just begun and Eduard was in the Russian army, vulnerable to every threat and pressure. Charlie supposed she would have compromised to protect her son, even though during their brief reunion in London she'd despaired at how the army had coarsened and brutalized the boy, turning him into the mirror image of the womanizing, drunken husband who had abandoned her.

So OK, she might have been part. Just. And reluctantly if she'd been forced to cooperate. But she would have warned him. There had been opportunities, difficult though it had all been, and she would have taken one of them to sound an alarm, if she had known what it had all been about.

What about himself? Charlie demanded. Simple. He'd failed her. He'd been unable to go the last mile — the last inch! — to ignore the instinctive self-preservation to keep the rendezvous: an escape rendezvous he'd seen her keep, but not left his concealment to complete.

Not just failed her. Lost her.

For what? The job? Charlie slumped back behind the desk, snorting the derision. What fucking job? Rejecting ill-considered, naïve assessments from analysts who'd got Double Firsts at Cambridge in International Political Science and never crossed the English Channel? Waiting for month

10

after month for the summons and the briefing for a proper, active operation that never came? Folding paper darts instead and playing kids' games, even awarding himself points!

What new reality was there going to be for his future? Hard reality, he guessed. Maybe a very uncertain future: perhaps no future at all. Sir Alistair Wilson's retirement from the Director-Generalship, after the second heart attack, had been a foregone conclusion and with Sir Alistair had gone a special relationship, a very special understanding. Which hadn't been favouritism or sycophancy or even friendship. It had been a complete professional recognition between two men born at either extreme of the English social divide, each respecting the other, each benefiting from the other, each never quite trusting the other.

In addition to all of which, Sir Alistair had served a magnificent Islay single malt whisky.

There hadn't been even supermarket whisky with the new Director-General. Only two meetings since the appointment of Peter Miller: both very formal, both introductory, each man circling the other to mark and scent the other's territory.

Miller was a professional appointee, transferred from internal counter-intelligence and showing it to someone able to recognize the signs, as Charlie could. The one characteristic so far picked up by Charlie was a taciturn, word-measuring suspicion about everything and everybody inherent in someone whose job until now had been to seek enemies within. Was Miller's transfer to ex-

11

ternal operations another naïve assumption of new realities, a belief that they didn't have to bother any more about hostile activity inside the country? Some of the opinions Charlie had read recently didn't make that suggestion as absurd as it might otherwise have seemed.

Charlie was curious how this third meeting would unfold. More than curious. Hopeful, too, that it could finally be a briefing, on something positive for him to *do*. Christ, he hoped so! He'd had the memorandum fixing the appointment a week before, which wasn't how he'd been briefed in the past, but he wasn't attaching too much importance to that. Miller was new and new people arrived with new ways. Not all assignments were urgent: most weren't, in fact. This could be one of those that needed time: careful consideration and proper planning. It could be . . . Charlie halted the speculation, recognizing another sort of kids' game, thinking himself into an optimism for which there was no justification. He was having his third meeting with the Director, that was all. Foolish, unprofessional, to clutter his mind with a lot of groundless hopes. Not the way to operate; certainly not the way *he* operated. Ever.

Charlie reluctantly refastened his laces, flexing his toes to ensure there was as much comfort as possible, and then straightened the clean shirt around his waist, where it had pulled out during the dart-throwing. He'd kept his freshly pressed suit jacket on a hanger, to prevent it becoming creased: couldn't remember the last time he'd dressed up so smartly.

The secretariat established on the ninth floor since his last visit was the most surprising innovation of all. There were outer office staff, but the inner sanctum was now controlled by just one woman. She was about thirty-five, guessed Charlie. Titian-haired, cut short. Nice tits. Not possible to see her legs beneath the desk, but probably good on the standard so far. Pity she was frowning so irritably at the internal telephone in her hand. She slammed down rather than replaced the unanswered receiver.

He smiled, brightly, and said: 'I've an appointment with the Director-General. Charlie Muffin.'

'I was trying to call you.' She didn't smile.

'Wanted to be early for a new boss! Make an impression!'

'He's not ready for you.' She nodded to a set of seats against the wall behind him. They were new, like everything else. 'You can wait there.'

'Rather stand,' said Charlie. 'How are you liking it here? Haven't had a chance to talk before.'

'I have been with the Director and deputy Director-General for some years.' She looked pointedly at the chairs she'd already indicated.

Director *and* deputy Director-General! 'Charlie Muffin,' he repeated, hopeful for a return introduction. He'd always made friends — sometimes even love — with Directors' personal assistants: insider knowledge was invaluable to someone who watched his back as carefully as

Charlie. The long-time P.A. of the Director-General *and* his deputy would be an incredible ally to cultivate.

'I heard you the first time.' There was still no smile.

Awkward cow, thought Charlie, smiling broadly: if at first you don't succeed, try, try again until they fall on their back. 'Be happy to point the way if you need help in a new department.'

She sighed, heavily. 'My name is Julia Robb. During the time I have been with the Director and his deputy I have been chatted up by a large number of operatives, usually far better than you're doing now. And all for the same reason you're doing it now, although getting into my bed was sometimes an additional ambition. I don't, ever, talk about things I hear or see or know about. And I don't screw round with the staff, either. Have I left anything out?'

Charlie decided that qualified as a rejection. 'Don't think so.'

The delayed summons to the inner office was a grateful escape.

It had all been changed from the London Club ambience that Sir Alistair Wilson had installed: gone were the faded, leather-topped desk, the sagging, well used leather chairs, the tub-shaped liquor cabinet, usually open, and the proud display of roses which it had been the former Director-General's hobby to grow.

Everything now was functional. The furniture

was far superior to that in his own office four floors below, but Charlie guessed it had all come from the same Ministry supply depot. There was a lot of hard-wearing metal and hard-wearing plastic and the wall decorations were mass-produced Ministry prints of scenes of Dickensian London. Charlie's impression was of an up-market doctor's waiting-room. Peter Miller looked a bit like an up-market doctor, too, although Charlie wasn't sure about a bedside manner. The hair was the reassuring grey of a man of experience. The glasses were heavily horn-rimmed, the left lens thicker than the right. A watch-chain looped across the waistcoat of a striped blue suit, which Charlie recognized to be well cut but not specially tailored. Harrods, ready-to-wear department, he guessed. Miller wore no rings, which mildly surprised Charlie: most of the other Directors under whom he'd worked had been able to wear a family crest. Whatever, Charlie didn't think Miller would be a grammar school boy, like himself.

Miller remained aloofly blank-faced behind the desk, gesturing towards a visitors' chair. Charlie took it, aware of another oddly placed to the side of the Director's desk. As he sat, Charlie realized the desk was sterile: there were not even framed personal photographs.

'I believe I've had sufficient time to settle in,' announced Miller.

The man had a flat, monotone delivery, the sort of voice that made public announcements in supermarkets about the bargain of the day.

15

Charlie decided it went well with the metal furniture. He wondered what he was supposed to say. 'Bound to take time.'

'I have decided upon some operational and command changes,' said the Director-General, a continuing metallic announcement. 'My predecessor involved himself very closely in active operations, didn't he . . . ?' There was a flicker of what could have been a smile. Alternatively, Charlie thought, it could have been pain. '. . . What our American cousins call a "hands-on" Controller?'

Charlie listened to gossip, never imparted it. And he certainly didn't intend discussing Sir Alistair with this Mechanical Man. 'Everyone works in different ways.'

Miller nodded, seemingly unaware of the evasive cliché. 'Quite so. I see myself as responsible for the organization as a whole: I do not intend to become immersed . . .' There was another grimaced smile. '. . . some might even say distracted, by one particular branch of the service, interesting — exciting even — though that branch might be.'

And as career-dangerous as those active operations might be, if they went wrong, mentally qualified Charlie. So Miller was a political jockey, riding a safe horse at prime ministerial briefings and Joint Intelligence Committee sessions. 'Always best to get the broadest picture.'

Miller nodded again. 'My recommendation for the post of deputy Director-General has been confirmed. I shall, of course, be ultimately responsible, but all decisions concerning you will be up to my deputy . . .' The man turned his head slightly towards the intercom machine. Without making any obvious move to activate it, he said: 'I'll see the deputy Director-General now, Julia.'

Charlie turned at the noise of the door opening behind him and managed to get to his painful feet just slightly after Miller at the entry of a woman.

'Patricia Elder, the new Controller under whom you will be working,' introduced Miller.

Natalia Nikandrova Fedova heard the familiar sound at once, hurrying into her bedroom: the cot was close to her bed, for her to reach out during the night. The baby was awake but not truly distressed: she decided it was most probably a wind bubble. The baby smiled when Natalia caressed her face. Definitely a wind bubble: Alexandras was far too young for it to be a smile of recognition. Natalia turned her on her side, still caressing, and said: 'Shush, my darling. Shush. Sleep now.'

The baby did.

Now Natalia smiled but ruefully, thinking how much more obedient the baby was than its father.

Two

The wind strong enough to bring the grey dust all the way to Beijing from the Gobi Desert hadn't been due for at least another two months. Jeremy Snow hoped it wouldn't go on too long. The grittiness was in his throat and making his eyes sore. Last year, when it properly came, it had affected his asthma, giving him a particularly bad attack. He could always wear a face mask, like the Chinese, but he was reluctant unless it became absolutely necessary. Snow was always very careful — because he was constantly warned to *be* careful — not to do anything that might offend. The previous year, when he'd worn one, he'd suspected some Chinese believed he was mocking them. A small point, perhaps: but during his time in China, Snow had learned the importance of observing small points. Observing things, large or small, was after all one of his functions, albeit unofficial, unrecognized and known by very few.

Snow hurried through the Beijing suburbs towards the former and now decaying Catholic church the authorities allowed to remain as an empty symbol of supposed religious tolerance, just as Father Robertson was retained as an even emptier symbol. Snow knew Father Robertson would have been terrified if he'd known of his second role, which he conceded was hardly surprising, considering how much the ageing priest had suffered during the five-year imprisonment through the final period of the Cultural Revolution. But Snow often found it difficult to curb his impatience at the old man's hand-wringing nervousness and constant warnings against offending the authorities.

The Jesuit Curia should never have allowed the Chinese government to use them as it had in allowing Father Robertson to remain, after his release, even though it provided the Order with a presence in a country where it had always been traditionally important for it to be and where Catholicism was still, officially, permitted. Father Robertson was no longer a proper Soldier of Christ, not like Snow knew himself to be: had known from the earliest childhood days in the seminary and would always be, prepared to fight like a soldier and suffer like a soldier if called upon to do so. As Zhang Su Lin had said he was prepared to suffer, after the massacre in Tiananmen Square. Snow often wondered about Zhang: the man had been the best dissident source he'd ever had. The only one, in fact. And he had disappeared with the complete suddenness of his arrival.

Despite the stinging dust and his desire to get into the protection of the church and its attached quarters, Snow halted abruptly short of the intersection, to allow as much room as possible between himself and the approaching nightsoil collectors carrying their brimming buckets of excreta from the non-flushing street stalls: the smell of untreated sewage in the strong wind was even more throat-clogging than the biting grit.

Snow coughed, as much against the memory of Father Robertson's reaction to Tiananmen as to the stink all around him. The broken man had actually confronted his outrage by quoting the Old Testament — *Shall not the Judge of all the World do right?* It had been one of the first times Snow had let his contempt show openly, quoting directly back from the Book of Proverbs. *Answer not a fool according to his folly, lest thou also be like unto him. Answer a fool according to his folly, lest he be wise in his own conceit.*

Even as he had uttered the words Snow realized he had gone too far — been blatantly insubordinate — but he'd said it and the harm had been done, perhaps forever. Father Robertson had asked for his folly to be explained, and Snow had made the necessary apology and tried to argue the evil of a genocidal regime that had to be swept away. Only to be answered by another quotation, on the futility of fighting might with might, which hadn't met the point he'd tried to make anyway and which rendered futile the whole dispute between them. As any political discussion between them would always be futile.

Had Father Robertson ever been a proper Jesuit? That was practically a sacrilegious doubt about a man who had served a five-year jail sentence ostensibly for his faith, but privately Snow

20

was frequently unsure. The old man could quote all the catechism and diktats of Ignatius — which was how he faced any dissent, by placating quotation from the Order's founder or the Bible or whatever tract he considered appropriate — but the man never seemed to have the fervour or commitment of other Jesuits Snow had encountered before his posting to China.

He had to stop himself becoming so irritated by the other man, Snow decided. He was a proper soldier, secularly as well as spiritually: that was all that mattered. If it hadn't shown the most arrogant conceit, he would have believed himself chosen, to perform a dedicated, committed task.

The smell of body waste lingered in the street as Snow crossed, able when he turned into the side-street to see the sagging shingled roof of the church buildings: their green was already dulled by the grey fall-out from the desert. Snow's aggravation switched from the man who was considered, by their Order, to be his superior to what he saw as the emptiness of his own position in Beijing. He was only accepted by the Chinese authorities as an instructor of English, not a priest. He went through the charade to justify his residential permission, but he decided, impatiently, that he was not truly performing any proper function, at any proper level. He needed to get out, into the provinces, to meet people hopefully less afraid than the majority seemed to be in the capital, to talk in the Mandarin or any of the three other dialects he spoke about anything they wanted to discuss. It was a suggestion to put to Father Robertson who, annoyingly, had the power of veto over him.

He was grateful to get inside the complex, out of the driving wind. Directly inside the door he shook himself, like a dog discarding water. He remained quietly in the hallway for several moments, waiting for the tightness in his chest to lessen before going into the church misted from disuse with a different, thicker dust. Quite alone in the echoing cavern, in front of an altar denied any ornamentation, not even the statues of adoration, he went through his devotions, praying as he did every day for special guidance in each role he performed.

Before going to Father Robertson, he splashed water from a prepared jug into a matching bowl in what had once been a robing-room, washing the grit from his hands and face.

Father Robertson was at his desk and quite motionless when Snow finally entered, head bowed so deeply over its scattered and dishevelled contents that he might have been asleep. From long experience, Snow knew that he wasn't. In the early days, Snow had waited politely to be invited to sit, but not any more: he even grated the chair over the bare boards, needlessly to alert the older man that there was someone else in the room.

It was still several minutes before Father Robertson stirred and looked sideways. It was not the Jesuit practice to wear any habit, and certainly not here in Beijing. Father Robertson wore bagged and shapeless trousers and an equally used shirt, open at the neck. His pure white hair was full and long and without any shape: Snow had never been aware of the man combing it, even on the occasions when they'd attended official or government events. The faded blue eyes were watery, in a lined face whitened by the years of sunless imprisonment.

'I've heard the wind.' The smile was distant, an attitude the man constantly conveyed.

'It's the Gobi,' suggested Snow.

'Not so soon.'

'So it won't last.' It was still too early for there to be the smell of whisky. That would come later.

'Where have you been?'

'An early morning walk.' Snow had been again to the main railway station. Three weeks earlier he'd witnessed a heavy troop contingent going north, on the Shenyang line. There'd been nothing on any radio broadcast or in any newspaper in Beijing, but then he hadn't expected there to be.

'It can't have been very pleasant.'

'I'm glad to be back.'

'Well in time for your school.'

At best the class comprised twenty people, but the attendance was irregular. Snow had wanted the lessons to be given in the church, but Father Robertson had insisted that would be provocative so they were conducted in the church hall. Snow said: 'I was thinking, while I walked. I would like officially to take leave owing me. To travel

23

around the country a little.'

'Where?'

Snow was surprised there had not been the instant rejection that had greeted previous suggestions of his moving around the country. He shrugged. 'Shenyang perhaps. Or south, to Wuhan or Chongqin.'

'I once travelled to all those places,' said the head of a mission that no longer existed. 'People were not frightened then.' The nostalgia acted as a reminder. 'You could endanger our position here.'

What position? thought Snow, cynically. 'Of course I would not think of openly discussing religion, not with anyone.'

'It still might be dangerous.'

'I would be extremely careful.'

Father Robertson was reflective for several moments. 'Make a general application, to see how it is received.'

Snow was more surprised by the acquiescence. 'I could get to the Foreign Ministry this afternoon.'

'Tomorrow,' decided Father Robertson. 'You're tolerated here as an English lecturer. So the school comes first.'

Fifteen people turned up for class. One was a man of about twenty who hadn't come before and Snow guessed he was sheltering from the dust storm. He spoke English well but had difficulty reading it. Snow didn't believe the man's promise to return the following week.

He considered disobeying Father Robertson by trying to reach the Foreign Ministry before it closed but decided against it. He'd wait until tomorrow, when there weren't any English classes scheduled. The necessary Foreign Ministry in the morning and probably the more important Gong An Ju, the Public Security Bureau, in the afternoon.

'Well?' demanded Miller. He reached out, brushing her hand, wanting the brief physical contact.

Patricia Elder shifted more fully to face the man, offering her hand to answer the touch, always with intimate gestures like that. 'It's difficult to believe he's been responsible for all that I've read in his files.'

Miller continued to frown, hoping the woman was not being over-cautious. 'I'm not sure appearance has got anything to do with it . . .'

'. . . I am,' she interrupted, confident of their relationship. 'I think everything about Charlie Muffin is calculated to mislead. And most certainly his appearance.'

'I thought you might have told him just now, in front of me. Make it clear that it is with my authority.'

She shook her head. 'It's important he realizes from the beginning there's no longer any special relationships: most definitely not with the Director-General. From now on he's simply an ordinary officer who's got to take orders, as and when they're given. *My* orders. We'll keep your authority for when he challenges me.'

'Have you chosen someone?' he asked.

She nodded. 'John Gower. University entrant. Incredibly keen. Scored the highest for interrogation resistance.'

'When are you going to brief Muffin?'

She smiled. 'When there's a benefit to be gained. Which isn't yet.'

Four floors below, Charlie Muffin was thinking: attempting a very personal — and therefore vitally important — assessment of where he stood. If he stood anywhere at all. A woman! He was to be ordered about by a woman! Why not? Why the automatic sexism? Because it had never happened before, that was why not. He'd never had to work this way. Nothing to do with her sex: it was to do with too many dismissive changes. He had no chauvinistic difficulty about the fact that Patricia Elder *was* a woman. Or that he was expected to do what she told him to do, when she told him to do it. He just hoped she was properly professional, that's all. Which *was* male chauvinism.

She'd worked hard during their brief meeting, to make it clear how much she was the superior and he was the subordinate. Why? The peremptory manner could indicate nervousness, a bravado effort to intimidate him. Or, on the other hand, to show a self-assured confidence and convey that from now on he *was* very much the subordinate. What about Patricia Elder herself? No wedding ring, which had to be kept in mind. No discernible accent, but obviously well educated private school delivery. No bust to get excited about but the suit jacket was high buttoned and might have hidden a surprise. Nice legs, crossed without embarrassment at his quick examination: strong-featured, the nose almost too big and not helped by the shortness with which she wore her slightly greying hair. Better to have grown it longer. Interesting, full-lipped mouth and unusual eyes, which were probably cosmetically described as brown but which he thought closer to black. She'd used them very directly, too, staring at him when she spoke, not dropping her gaze when he'd stared just as fixedly back, curious if he could face her down. But always an uncertainty. Charlie couldn't understand that inference: couldn't understand it at all.

What else?

Possibly that Peter Miller was a sneaky bastard. And that Julia Robb might not be the robotic ball-breaker she'd appeared. Charlie was sure Miller hadn't used any foot button to activate the intercom. So it could have been on and relaying his arrival conversation with the girl. So she could have been protecting him, against betraying himself as . . . Charlie stopped, seeking the word, grinning when it came. Against betraying himself as a sneaky bastard, he supposed. Whatever, he'd have to be careful around Miller's suite if he were ever allowed entry from now on, until he discovered if the Director-General did play eavesdropping tricks.

What about the meeting itself? Confusing, Charlie judged. There hadn't been any real purpose in it: at least not one that he could find. It hadn't needed a personal encounter for Miller to announce how he intended running the organization in the future. Or for the introduction to Patricia Elder to be made personally, either.

There had been no mention of anything positive for him to do. Despite the self-admonishment against expecting things in advance he *had* anticipated being given something today: something that would have broken this stultifying, paper-dart-throwing inactivity.

Analysed completely, what had taken place today was nothing more than his being summoned for examination, like a museum exhibit or maybe a laboratory specimen, to see how he would jump when the acid dripped on the nerve ends. Which had they considered him to be?

The musing began idly, his mind drifting, but abruptly Charlie began to concentrate. Couldn't that be *precisely* the purpose: for them to study him, for some reason? It certainly hadn't appeared an intense examination, from the quickness of the meeting, and the short conversation hadn't given any indication, but it was the reason that made the most sense. Charlie liked things to make sense.

Examined for what? An impossible question, at this stage. Maybe not even a question. Maybe he was again mistakenly anticipating things, when there was nothing to anticipate. All he could do was wait. As he had been waiting, for far too long.

In Beijing, the *People's Daily* carried a lengthy diatribe warning of foreign reactionaries encouraging counter-revolution within the country, pledging that any such activity would be sought out and crushed, with its perpetrators put on trial.

Three

Jeremy Snow never expected the length or the intensity of Father Robertson's lecture upon every possible pitfall and disaster after the favourable reaction to his travel application. More specifically than ever before, the old man talked of the prisons and even the two re-education installations in which he had been incarcerated, regimes of rifle-butt discipline and brainwashing propaganda.

Always, however, Father Robertson declared personal suffering unimportant. The need, always, was to retain a mission in a country where Jesuits had lived and worked for hundreds of years. Throughout Snow gave repeated assurances that he would do nothing to jeopardize their tenuous position. On this occasion the man quoted from the Epistle of James: *Ye have heard of the patience of Job.*

Snow would have welcomed more the chance of a proper briefing with Foster: he'd suggested it, in the letter drop through which their communication was imposed and limited by the liaison officer, when he'd learned he was getting his travel permission. But Foster had predictably refused, arguing there were no embassy or other convenient gatherings of Westerners to disguise an encounter.

Snow had become increasingly frustrated in the nine months he'd worked under Walter Foster. The red-haired, freckle-faced man looked and behaved like a timid clerk: even when there was virtually no risk at embassy gatherings of diplomats or Western enclave people, Foster was always twitching over his shoulder, inviting the attention they forever sought to avoid. So very different from the others. Bowley had always managed personal meetings in the early, first-arrival days. And George Street, too, using the flamboyant eccentricity of handlebar moustaches and floral waistcoats and an imported Rolls Royce to hide behind, deflecting any official interest by drawing it upon himself.

After three and a half years Snow didn't have to be told to get everything, which was what Foster had said. He *always* got everything. Photographs, whenever possible. Any scrap of conversation, no matter how inconsequential. Twice he'd even supplied names of men at the time unrecognized at the middle level of the government both of whom subsequently achieved influential appointments, marking them as people to watch and monitor. And from Zhang Su Lin, when he'd had the man as an informant, he'd provided the virtual framework of the dissident movement that survived Tiananmen.

Fleetingly Snow regretted not being able to complain about Foster: get something done to improve the communication through the embassy. Was it so unchristian to think as he was thinking?

31

Maybe, if any complaint affected the man's career. But didn't it go beyond Foster's career, to his own personal safety? He was taking all the risks. Foster had the protection of diplomatic cover. Snow accepted he had nothing. Not true, Snow decided, in immediate contradiction. Didn't he have the protection of God? Spiritual protection, unquestionably: just as his spiritual conviction was unquestionable. But this was temporal. Still not a difficulty. After three and a half years he was sure he had completely assimilated into a Chinese way of life, far more adjusted temporally than in any other way.

Snow planned his itinerary with infinite care. Every route he suggested took him into closed areas — because obviously these were the cities and places of interest — and he discerned from beginning negotiations at the Foreign Ministry that to press for the north might lead to a straight-forward refusal. He instantly switched the per-suasion to a southerly route.

It took a lot of discussion to finalize a route. It allowed him as far south as Chongqin, to return eastwards through Wuhan up to Shanghai before going more directly north, back to Beijing. It put him close to at least five restricted areas and maybe six closed cities. It would have been naïve to hope to get into all, but if he penetrated just one or two the trip could be more than worth-while. An additional benefit was that for the first few days he could travel alone without any official supervision.

It was not until Zhengzhou, on the sixth day, that he was scheduled to meet an escort to take him through the restricted areas. The guardian's name was Li Dong Ming. His photograph showed a bland-faced, bespectacled man with rather large ears. Snow guessed him to be about thirty years old. If he was, they would be exactly the same age.

Natalia Nikandrova Fedova accepted that professionally she had been extremely fortunate.

She had been exonerated from any responsibility for the ultimately failed operation in England, which, incredibly, had turned out to be a personal affair for the ego-inflated satisfaction of the Directorate head, Alexei Berenkov. And then escaped completely the KGB reorganizational purges after the failed coup of 1991. Not just escaped: positively and materially benefited, when the KGB had been transferred to the jurisdiction of the Russian Federation, still headquartered in Moscow, but renamed as an internal security agency now. There had, of course, been the advantage in those early days of her being an officer in the external First Chief Directorate, not attached to any internal part of the oppressive apparatus which deservedly bore the brunt of the mass sackings, blood-lettings and even elimination of entire departments.

Natalia supposed there was a supreme irony that with her elevated rank of Major-General she now occupied the position once held — and finally abused — by Alexei Berenkov, who had been prepared to sacrifice her in his personal vendetta against Charlie Muffin, an adversary for whom one-time admiration became unreasoning competitiveness. Now Berenkov was disgraced, dismissed and stripped of all rank and privilege. And Charlie, who'd beaten Berenkov first with a phoney defection to Moscow and then again by refusing to fall into the London trap as a supposed Russian agent, was . . . was where? She wished, how very much she wished, that she knew. Whatever and wherever, he would still be in intelligence. He was too good to dump.

Natalia slowed the car at the traffic intersection at what she still thought of as Marx Prospekt, despite the Communist-cleansing name change which had altered the street maps of Moscow. She turned almost instinctively at the pause, looking into the rear of the car, annoyed with herself for forgetting to leave the bag with the clothes change and fresh nappies at the crèche: she knew there would be spare things available at the nursery but she'd still telephone as soon as she got to the office.

Was it allowing too much self-pity for her to think she *had* been sacrificed, personally? Yes, she decided at once. Charlie had acted the only way possible — the only way he knew — as a professional intelligence officer. The setup was wrong and they'd both known it. She'd decided to take the chance. He hadn't. And in the event she'd managed to rejoin the Soviet visiting group from which she had been prepared to defect without being missed, so there had been no inquiry or punishment.

The traffic began to move and Natalia looked away from the back of the car. Sasha couldn't be considered a factor: neither had known then. Would it have made a difference, if Charlie *had* known? Perhaps. She liked to think it would. But she could never be sure. Determinedly Natalia rejected another reflection, this one probably more pointless than the rest. Whatever there might have been — could have been — for her and Charlie Muffin had ended: closed off forever, with no possibility of ever being opened or restored.

She had a baby whom she adored. A privileged life, despite the democratization which was supposed to have swept privilege away. And a high executive position, providing everything she could conceivably need, in addition to privilege. She was a lucky woman.

But not complacent. She could not afford to be, with Fyodor Tudin at her back. She'd made a mistake, agreeing to Tudin remaining as her immediate deputy. He was an old-timer, a relic of as far back as the Brezhnev era. Natalia knew she would always have to be wary of the depths of Tudin's resentment of her being the Directorate chairman, rather than him.

As Natalia edged off the ring road at Yasenevo, into the skyscraper block of the original and still retained First Chief Directorate, she wondered if Charlie was as fortunate. She hoped so.

Just over fifteen hundred miles away, Charlie Muffin stared down at the summons that had finally arrived from the deputy Director-General and hoped exactly the same thing.

Four

Patricia Elder's suite came off the second arm of the new triangular ninth-floor layout at the centre of which reigned the starchily formal Julia Robb.

But the deputy Director's room had none of the sterility of Miller's. There were two flower arrangements, one on a small, elaborately carved cabinet of a sort that Charlie had never seen before in a government office. There was a display of art deco figures on the same cabinet and on a mantelpiece in the centre of which was a gold filigree and ormolu clock. There were screening curtains of festooned lace at the window, which had a partial view of the Big Ben clock and the crenellated roofing of the Parliament buildings. The deputy Director sat in front of the window, at a proper wooden and leather desk, not something fashioned from metal and plastic which looked as if it had popped out of a middle-price Christmas cracker. The only similarity Charlie could find with Miller's quarters was the complete absence of any personal photographs. There would have hardly been room on the desk anyway: there were two red box containers and a string-secured manila folder Charlie recognized from the three — or was it four? — disciplinary hearings he'd endured over the years.

The woman's suit was as formal as that of their initial meeting: today's was grey, high-collared and as figure-concealing as before. Charlie automatically checked her left hand: there was still no wedding ring.

She studied him just as intently with her black-brown eyes, and at once Charlie felt like a schoolboy called to explain his hand up a knicker leg behind the bicycle sheds.

Patricia breathed heavily, before she spoke: the sigh, dismissive, remained in her voice. 'So now we come to talk about Charles Edward Muffin . . .'

Charlie easily remembered the last two occasions he'd been addressed with such formality: both times at the Central Criminal Court at London's Old Bailey. The first a set-up prosecution and an escape-intended imprisonment, all to create a phoney defection to the then Soviet Union: the unsuspected beginning of so many things. The initial encounter — his debriefing — with Natalia that had led to a love neither of them had foreseen and which he, ultimately, had ruined by not going to her in London. The operation — the purpose of which he'd never known until he'd innovated his own special self-protection — to discredit Alexei Berenkov. Which had nevertheless partially succeeded and led to Berenkov's close-run retribution, involving a manipulated Natalia again. The second court appearance had been phoney too, like the announced ten year sentence, to convince the Russians his entrapment had succeeded in part. It should have protected Natalia, as well. There was no way of knowing if it had. Double disaster. Double abandonment. Belated double despair. So many things . . . Charlie stopped the nostalgia, forcing himself to concentrate, although the recollection of the trial stayed with him. 'That sounds very official: should I stand to receive my sentence?'

There was no facial relaxation. She patted the box files and said: 'There's enough to merit a sentence.'

'A man is always presumed innocent until proven guilty by the weight of evidence. I was always innocent!' said Charlie, brightly, trying to build bridges between himself and his new Controller.

'There are parts that are impressive,' she said. 'But the bad outweighs the good: Charlie Muffin, forever making up his own rules but to whom no rules ever need apply.' She paused. 'Right?'

'I've never failed, when it mattered,' Charlie fought back. 'When operations went wrong, it's because they would have gone wrong anyway: they were impractical or incorrectly planned. Or I needed to innovate to survive, not having been properly briefed.' What the fuck was this? It *was* like having to explain himself for being caught behind the bicycle sheds!

'One of the central themes,' isolated the deputy Director. 'Your personal survival.'

A poor shot, seized Charlie. 'I've always thought

personal survival is a fairly basic principle; a blown intelligence officer is a failed operation and invariably an embarrassment, to be explained away. There aren't any embarrassments in those files to be explained away.'

'Not publicly.'

'All that matters,' insisted Charlie. 'What the public *don't* know doesn't concern them. They can just go on sleeping safely in their beds while the shadowy people clean up the shit.'

She nodded, seemingly conceding the argument and giving no reaction to his swearing. 'What comes first, for you? Personal survival? Or the operation?'

He didn't have to be defensive about that. Charlie nodded to the files. 'If you've read those thoroughly you don't have to ask me that!' The indignation was genuine.

'You're offended?'

'With justification.' Charlie still wished he didn't feel as if he were explaining himself to a school principal.

'Maybe it's all semantics anyway,' she said, dismissive again. 'All in the past. The dinosaur age. Cold War, white hats, black hats.'

Quite a bran tub of mixed metaphors, thought Charlie: he didn't believe dinosaurs existed in the Ice Age. Expectantly he said: 'Now we're looking into the new and different future I've been reading so much about in the last few months?'

'Some of us are,' she said, heavily. She extracted some obviously new and therefore recent sheets from the manila file. 'You don't seem to agree with a lot of what you've been asked to comment upon.'

Charlie regarded her cautiously. Again he'd tried to avoid anticipating this encounter, but he had not expected it to be like this, so openly and consistently hostile. 'In a Europe more unstable than it has been for fifty years, I considered many of the opinions naïve.'

'Explain naïve!'

'There were suggestions, in at least three theses, that because of the end of the Cold War — whatever that was — intelligence services could be scaled down.'

' "Whatever that was",' she quoted, questioningly.

Quick on her feet, judged Charlie. 'Why don't you define the Cold War for me?'

'Why don't *you* define it for *me?*' she came back, easily.

Shit, thought Charlie. 'Simplistic, because there was a Wall dividing Berlin and physical barriers between Eastern and Western Europe. Newspaper shorthand: spy-writers' cliché.'

'What did you think it was?'

Shouldn't have let her be the first to speak. 'I didn't think it was anything,' said Charlie, lobbing a difficult return.

She frowned and he was glad. 'You're not making sense.'

'You know I am,' insisted Charlie. He'd had her running about: not exactly broken her serve but getting some of the difficult returns back over the net.

'The coming down of the barriers doesn't matter, in reality?' There was an uncertainty in her voice, beyond it being a question.

'Not *our* reality.'

'Tell me what our reality is,' she demanded, gaining confidence.

'What it has always been,' said Charlie. 'Finding out the intention of other governments and other world leaders, in advance of it becoming obvious, so that *our* leaders are not wrong-footed. Which means we now have to learn the intentions of more than a dozen separate governments of countries that used to be the Soviet Union but now consider themselves independent: the Russian Federation — which is also splitting up internally — most of all. And Czechoslovakia. And Poland. And Hungary. And Bulgaria. And how East is *really* going to integrate with West Germany. And whether communism is going to collapse in China, as it's collapsed everywhere else. And what a close-to-bankruptcy America that thought it was the world's policeman until Vietnam is going to do, now that it's lost the black hat, white hat simplicity. And which bulging-eyed, Third World despot is going to channel the four or five million he hasn't already put into his Swiss bank account into buying a nuclear device to threaten the next door neighbour Third World despot too busy at the time putting United Nations and pop concert famine aid money into another Swiss account. And then there's the Middle East . . .'

She didn't bother with an answer. Her sigh was dismissive enough. 'The Director told you there were to be changes? That there was no longer room — nor intention — for special relationships?'

'Something like that.'

'So this is reorganization time.'

Charlie abruptly felt a deep, gouging hollowness. 'Am I being retired?'

Patricia Elder held his look for several seconds before lowering her head over the written account of Charlie Muffin's entire career as an intelligence officer. Remaining head-bent, she said: 'We couldn't risk your being retired. Beyond our control, until it was too late.'

There was a distant snap of hope, a spark in the darkness. 'What then?'

The dossiers got another momentary pat. 'You were good: bloody good.'

Past tense, Charlie noted. 'So?'

'You've still got something to contribute. By teaching others.'

'Teaching!'

'Not the manual stuff: there are staff colleges for that. Or your insubordination, either. There's no place for that in the sort of service the Director-General and I envisage. I want you to teach selected officers what *isn't* in the manuals . . .' She allowed herself a smile: one tooth crossed slightly over the other in the front. 'You're so very proud of being a survivor. Instruct the new people how to survive, as you did for so long.'

Charlie was listening, of course — to every word — but his mind was way ahead of what she was saying. Over, he realized: his operational life was over, being ended right here with matter-of-fact efficiency by a woman who considered him an anachronism. A dinosaur. The hollowness was still there but different now: it was an empty helplessness, at having taken away from him something he never thought he'd lose. Charlie had never liked feeling helpless.

'I'm not sure I'd be any good at it.'

'You'll have to learn,' she said, impatiently.

'I could decline?' suggested Charlie, who never in his life had refused any assignment, because the job was not one in which a person *could* refuse.

She pushed the files to one side of the desk, with further impatience. 'In which case you could be assigned to Records: see a lot of boxes and folders like these. Or Archives. Same job except that the boxes and folders are older. Or department or safe-house security, the sort of thing usually allocated to retired military personnel. You've probably met a few of them in the past.'

He had, Charlie remembered. Upright, polished-booted men in gate-houses or hallway cubby-holes, trying to imbue a meaningless existence with a sense of urgency, automatically calling everyone 'sir' and standing to attention. Charlie had actually thought of them as dinosaurs.

44

'Or I could retire, if you've no further use for me.'

'You haven't been listening!' she said, curtly. 'I didn't say we've no further use for you. The opposite. I said you still had something to contribute. You're not eligible for retirement, which we wouldn't accept in any case. I also said I want you in a position I can control. I'm not risking you as a wild card: offering yourself as some sort of commentator on intelligence on television or in newspapers, like all those supposed experts who emerge whenever espionage becomes newsworthy and don't know what the hell they're talking about.'

Charlie opened his mouth to argue her wild-card nonsense, but changed his mind because there wasn't any point: she wasn't going to be persuaded to any opinion other than her own. Instead he said: 'I thought Henry Wilberforce got slavery abolished in the 1800s.'

Patricia Elder gave another of her heavy sighs. 'I've told you what your new role is to be in this department.'

There *was* no point in arguing. He had to take it: give himself time to think. It didn't necessarily have to be permanent: Director-Generals and deputies with newborn theories came and went, so there was always the chance of recovering. 'Selected officers?'

She nodded. 'On a one-to-one basis. They will have graduated from all the usual instructional courses: this is going to be something beyond the normal . . .' There was another frigid smile. 'You tell *me* how long it will take to pass on your particularly special expertise.'

He couldn't teach instinct: how to know that something was wrong, without anything apart from a feeling on which to base that judgement. 'It'll depend, upon your selected officers.'

'You'll like your first apprentice. He's good.'

'I wouldn't consider liking him!' said Charlie, instantly.

'That was thoughtless,' she apologized at once. 'I shouldn't have said that.'

'I'll operate from here?'

'Yes.'

'Let's hope it works,' said Charlie, rising to leave.

'It's got to work,' said the woman, as if she were affronted by the suggestion of failure. 'And it was William.'

Charlie stopped at the door. 'What?'

'The Member of Parliament who campaigned against slavery in the 1800s. It was *William* Wilberforce. Not Henry.'

Charlie had been worried she wouldn't respond. He smiled and said: 'Well done.' Her face tightened, in belated realization. Not much of a victory, decided Charlie. But something at least. He was a schoolmaster now: schoolmasters knew things like that.

At her control post at the apex of the triangle Julia Robb scarcely looked up as he left. Bugger you, too, thought Charlie.

Miller personally poured the tea, offering it across his desk to the woman. 'How did it go?'

'As I intended,' she said, which was a slight exaggeration.

'He's got to do the job properly. Believe in its importance.'

Patricia Elder shook her head. 'His feeling is against me. I've read everything that's ever been written about the man. Know him. He'll do the job, to the very best of his ability. And it's a pretty damned good ability. He out-argued me, a couple of times.'

'Everything set up with Gower?'

The woman nodded this time. 'I've fixed the meeting.'

'Let's hope it works,' said the Director.

Patricia Elder laughed, abruptly. 'That's what Charlie said. It was interesting, listening to him. His views about the future of intelligence are exactly the same as ours.'

'I hope he doesn't think we're fools.'

'Of course he does! How can he think otherwise?' She paused. The conversation about Charlie Muffin was over. 'Is Ann coming up from the country?'

'I'm sorry.'

'So am I.' Increasingly Patricia Elder was regretting the absolute commitment she'd made to their relationship, neglecting and finally abandoning other friends and acquaintances until Peter was the only person she had now. There was nothing she could do about it: nothing she wanted to do about it. He'd make the decision. She was sure he would. Dear God how much she wished he'd make it soon.

Five

John Gower bet himself she'd say something by the third crossroad and lost, because they'd gone through the frustration of hay-hauling tractors and school-pool Volvos and were five miles up the motorway towards London before Marcia finally spluttered and broke into laughter. 'I just couldn't believe it!'

'She's old-fashioned!' Gower said, defensively. He didn't really think of his mother as old-fashioned. Not *old* at all.

'It was like something out of a Noël Coward play, creeping from bedroom to bedroom!' Marcia protested.

'I'm sorry.'

Marcia Leyton felt reassuringly for his hand. 'I'm just playing with you! It was a wonderful weekend. And I like her . . .' There was a pause. 'Do you think she liked me?'

Gower accelerated past a crocodile of lorries and said: 'I know she did.' It had been the first time his mother had met Marcia: he wasn't sure which of the three of them had been more anxious.

'You don't sound convinced,' Marcia said, wanting more.

'I am,' said Gower, honestly. 'She loved you.' He coasted into the cruising lane, looking across at her. They had the sun-roof open: a stray flick of blonde hair had escaped from beneath her head-scarf but was blowing backwards so she wasn't bothering to restrain it. Her face, devoid of make-up, shone in the morning light: she wasn't looking back but staring straight ahead, so that he could see her sharp, nose-tilted profile. He guessed many girls — probably *all* girls — with such perfect features would have intentionally sat as she was sitting now, displaying themselves for admiration. But not Marcia. She was the most exquisitely beautiful girl he had ever known, but someone completely and ingenuously unaware of it. He found it difficult to believe she loved him as much as she said she did; it was like stealing, taking something that didn't belong to him by right.

His weekend for meeting her parents had been a month before, and much more difficult than the one just past, even though he and Marcia had not stayed in the family house because it had too few bedrooms: Marcia's much younger, electronically crazed brother lived in one com-puter cave and her father's bed-ridden sister was regally suspended in the other spare room in a miasma of disinfectant and lavender perfume. Marcia's father, a retired bank inspector, had spent most of the time trying to initiate a debate about the intricacies of the European Exchange Rate Mechanism and European monetary union. The mother had baked a cake with nuts in it and Gower didn't like nuts. He was worried his ignorance of finance and small appetite at tea had been misunderstood as lack of interest.

'I don't expect to be back from Manchester until Wednesday,' announced Marcia. She was a visual display director for an advertising agency, which involved a lot of travelling, particularly to exhibitions.

'I've no idea what this new course is about,' he said in return. 'I'll probably be busy: certainly until it settles down.' Closer to London the motorway was becoming more congested and Gower wished he had given himself more time to get ahead of the rush hour: he hated being late for appointments, especially first-time encounters.

'I've been thinking,' she said, slowly. 'Don't you think it's stupid, us living like we do . . .' She squeezed his hand again, in further reassurance, and said quickly: 'OK! I'm not getting heavy. I am not sure I want the absolute commitment of marriage, either. I'm talking simple practicality. Keeping two separate flats is bloody mad: if I'm not out of town, like I'm going to be the next few days, we're with each other all the time. There's no point in living apart, is there?'

The traffic was getting heavier: Gower could see it at a standstill, far ahead. 'I suppose not,' he agreed, reluctantly, suspecting she had steered their conversation. Gower was frightened of their being permanently, more constantly together, although for none of the normal reasons that might make a person apprehensive of a stable relationship. His statutory inability to discuss his job with her would inevitably create a gap between them. And he didn't want anything between them. The paradox was that he *wanted* to be with her all the time, probably surer of their relationship than she was.

'That was begrudging,' she said, disappointed.

'Look at the bloody traffic!'

'We've got all the time in the world,' she said. truthfully. 'And we're not discussing the traffic. We're discussing living together because it might be nice. At least I am. If you don't want to, why not say so?'

'You know I want to.'

'Fine!' she said, a person of quick decisions. 'So let's do it! Whose place? Mine or yours? I think yours is more convenient but my flat is in a better area. My lease has some time to run . . .'

'Wait a moment!' halted Gower. 'Where's the panic?'

'Where's the reason for delaying?'

'I'm still going through courses: you know I'm starting one today.'

'You're already *in* the Foreign Office. There's job security, carved in stone, for the rest of your life. Why should a course affect our living to-gether?'

'I'm not sure,' he said, unhappy at not finding more convincing avoidance.

'I think I know what you're not sure about.'

He finally had to stop. Ahead the road was

clogged as far as he could see. They had only just passed the airport turn-off, so he estimated he had at least another eight miles of jammed motorway. 'That's not so.'

'Let's forget it.' She was staring straight ahead again.

'Why have we got to make a decision now, in the middle of a bloody traffic jam? Let's talk about it when you get back from Manchester.'

'What's there to talk about, apart from whose flat it's going to be?'

'You trying to make a row?' They rarely argued: he couldn't remember the last time.

'No.'

'We'll sort it out when you get back,' he insisted. He was glad the traffic began to move. He could at last see the reason for the blockage, a single-line crawl past three cars in a nose-to-tail accident, each driver blaming the other in a hard-shoulder shouting match: beyond the cars were moving fast again.

'Is this the last course there'll be?' asked Marcia, trying for neutral ground.

'I think so,' said Gower, uncomfortably. He'd been schooled for conversations like this, actually lectured on the responses and convenient answers.

'Then something permanent?'

'That's the procedure.'

'I would have thought by now you'd have been given some indication of what it will be.'

'Probably something in administration.' Always dismissive, he remembered, from the how-to-reply lecture. 'It'll give me time to look around and make my mind up about a definite division.'

They left the motorway and Gower turned through the Chiswick back streets to avoid any more main road crawl: he was taking her directly to the station for the Manchester train.

'I'm ambitious for you,' she declared.

'I'm ambitious for myself.' And nervous, he privately admitted. Despite all the exhaustive training and tuition and one-to-one lectures, just as it had been with his tutor at Oxford, Gower couldn't visualize what it was *really* going to be like. He'd actually mentioned it to his last instructor, seeking some guidance. Instead the man had nodded in quick agreement and said it wasn't a profession for which there was any sensible, practical apprenticeship.

'I'll phone tonight,' promised Marcia, as they stopped at the station. She leaned back in through the door, intending to collect her cases from the rear seat. 'Best of luck with the course.'

Gower kissed her and said: 'You're wrong: you know you're wrong, don't you?'

'About what?' She knew, but wanted him openly to commit himself, to make her the clear winner of the dispute.

'Me not being sure. About us. I've never been more sure of anything. I *love* you.'

It only took him half an hour to reach the headquarters building in Westminster Bridge Road and the boxlike fifth-floor office. 'Good morning, sir,' he said, politely, as he entered.

'Gower. John Gower.'

Charlie Muffin wondered if being called 'sir' would be the only tangible benefit of his new job. 'Your first mistake,' he said.

It was so unusual for a foreigner to travel hard-seat — the lowest, cheapest class on Chinese trains, on wooden benches without upholstery and which did not convert into sleeping bunks — that Snow attracted even more attention than he might normally have done, simply by being a *waiguoren,* a foreigner. Snow attracted attention not merely by being a foreigner. He was an unnaturally tall 6' 5", a spindly-limbed man whose long-ago purchased chain-store clothes never seemed to fit but to hang upon him, too short at the legs and arms.

From experience he didn't try to force any conversation, waiting for the other travellers to practise their English upon him, which several did, from the moment he left Beijing. Again from experience, he let the talk range at the whim of those who approached him, never asking a direct question. Always, however, he quickly disclosed his ability to speak Mandarin, to avoid offending anyone into thinking he was trying to be superior or eavesdrop on the birdlike chatter fluttering around him. Before the first overnight disembarkation he thought two passengers — a young girl student from Shanghai and a middle-aged man who said he was a doctor — were going openly to criticize the government, but although he encouraged further conversation neither, ultimately, did so.

On that third day he saw on its way northwards a long convoy of army trucks carrying soldiers along a road parallel to the railway track. The trucks looked new and not of Chinese manufacture. In such crowded, unknown surroundings — unsure of informers among his fellow passengers — Snow held back from taking photographs. He counted a total of forty-seven lorries.

Later that same day the train stopped for water almost directly opposite a series of camouflaged but obviously newly erected factory buildings. On that occasion, pretending to photograph the steam-skirted railway engine in the foreground, Snow managed three exposures.

He was going to be very restricted, accompanied by an escort: possibly unable to achieve anything worthwhile at all. But already he felt he had enough to justify the journey. So London were going to be very impressed. The self-judgement stayed in his mind. If they *were* impressed — which they really couldn't fail to be — he'd be in a position to seek favours: make demands even. So he *would* protest against the entirely unnecessary way he was being forced to operate. Foster said it was upon London's insistence, but Snow didn't believe him. He was sure London would be guided by what they were told, not try to impose unworkable difficulties from afar. So it was Foster's doing, nobody else's. So it was Foster's fault if enquiries were made, after the protest.

56

Not unchristian, Snow repeated to himself, needing the reassurance. Simply common sense, that's all. And he'd make his case sensibly and truthfully, not going behind the man's back.

Six

There was a lengthy period of mutual examination, when Charlie thought Gower's eagerness was practically flashing like a neon sign: *like me, like me*. Charlie wondered if he would. Gower was an averagely tall, averagely built man: maybe 5′ 9″, possible eleven and a half stone — perhaps a little heavier — and clearly fit, although not in a hand-clenching, chest-thrusting way. His dark hair was closely cropped although very full: if it hadn't been well barbered it would have fallen untidily about the man's face. That face was square-chinned and rather long, the nose aquiline. The mouth was full, made more so by the hopeful, please-like-me smile: the clearly new and still untrained moustache didn't help. The eyes had the same anxiety, beneath heavy eyebrows. Good enough, judged Charlie, ticking off a mental check-list like a motor-car mechanic going through an approved service manual. The clothes were a problem. The suit was dark blue but with a heavy chalk stripe, waisted for the jacket skirt to flare immaculately. The sleeves were short enough to half-reveal the personal initial monogram on the left cuff, which was secured by heavy gold links, of a pink shirt that was fronted by a striped blue Eton tie. Obviously hand-made brogue shoes gleamed from a lot of daily polishing. Charlie guessed, enviously, that they were very comfortable: concealed beneath the desk, he'd eased the Hush Puppies off completely.

On the little finger of Gower's left hand was a family-crested signet ring of the sort Charlie had expected but failed to discover on the new and remote Director-General.

Gower was completely disorientated by the appearance of the man confronting him — as well as by the greeting — in what didn't look like an office at all, more a caretaker's booth. Gower's physical training instructors had worn track suits but his other lecturers had invariably been neat, precise men even when they wore the tweeds or sports jackets of academics.

Gower couldn't find an appropriate description for this man. That much of the suit Gower could see was subdued green, with possibly a muted check although he wasn't sure. It was bagged and shapeless and clearly cheap from the way the jacket reared away as if in embarrassment from the crinkle-collared shirt. The tie, a clashing blue, had two spotted motifs: the white the designer had intended and the darker stains of long wear and mislaid food. There was no style to the man's grey-flecked hair, which looked as if it had been chewed rather than cut and that, whatever the method, a long time ago. The face was round, and here Gower was further confused because the expression was of unlined, open innocence: practically naïvety. That same impression was carried by the brown eyes, which Gower saw flick over him, in one encompassing examination, and then come back directly to his.

'I was told to report here, sir. This room.' Gower offered the appointment chit that had been endorsed at the ground-floor security check, listing the office number.

Had he ever been as uncertain as this, wondered Charlie: called instructors sir? He probably had: it had been a long time ago. 'What reason were you given, for coming here?'

'I wasn't.'

Charlie nodded, pleased the man hadn't had time to clutter his mind with preconceptions. 'Told by whom?'

'The deputy Director.'

Charlie gestured to the side of the room to an upright, wooden-backed chair with a plaited-cane seat bowed by age. 'Don't tilt back on the rear legs. It's buggered: it'll collapse under you.'

Gower brought the chair slightly nearer the desk and sat cautiously. Was this man being intentionally rude? Or just naturally brusque? Gower was reminded of a Classics tutor at Oxford with an offensive manner, like this man: his Year had decided it was caused by the sexual frustration of being a bachelor until the tutor was arrested for importuning in a public lavatory near Balliol College. 'I wasn't given your name, either.'

Charlie frowned. 'Were you, of other instructors?'

Gower hesitated, unsure of his reply. 'We came

to know each other, naturally.'

'By name?'

'Of course.'

'Christian name? Surname? Or both?'

Gower's uncertainty grew. 'Both, I suppose.'

'You underwent arrest training? How to respond to interrogation? Physical pressure?'

Gower permitted himself a different smile, this time of satisfaction. 'I achieved the maximum, every time.'

'Would you disclose the identities of your instructors if you were detained? Put under intensive interrogation: tortured, even?'

'Of course not!' said the younger man, indignantly.

'What *would* you do?'

'Refuse, of course! Resist! I know how to do that.'

Charlie nodded, briefly looking down at his desk. Eyes still averted, he said: 'That a family ring you're wearing?'

Gower was so accustomed to the platformed gold band that he looked at it as if surprised to see it on his finger. 'Very minor. No proper title: no money either.'

'But there's a family crest?'

Gower frowned again. He didn't want it to show but he was growing angry. 'Yes.'

'What do you think of that poster on the door behind you?' demanded Charlie.

Gower swivelled his head: the uncertain chair creaked precariously. Groping for comprehension he said: 'Very nice.' It was a mountain scene, with long-haired Scottish cattle.

'I think it's dreadful,' said Charlie, who'd put it up minutes before Gower's arrival. 'You're right-handed, aren't you?'

'How do you know that?'

Charlie ignored the question. 'And you came here by car, didn't you?'

Gower had to hold tightly on to his temper. 'We spent the weekend in the country with my mother: came up this morning. Why?'

'So clothes are important to you?'

Gower regarded Charlie with total confusion. 'I don't understand any of this!'

'What's the name of the deputy Director-General?'

Gower blinked across the cramped office. 'Patricia Elder.'

'She tell you her name?'

Gower made a vague movement of his shoulders. 'I . . . I can't remember. Yes . . .' There was a momentary pause. Then, in immediate contradiction, he said: 'No. It was Personnel. When I was told to go to see her, to be told to come here, they said her name was Patricia Elder.'

'Let's go back to your being detained. Would you disclose her identity, under questioning?'

'Of course not!' said Gower, as indignantly as before.

'You'd refuse? Resist?' said Charlie, offering the words back.

'Yes.'

'How many times have you been here, to Westminster Bridge Road?'

Gower paused. 'Four times.'

'You know it's the headquarters building?'

'Yes.'

'You wouldn't disclose it, under duress?'

'Am I under interrogation now?' demanded Gower, trying to get some sense into the bizarre encounter.

'Would you?' persisted Charlie.

'I think you know the answer to that, without my telling you. But if this is something for the record, no I wouldn't disclose it. That would be unthinkable.'

Charlie made a grunting, reflective sound. 'There isn't any record being made. Perhaps there should be.' There was certainly a memorandum he had to send. They'd probably disregard it, as they'd disregarded everything else he'd sent upstairs to the rearranged Executive echelon on the ninth floor, but that didn't matter. There were lapses that had to be corrected.

'I think I'm entitled to know what's happening here!' said Gower, finally giving way to the annoyance. 'I haven't understood a moment of it: it's been ridiculous!'

Charlie gave another reflective grunt. 'And you achieved the maximum in interrogation techniques?'

'Yes!' said Gower, his voice too loud in his anger.

Charlie sat intently regarding the other man for several moments. 'You're entering the external intelligence service. And you've been through all the training? You know all that's involved?'

His uncertainty in the car, remembered Gower: the uncertainty a previous instructor hadn't helped him resolve. 'No,' he said, honestly. 'I don't think I do know what's involved: not *really* involved. I was told there's no apprenticeship I could properly go through. Just training.'

Unexpectedly Charlie smiled. 'There's some,' he disagreed. 'That's what this is about, to answer your question a while back . . . the first lesson.'

'I don't . . .' started Gower and then stopped.

'. . . Know what you've learned?' anticipated Charlie. 'Nothing yet. Let's hope you will, when I explain.'

'I wish you would.'

'You've just had a very small indication of what is necessary to be a professional intelligence officer. Very small. Childlike, compared to the level you've got to achieve. *Will* achieve, before we're through.'

'I'm still not properly following you.'

'What was the first thing I said to you, when you came into this room?'

'Ah . . .' Gower hesitated, unsure. 'Something about a mistake.' He smiled, hopefully.

'What, exactly?'

There was another hesitation. ' "You've made a mistake." '

'My exact words were "your first mistake",' corrected Charlie. 'You were entering a completely unknown situation, with no idea what you were here for. You admitted that very shortly afterwards, which was another mistake because you never admit anything you don't have to in an unknown situation. And in an unknown situation you remember *every* word that's said: not *something* like what's said. *Everything.*'

'I see,' said Gower. He thought this *was* child-like: stupid and unnecessary. He didn't think he liked this man who would not even introduce himself.

'As someone who achieved his maximum in interrogation technique, tell me what your first mistake was.'

There was silence. Then Gower admitted: 'I don't know.'

'You offered your name,' said Charlie, simply.

'This is an officially arranged meeting, for God's sake! We had an appointment! I assumed you'd know my name.'

'All the more reason for not offering it. In an unknown situation, you take, never give.'

'I was personally told to come here by the deputy Director!' Gower fought back. 'And this is the headquarters building! Surely it's safe to think . . .'

'. . . Nothing's ever safe,' interrupted Charlie, urgently. 'You've got to behave *instinctively:* in a real life situation there isn't time to work everything out . . .' Immediately putting advice into practice, he demanded: 'Why do you imagine it was important for me to find out you were right-handed?'

Gower hunched his shoulders, head bowed to avoid the older man detecting from any facial reaction the continuing annoyance. 'I don't know.'

'*How* did I find out?'

'I don't know that, either.' Pompous bastard, Gower thought.

'I put the chair so you'd have to move it. You did it with your right hand, the same hand with which you offered the appointment docket. Then I told you to look at a poster behind you: you turned over your right shoulder . . .' Charlie hesitated. 'Mean anything?'

'Absolutely nothing.'

'Then either you were badly taught, or you've forgotten evasion techniques, if you suspect yourself to be under surveillance that you have to lose. It's automatic if you are a right-handed person to move to the right: take right turnings, check to your right more than to your left. Learn to check both ways. Never stick to any pattern.'

'I was told about avoiding patterns.'

'But not about right or left?'

Gower wanted very much to say he considered it a meaningless trick. He didn't. 'I'll remember,' he promised, emptily.

'If I had you under surveillance out there somewhere on the streets, without any idea where you lived or what your name was, how long do you think it would take me to discover both? Just from how you appear today?'

Another trick, anticipated Gower. 'I don't

know.' He wished he didn't have to keep admitting that.

'Less than a day,' insisted Charlie. 'I knew you'd come up by car, remember? That was obvious from your suit jacket *not* being creased: even if you'd taken it off on a train, you would have kept it on in a taxi or a bus, showing some signs of recent wear. So you took it off for the drive back from the country. With your own car, there's a more than fifty percent chance you would have parked it on a two-hour meter to which you would have to return. When you did, I could have got the vehicle registration number. Your name and address is recorded by the registration authorities: they respond to apparent official enquiries about vehicles possibly involved in unreported accidents. Remember if you're under official surveillance — *anywhere* — there are official facilities that can be utilized. The initials on the left cuff of your shirt would be an immediate confirmation, of course. Your ring has a halved shield, the left half blank, the opposing half crossed with swords or possibly lances. I could locate that crest at the Office of Heraldry. Having identified the family name, I could get your full family history from *Who's Who, Debrett* and *Burke's.* I would expect to find that your father is dead or that your parents are divorced: you qualified spending the weekend with your "mother". And you weren't alone. You said "we". So it was either a girlfriend or wife. If it was a wife, there'd probably be an indication in the listing in the reference books I've mentioned. Then there's the Eton tie. From Eton records I could trace the university you went to: Oxford or Cambridge would be the obvious first choices. The Old Boys' clubs and societies of either would be another check, whether you were married or not.'

Gower still regarded it as a trick, but at the same time it was unsettling, like having someone spying on him through a hole in a lavatory wall. 'What, exactly, am I supposed to be understanding from all this?'

Charlie paused, isolating a continuing fault that he wasn't yet prepared to discuss. 'The value of proper observation. And the disadvantage of being so noticeable. Your suit is too good: and therefore too distinctive. Your shoes, too. The shirt's too obvious and shouldn't be mono-grammed. You shouldn't wear your ring: you'd probably get away with it in France and in a few rarefied surroundings in Spain and Germany but there's no guarantee you'll ever work in rar-efied surroundings and even less that you'd be doing so in France or Spain or Germany. So the ring would pick you out — to a properly trained observer — as a foreigner in a country in which you were trying to assimilate, particularly if that country was in any part of Eastern Europe or Asia. The tie is identifiable and wrong, as well, for the reasons I've already spelled out.'

Gower was hot with annoyance. 'What the hell are you saying, then?'

'I've given you the best piece of instruction you've had since you got accepted into the service,' said Charlie, evenly.

Gower studied the other man from the chair that really did seem about to collapse, wishing he'd concentrated more — instead of making angry judgements — to have avoided the need for yet another question. 'What's that?' he asked, with no alternative.

'The definition of a perfect intelligence officer,' said Charlie. 'The perfect intelligence officer is the sort of man that crowds are made of. Which is what I want you to become.'

Gower wished he didn't feel so inadequate in front of a man he wouldn't have even noticed in the street: and then the full import of the thought, against the immediately preceding definition of the perfect intelligence officer, came to him. He only just avoided smiling, not so much in amusement as in acceptance of the lesson. 'I haven't done very well, have I?'

'I didn't set out for you to do well. Or badly. Just for you to realize, from the absolute basics, what your job involves.' Was this how schoolmasters conducted lessons?

Which was what he'd wanted so much to discover, conceded Gower: he'd been stupid, allowing the resentment. 'Anything else I did wrong?'

'Your other instructors didn't mind you knowing their names?'

'They didn't seem to.'

'Then why should you bother to conceal their

identities, in a hostile interrogation? Cause yourself unnecessary pressure?'

'You mean name them!' Gower was astonished.

'Why not? They let their names be known:
why should you try to hide them?'

'But that's . . .'

'. . . treasonable? It would be an arguable point.
But in the circumstances we're discussing, you'd
have to reduce as much as possible what was
being done to you. Use the names, if it's necessary.'

Gower was concentrating now, not absolutely
convinced — but growing increasingly so — of
what he had to do. 'What about the identity of
the deputy Director-General, in such circumstances?'

'The same, once your interrogators prove
they've definitely identified you,' insisted Charlie.
It was looking hopeful.

'And the location of Westminster Bridge Road
as the headquarters of our service?'

'Do you really think there's an intelligence organization anywhere in the world that doesn't
know where every other organization lives, in
its own country? Paperback spy writers identify
this place!'

There was silence between them for several moments. Gower said finally: 'I think I've learned
a lot.'

'You haven't,' Charlie contradicted. 'You've
gone through a good three-quarters of this meeting at varying stages of anger. Which I set out

to achieve. So that's something else you either didn't learn or don't remember, from your interrogation resistance lectures. You've lost the moment you let your temper go. Dead: maybe even literally. Don't you ever forget that. Don't you ever forget anything I try to teach you, but don't forget that most of all.'

'Every other training session had a title,' said Gower.

'This has, too,' said Charlie. 'It's called survival.'

Charlie wrote three memoranda.

The first pointed out the obvious dangers of instructional staff allowing their names to be easily known to trainee officers and the even greater danger of the identity of the deputy Director-General being disclosed by the Personnel department, in inter-office correspondence.

The second was a detailed account of his initial meeting with John Gower.

The third official letter to Patricia Elder asked to be informed of any communication John Gower sent to her. It was, Charlie insisted, a particularly important request.

The official communication completed, Charlie tilted himself back in his chair, reviewing the first day in a new job he disliked intensely. He'd shown off like a bastard, he decided. But then, legally he was a bastard. It reminded him he had to visit his mother very shortly.

Seven

Natalia Fedova lived in confused guilt about Eduard. Her son had grown up — until the age of nineteen at least, the last time she had endured his being with her — to be a replica of the father who had abandoned them both when Eduard was barely three years old.

All the bad memories — memories she'd erased from her mind — had been brought back by the official notification of her husband's death, just over a year earlier. Memories of the drunkenness and the beatings and the whoring — he'd been in bed with a prostitute the night she'd actually given birth to Eduard, prematurely — had all flooded back.

But at least, in the first year, he had carried himself with some danger-hinting charm, helped by the dash of a naval officer's uniform. Initial charm was the saving trait that Eduard had failed to inherit. It hadn't been so obvious when he had been at university: none of it had been obvious then. It had all emerged, once he'd joined the officer cadet school: considered himself a man, able to do anything a real man could do. A large-for-his-size, perhaps overly confident teenager had left her. The person who returned from the academy had been an army-coarsened, foul-behaved, even fouler-smelling stranger interested only in the material benefits she could provide. Like the car and the apartment at Mytninskaya which he'd literally invaded with other army cadets as ugly and as frightening as himself and who he said were his friends she had to like. Later they had invaded with their whores when she was away, doing to her carefully maintained home whatever they liked, breaking and smashing and soiling. She shuddered at the last word, insufficient to describe the blood and stains and filth she'd found in her own bed, when she'd returned.

Despite which, despite everything, he was *still* her son, a son she felt — and could never stop feeling — she had abandoned.

She had tried so very hard over the months that now stretched into more than a year, to rationalize how she felt. But never fully succeeded. It was, maybe ridiculously, not enough for her to convince herself of the true situation. That it was Eduard who'd abandoned her: never ever making contact — never a letter, never a telephone call — until he was about to arrive in Moscow. When he needed the things — showing them off to the coterie of grabbing, snickering hangers-on — that her official position could provide. Even those sickening, impossible-to-avoid visits had ceased during her last year at Mytninskaya.

And now she was no longer at Mytninskaya. One of the benefits that went with her promotion

— in a country and a city where there were no longer supposed to be elitist benefits but where there always would be — was a much more opulent, better-equipped and more comfortable apartment originally designated for members of the now discredited Communist Party, on Leninskaya Prospekt.

Without needing a reminder of the time, Natalia went to the chrome-glittered kitchen to begin preparing the baby's bottle: from the window over the disposal-equipped sink she could see the monument to Russia's first astronaut, seemingly so long ago, in terms of history little more than yesterday.

So much of her personal history seemed just like yesterday. And not just the Mytninskaya apartment, with its kitchen fittings so very inferior to this. An apartment she no longer occupied, she remembered, forcing herself to concentrate to get some cohesion into her mind. But the only address Eduard had: the only place he knew where to reach her. Yet it was still controlled by the Russian intelligence service. So this new address would not be divulged if Eduard tried to find her from the old apartment. Would he have tried since she'd left? Inevitably if he'd wanted something. Should she order that he was to be told where she was, if he enquired? Or try to locate him herself? With the power she now had — a degree of power which, after more than a year, she was still sometimes bemused to discover — she should be very quickly able to locate him and his unit or group or whatever it was called.

If he had a unit or a group. All the military had been withdrawn from the satellites and the no longer linked republics: the army was being decimated, destroyed more quickly and effectively than if there had ever been a war. Would Eduard still be *in* the army? He'd enlisted on a commission — not been a conscript — so there would have been some protection, but if the military reductions were anything like those already announced the cutbacks would have gone far beyond, biting deep into the structure of the regular army. Eduard would still be the most junior of officers, even if he had passed the promotion examinations. The most junior of officers would be the first to be dismissed under such reorganization.

Natalia completed the bottle preparation, leaving it to cool until Alexandra awoke. To what would Eduard be dismissed, she asked herself, brutally. Nothing, she knew. No home, no job, no monetary support. Nothing. So he could be one of the destitutes on the streets of Moscow, one of those shuffling, head-bent, sunken-cheeked men whom she drove by each day but never properly saw, or bothered to see, not thinking of them as individual people at all.

Should she agonize about someone who had treated her as badly as Eduard had done: and who would doubtless treat her as badly in the future if they restored contact? It was difficult for her not to. But she didn't *want* Eduard intruding into her life any more. Biologically he was her son, maybe. But nothing more. Therefore hardly enough. She had her own territory: her own peace. She was finally settled. She was in charge of an entire Directorate — perhaps the most *important* Directorate — of the reformed Russian security agency. Untouchable. Secure. There was a quick qualification: untouchable and secure providing she did not give Fyodor Tudin any opportunities. Which she had no intention of doing. And most of all she had Alexandra — always shortened, of course, to Sasha.

A peaceful, settled existence, she determined, letting the reflection run on in a familiar direction. What she *didn't* have, she *couldn't* have: absolutely impossible. And because it was impossible it was easier to live with than her dilemma over Eduard. Not true, she denied herself once more. Not easier to *live* with: easier to confront because there was no possibility of her ever seeing Charlie again. The baby murmured and Natalia got the cooled bottle before picking her from the cot to feed.

'Wonder what Daddy's doing, Sasha? He'd love you very much, if he knew. Be very proud. I know he'd be proud. He told me once he had always been frightened of having a baby but I don't think he would be frightened if he knew about you. No one could be frightened of you.'

Natalia looked up from the contented baby, out into the darkening night enveloping Moscow. How *would* Charlie feel, knowing he had a baby daughter?

John Gower picked up the telephone expectantly on the second ring, smiling in anticipation.

Marcia didn't make any greeting. She just said: 'I'm missing you.'

'I'm missing you, too.'

'Enough to set up house, so we don't have to be apart at all when I'm in London?'

Gower hesitated. 'You win.'

'It isn't a game. Or a battle.'

'I can always kick you out, if we don't get on.'

'Who said we've decided on your place?'

'You can always kick me out,' he said. He had to learn how to be permanently with someone, just as he had to adjust to everything else.

'How's the course?' asked Marcia.

'OK.' His pause was longer than before.

'What sort of course *is* it?'

Another hesitation. 'Difficult to define, really. I suppose it's to see how well I've learned everything else.' Gower wasn't at all sure that was correct, but it was the best he could offer.

'What are the people like?'

It was obvious she would expect there to be a classroom group. 'Odd,' he said, honestly, giving his personal judgement on his instructor with shuffling shoes.

'Like them?'

'Too soon to say.' He'd done what had occurred to him at the first meeting and was apprehensive now at the outcome. Whatever, he knew he'd made the right decision. 'How's it going in Manchester?'

'I've had two invitations to dinner tonight. One guy has a gold tooth and claims he owns a Rolls Royce.'

'Accepted either?'

'Do you want me to?'

'If I said no it would mean I didn't trust you. As I do trust you, I don't think it's my decision.'

'But do you want me to?' she persisted.

'No.'

'I didn't think you would. That's why I refused both.'

It had taken Charlie days of trying to catch the same downward elevator as Julia Robb. She showed no sign of recognition.

'I've been meaning to thank you for the other day.'

'For what?'

'Miller keeps his intercom live, so he can hear what happens in the outside office, doesn't he? Could have been embarrassing for me. So thanks.'

She gave no confirmation but she did smile, very briefly.

'I think I owe you a drink,' pressed Charlie.

'I thought we'd covered all this already?'

'For the benefit of the open intercom.'

Julia smiled more broadly. 'Just for a drink?'

Charlie looked open-faced at the joint personal assistant for both the Director-General and his deputy. 'What else?'

'I'll think about it.'

Sometimes the old tricks were the best, reflected Charlie.

Eight

For long periods — as long as a total of six months on one occasion — Charlie's mother had retreated from any reality, unreachable in total catatonia. It had all changed with the development of new drugs. Now she was invariably brightly alert, chattering constantly, although the senility was still well advanced. The largely one-sided conversations were confused and disjointed, the names of the men of whom she boasted so proudly more imagined than properly remembered any more. That afternoon she'd identified Charlie's father by two different names, neither of whom he believed responsible for his conception and twice called him William instead of Charlie. He remained at the nursing home for an hour, leaving with the usual assurance to come again soon, which he repeated at the matron's office on the way out, without stipulating a positive date: it was automatic for him to avoid creating the most innocent of patterns, even in something as mundane as visiting a bedridden mother suffering Alzheimer's Disease. It was automatic to check the car park for occupied, waiting vehicles when he left. Abruptly he stopped, just as he immediately afterwards consciously avoided the instinctive pursuit check on the twisted and curved road leading from the home.

He didn't have to bother any more. He was no longer active: no longer an operational officer who had always to be alert to everything around him, never able properly to relax. Charlie accepted he was effectively retired: like those sad, mentally eroding people he'd just left, sitting motionless in chairs, living in yesterday.

Charlie took the hire car out on to the main road, coming to the big decision of the day, where to have lunch. There was the Stockbridge hotel which didn't let rooms to the general public ahead of one of Britain's most exclusive fishing clubs. Or a country pub further on. Or wait until he got to London. A country inn, he decided. He still hadn't found anywhere he really liked around the new flat in Primrose Hill: all wine bars and mobile phones that never rang. Charlie had been much more at home south of the Thames: like an animal, knowing its own warren. Denied him now though, even for a casual return visit to the Pheasant with the best pork pies in London, beer from the wood and Islay malt whisky always available.

Was it still denied him? Hadn't he already decided he didn't have to bother, no longer being operational? Yes. No. Confused self-pity, Charlie decided, annoyed. Of course he had to stay away, even for a casual pub visit. There was no doubt — there was proof! — the Russians had located the Vauxhall flat, in the targeting operation that had included Natalia and which he still didn't understand: whatever their failed objective and the now much changed circumstances of Moscow, he couldn't go back.

The inn was alongside the river on which the exclusive club had its rods and which still had some of the best fishing in England, despite — ironically — the pollution of the bankside fish farms breeding trout the size of small whales. The menu insisted the salmon was locally caught so Charlie took a chance. The beer was good — not as good as the Pheasant, but good enough — and he got a seat at an outside table, overlooking the hurrying, insect-swarmed river.

The self-annoyance at thinking as he had about his old apartment at Vauxhall stayed with Charlie, becoming more specifically focused. What the fuck was this self-pity all about? OK, so his pride was hurt. But it *was* an assignment. He was — for the moment or maybe forever — a schoolmaster. Which on the surface he hated. He'd never liked schoolmasters who'd always, in his experience, been bullying bastards. But hadn't he been a bullying bastard in the first encounter with John Gower? Why didn't he properly fulfil, to the absolute best of a personally never doubted ability, the job he'd been given? Which would be to instil the attitude and aptitude always for self-preservation, *by* John Gower, *of* John Gower. To make John Gower as good as he'd been himself, in the past.

Deep within the bar the number of his food order was distantly called, breaking Charlie's reflection while he collected and carried it back to his waterside place: the salmon was properly sized, not a fish farm freak, and tasted earthily fresh. He was outwardly content.

Could he make John Gower — could he make *anyone* — his alter ego? Charlie felt the challenge stir, the self-pity receding further. He didn't know: couldn't know, until he tried. But he determined *to* try: to accept the function he'd been given, maybe still hoping in the far back reaches of his mind that it was only temporary and that he might one day go back on to the active roster. In the meantime he'd give everything he had to turning Gower and whoever else might follow into the best intelligence officers possible.

Having made the positive decision Charlie felt . . . felt what? Illogically the emotion seemed to be relief, which didn't make any sense but was the closest description he could find. Even more illogical, it seemed that only now, on a Hampshire river bank in the early spring sunshine, picking his way through a perfect fish, had he properly realized what he'd been ordered to do. Not properly realized: properly *accepted*, professionally putting all his pride and resentment aside to start thinking like the teacher he had become. He would genuinely try to teach John Gower everything he'd ever learned in a bruised and battered life in the very specialized art of saving his ass. Or at least not getting his ass too badly burned.

Charlie had intentionally introduced a day's gap

before his next contact with Gower, hoping for something to emerge from his initial encounter with the man. There was nothing official from the ninth floor when he got into his office the following day, and Charlie was disappointed, although he supposed it was too much to expect it to have happened the first time. He still wished it had.

It was not until late into the afternoon, gone four, that the summons came from Patricia Elder. It was a different suit today, blue, but still severely businesslike. The greying hair seemed neater than the last time, and Charlie guessed she'd had it cut again. He still thought it was a mistake. The new shortness made even more pronounced the already strong features that didn't need accentuating. There were still the two flower arrangements, although the blooms had been changed: they looked fresh. There were no folders on this occasion.

'You seemed to find a lot to write about, after just one meeting with Gower,' she said at once.

'It's a new job: I'm not sure what's expected of me.'

'The best you can do.' The black eyes bored into him.

Bitch, thought Charlie. 'I considered it a security lapse, instructors at training facilities disclosing their names. Don't you?'

The woman lowered her head, in unspeaking concession. 'I have already issued a memorandum, correcting it in future.'

'How long has it been allowed? How long has it gone on?'

There was another head movement. 'I've begun an inquiry into that, too.'

'There'll be a lot of lying. You'll never get an accurate figure. If I were you I'd try to find out the other way around: enquire from officers who have passed out in . . .' Charlie hesitated, seeking a sensible period. '. . . maybe the last four or five years.'

Patricia Elder sighed. 'I've gone back six years.'

'Good,' said Charlie, feeling satisfied.

'I am impressed, if that's what you want to hear.'

'It's not,' said Charlie, which wasn't completely true: he *was* trying to impress this woman who for the moment had power over him. 'What about Personnel bandying your name all over the place?'

'Reprimands have been issued. It won't happen again.'

'You having every single memorandum checked, since you took up your appointment?'

'*I'm* not the person you're supposed to be training!'

Charlie noted, pleased, that there was no outrage in the protest. 'I sent a third memorandum.'

'I read it.'

'And?' Charlie prompted.

'According to the security log, your meeting with John Gower ended at 3.39 pm. I received that afternoon a memorandum from John Gower timed at 4.20 pm, warning me that you had ad-

85

vised him, in the event of hostile interrogation, to disclose the names of every one of the instructors who had allowed him to know their identity, my own identity, and the location of this building.'

Charlie smiled, broadly, in increasing satisfaction. 'That's excellent! Did he make any recommendation? Suggest I was a security risk?'

Patricia Elder frowned, coming slightly forward over her desk. 'Was that what it was? A test you set up, to see if he would respond?'

'Of course it was a test!' said Charlie. 'And he passed it.'

'What if he hadn't reported you?'

'It would have put a doubt in my mind of his ever completely becoming the sort of officer he should.'

'Would you have disclosed the information, under forced interrogation?'

'Every one.'

'You *really* mean that?'

'Of course I mean it. If instructors are stupid enough to let their names be known, it's their fault if they get a hostile file created on them. If security here is so lax your name is openly used on memoranda, then your identity deserves to become public knowledge as well. And what I told him about this place is true: this address is probably on lavatory walls in outer Mongolia. Why should anyone with their balls in a vice suffer more than they have to, because there aren't professionals back here training them?'

'The old Cold War warrior!' mocked the woman. 'And I'm not sure people get their balls put in a vice during interrogation any more.'

Charlie wasn't offended by the sarcasm. 'They will, if the interrogators think there's something important enough to find out. And you agree with me about poor security: if you hadn't, you wouldn't have ordered the tightening up you've already told me about.' Charlie wasn't sure but he thought she was colouring slightly, as if she were embarrassed at being so easily caught out.

'So it's begun well!' she said, briskly, wanting to move the conversation on.

'Well enough.'

'Any idea how long it's going to take?'

'Not yet,' frowned Charlie. 'There's no hurry, is there?'

'None whatsoever,' smiled the woman.

In one of those illogicalities of Chinese life to which Jeremy Snow had long ago become accustomed there was no *luxingshe* tourist bureau on Zhengzhou station, even though it was a large terminus. The first station official claimed not to know where the Jasmine Hotel was: from the direction from a second, it seemed too far to walk. Snow took a pedicab, instantly immersed in a shoal of bicycles weaving and darting all around him: just like the fish of which they reminded him, they always appeared on the point of disastrous collision but never quite hit each other. He saw that several riders were wearing pollution masks and wondered if he would soon have to use his.

Li Dong Ming was sitting patiently in the hotel foyer when Snow arrived, hurrying forward the moment the priest identified himself to the receptionist. There was no smile of greeting from the official escort, just the vaguest of bows. The spectacles added to the expression of seriousness: the man's ears stuck out as prominently as they had appeared in the photograph provided in Beijing. He was extremely short, hardly more than 5′ tall, creating an almost ludicrous comparison between their respective heights.

The dormitory that had been allocated was small, fitted with only two beds.

'I have the other one,' said Li. 'It seemed best, don't you think?' He had to strain to talk to the priest.

'Yes,' said Snow, not quite sure to what he was agreeing.

Nine

The next session began well. Everything Gower wore was subdued. The shirt was plain white, with no monogram, the tie a bland blue and the chain-store suit nondescript. He'd left off the signet ring. He continued to call Charlie 'sir'. Charlie supposed the man had to address him in some way.

Charlie carefully chose the centre at Berkshire where he knew Gower had *not* been instructed: he didn't want identification by association from instructors careless of security.

Charlie selected the motorway route. After half a mile he demanded the number of vehicles Gower had overtaken since they'd joined and which cars that had been behind from the beginning were still close.

'Someone's following! It's a test!' exclaimed Gower, snatching a series of hurried looks into the rear-view mirror.

'Soon it isn't going to be training. When you're operational and it's got to be an automatic reflex to check. And check and check again. You've *always* got to know what's happening around you.'

'Even when I'm not on assignment.'

'*Always,*' insisted Charlie. He wasn't happy with

the slight head movement of disbelief from the other man.

'Are we being followed?'

'You tell me.'

Gower was silent for several moments. Then he admitted: 'I don't know how to identify pursuit in this sort of circumstance.'

Charlie was glad Gower's admission hadn't taken longer: the turn-off was already indicated. 'Slow, into the inside lane. Mark the cars behind. And those ahead, too. In a moving vehicle it's as easy to watch a target from the front as from the back; all you need to do is maintain speed.'

Gower did as he was instructed, nervously checking both directions. 'I take the turn-off?'

'Don't indicate until the very last moment: without a warning you can lose anyone in front. Take the turn. See who's behind you . . .' There was a protesting blare of a horn from the rear at the lateness of the indication. 'Fuck him,' dismissed Charlie. 'Get on to the roundabout underneath the motorway: here's your learning point. Everywhere in the world major highway slip-roads go into roundabouts from which there's always another slip-road to rejoin as well as leave. Go completely around . . . watch your back. Anyone?'

'A red Ford . . . no, he's turned off.'

'Now go up the connecting link to get back on to the motorway in the same direction we were originally going.'

'What about a real operational situation? What

should I do if a recognizable car stays with me?'

'Abort,' declared Charlie. 'But sensibly. Don't panic and go dashing back to where you started: panic is proof of guilt. If it had been operational, we'd have taken the next turn-off to whatever reasonably sized town was signposted. That would have been an explanation for the first suspicious manoeuvre: we'd made a mistake and came off too early. Every town has something historical it's proud of. We'd have been tourists, looking at the sites. After which we would have made our way back leisurely.'

'And then?'

'I told you. Abort.'

'Abandon an assignment?' Gower seemed surprised.

Charlie frowned across the car at the other man. 'What's the alternative? Leading whoever is watching you to whatever that assignment is?'

'That seems . . .' began Gower slowly, searching how to explain himself. Charlie talked across him. 'What was the final thing I said to you at the last meeting?'

'Something . . .' Gower stopped abruptly, suspecting another test and remembering the instruction to recall everything, word for word. 'I asked if what we were doing had a title. You said "It's called survival." '

Charlie smiled, pleased. 'If you as much as think an operation is blown get out: save yourself and maybe the operation. Let someone else come in after you to take it over . . .' Charlie saw the other man prepare to speak. 'That's not failing: giving up. That's being professional.'

'It's not been explained to me like that before.'

'For Christ's sake lose your public school pretension. You haven't joined a club your father put you down for at birth. Road-sweepers and refuse-collectors go around the streets, picking up the shit and muck that people cause. Our job is picking up the shit and muck that governments and countries cause.' He remembered virtually the same exchange with Patricia Elder: she hadn't appeared to accept it.

Gower took the proper turning off the motorway, heading into Berkshire.

'Isn't there some inverted snobbery there somewhere?'

'Complete objectivity,' insisted Charlie. Not completely true, he conceded. Always a problem: always a self-admitted fault. He was uncomfortable the inherent attitude had shown through.

At the creeper-clad Georgian mansion they had to sign in at a reception desk to one side of the huge entrance hall. The straight-backed man who recorded their arrival would have medals at home, guessed Charlie, recalling Patricia Elder's threat: being a teacher was definitely better than being part of the security staff at a safe house. Charlie chose a preparation time of fifteen minutes, ignoring Gower's questioning look, leading the way into a small but immaculately maintained drawing-room.

There was a bowl of roses on a piano set in

the larger of two window areas, with a low table and two easy chairs to the right. There was an arrangement of magazines on the table. Near the door was an open-fronted display case, showing a series of miniature porcelain figurines set out on the shelves. There was a spray of dried flowers filling the cold fireplace. At either end of an elaborately carved marble mantelpiece there were porcelain statues of red-coated Georgian military figures. Between the figures there was a porcelain-cased clock, the bottom half-glassed to show the wheeled movement. A large couch fronted the fireplace, with matching chairs either side. A padded leather fender sealed off the fireplace, with a magazine lodged on one corner. There were two bookcases, one open, one glass-doored and closed, to the left. The open bookcase had a protruding reading ledge. There were books on it, one lying open. A telephone stood on an adjacent glass-topped table. The curtains in the second window annex were draped almost to meet at the top of the rail, looping down practically to the floor. They were held back by plaited crimson cords.

'Room intrusion!' recognized Gower.

'Standard rules,' acknowledged Charlie. 'It's a room you've been allocated, possible in unfriendly surroundings. You occupy it briefly, then leave. You've got to itemize the indications of it having been searched.'

Gower walked carefully around the room just once before announcing that everything was registered in his mind and that he was ready. They left the room for the ex-army duty officer to go through the pretence of a search. When the man recalled them, Gower repeated the examination he'd made to imprint everything in his mind but this time turned back on himself, retracing the route to return to the centre, by the couch. He missed ten items that had been rearranged by the duty officer.

'Shit!' said Gower, viciously, when they were pointed out to him.

'Your advantage was knowing there had *been* some rearrangement: you'll never know that for certain, in a genuine situation,' lectured Charlie. 'Your mistake was looking for the probable tricks. Play your own. Leave something ajar when you leave a room. A searcher invariably *closes* a door, after looking to see what's inside. You can even extend it. In a hotel room you'll have a suitcase, which would have to be looked at by anyone going through your things. Leave one lock secure, the other one open, and remember the sequence. Again it's instinctive for anyone looking through to resecure the locks. Keep that in mind if you're *doing* the searching: always remember what's open and what's closed.'

'I missed too much,' insisted Gower.

'In an operational situation you only have to realize *one* thing is out of place to know you've been turned over. You're not expected to score a hundred per cent.'

Charlie took the duty officer's recommendation

of a pub with outside tables in an orchard with chickens running free, pecking at the fallen apples. Gower ordered beer, like Charlie, and drank with obvious enjoyment. Charlie eased his shoes off. Each was well into the first pint when Gower said suddenly: 'I'm quite nervous, you know.'

Charlie frowned across the rough wood table. 'About what?'

'The job. What it will be like. Because that's the trouble: there's no way of knowing what it will be like, is there? Not *really* like. I wish I wasn't. Nervous, I mean.'

'I'm glad you are,' said Charlie. 'It gives you the right edge. I've never known an over-confident intelligence officer who was good at his job.'

'You were operational?'

Charlie swallowed at the use of the past tense, nodding again.

'Tell me what it's like!'

At once aware of the man's need, Charlie said: 'There are some generalities. You'll usually be working alone. So you'll be lonely: miserable. It's not uncommon, if you are sent in to a foreign capital, to be ordered to keep away from the embassy, to avoid it becoming compromised if anything goes wrong. If you *are* attached in any way to an overseas embassy, you'll be unwelcome: diplomats are always frightened of people like us. You'll make mistakes. A lot of the things you'll be sent to do won't work: most don't, in fact. A success rate of twenty per cent is excellent.'

'A failure rate that high isn't going to look good on a personnel record.'

'Hold it, now!' cautioned Charlie, glad of the conversation. 'We're back to public school now, without the pretensions. Don't *ever* look upon what you're doing like it earns high or low marks to be totted up for a good end-of-term report.

'Always remember an operation aborted or simply walked away from is better than a diplomatic incident that requires ministerial apologies to foreign governments and statements in the House of Commons. If anything goes wrong, you'll be disowned: become a non-person.'

'You're not painting a very pretty picture,' complained Gower.

Charlie had to put his shoes back on to go inside the pub for more drinks. When he returned to the table he didn't immediately sit. Standing over Gower he said: 'It isn't a pretty picture. Ever. It's not even exciting. Nine times out of ten it's boring, dull routine: checking files or official registers, conning your way past officialdom, trying to make sense out of nonsense.'

'You married?' demanded Gower, suddenly. He held up both hands, in a shielding gesture. 'All right! I know it's a personal question, which isn't allowed. But it's important to me.'

Charlie hesitated, finally sitting down. 'I was once.'

'Divorced?'

Charlie shook his head. 'She was killed.'

'I didn't mean to bring up unpleasant memories.'

'It's OK,' said Charlie, which was a lie. It would never be OK: there would always be the guilt that Edith had intentionally put herself between him and the gun of the deranged CIA official whom he'd exposed in retribution for an earlier joint-service decision to sacrifice him. The long-ago time of the Cold War, recalled Charlie, without any nostalgia: it had been an actual crossing through the Berlin Wall, with final proof of a Russian espionage ring operating out of London. 'Why's it important for you to know?'

'How can you live with someone — get married, have kids — without ever telling them what you really do?' demanded Gower. 'It's got to be unnatural: impossible. People talk about their jobs. Go to the firm's events, stuff like that. How can you go through life living a lie with someone whom you're supposed to love? Cheating them all the time?'

Charlie sighed. 'When I married my wife she was the personal assistant to the Director-General: she knew what I did. Her knowing made it more difficult. Whenever I was away on assignment, she went through hell.'

'You saying it goes beyond security: that it's better if a wife doesn't know?'

'*Are* you married?'

'Not yet. There is a girl.'

'I'm saying it's something everyone has to work out for themselves.' Charlie paused. 'Any of your

97

illustrious other instructors teach you properly how to lie?'

Gower gazed back at Charlie across the table. 'No!' he said, close to indignation.

Charlie sighed again. 'Christ, I've got an awful lot to teach you, haven't I?'

The transfer of much of the KGB to the Russian Federation after the Commonwealth of Independent States was formed from the old Soviet Union meant that as the head of the old First Chief Directorate Natalia Fedora inherited practically intact the entire overseas network of the renamed external security agency. And a lot more responsibility besides.

In addition to what she had controlled in the past it was now necessary to have intelligence facilities in the former satellite countries like Poland and Hungary and Czechoslovakia of whose intelligence services the KGB was no more the overall controller, but instead despised, no longer accepted interlopers. Added to which was the need to establish completely new networks in the republics of the new Commonwealth, now technically foreign sovereign states in which any legacy of the old KGB which once ruled them by terror was not merely despised but considered criminal intrusion.

The only practical way for Natalia to run such a sprawling empire was to delegate, which she did both to create the service she wanted and, equally important, in the hope of forestalling any danger from Fyodor Tudin, whom she objectively regarded as an enemy whose every move had to be anticipated and watched, at all times.

She had appointed the man head of the Commonwealth republics division. It was unarguably a prestige position of real and proper power, impossible for Tudin, one of the few old guard KGB survivors, to perceive as a demeaning secondary post. So demanding was the creation and supervision of such a division that Natalia intended the man to be occupied to the exclusion of everything else, certainly any conspiracy against her.

But Fyodor Tudin was a resourceful and energetic man, a very bad enemy to have.

Walter Foster was surprised the query had come by wire and not in the diplomatic bag, because there didn't seem any reason for urgency. And airline-carried diplomatic mail only normally took two days between London and Beijing. The resident intelligence liaison officer shrugged, long ago having given up trying to make sense from a very great deal of what London asked.

It was a short reply, taking him only minutes to encode. Because the message had come by wire, it was regulations that he reply by the same route. That also took only minutes.

His message said: *Hunter journey ends two weeks.*

The following day the *People's Daily* carried a leading article threatening the strongest measures against foreign interventionists fomenting counter-revolution within the country.

Ten

Li stayed closer to Jeremy Snow than a second skin. In every hotel the reservation was for a shared, two-occupancy room. Always Li chose as their restaurant setting small, two-place tables away from any chance encounter with other Chinese. The man invariably positioned himself on buses or trains to create a physical barrier between Snow and other passengers. The initial morning in Zhengzhou — and at every subsequent hotel — he accompanied the priest to the communal shower facilities, outside the washing cubicle when Snow entered, damply on duty when Snow emerged. No conversation between them was ever interrupted by Snow needing a lavatory: every time, Li seemed to feel the same need and occupied the adjoining space. He waited dutifully outside of lavatory cubicles. Each day he offered to dispatch any correspondence Snow wanted sent during their journey, while they travelled. Each day Snow said he did not intend to send any. Li kept asking.

It was Li who established the regime for their conversations: Mandarin when they were sufficiently away from the possibility of other Chinese joining in, English when they were among people, but loudly spoken and with many official references, proclaiming his escort function to create the block against the frequent Chinese eagerness to practise the language with a foreigner. At the beginning in Zhengzhou, Snow had feared the usual approach from money-changers, convinced from the outset that Li would have summoned a plainclothes policeman or detained the man himself, but so obvious was Li's authority that they were never once solicited.

Li was also a diligent questioner, but too eager. The man started, with seeming innocence, by praising Snow's command of Chinese but alerted Snow at once by asking why he had perfected the language and why he was in China. In Beijing, which had appointed Li his escort, all those details were listed on his Foreign Ministry accreditation, to which the Chinese would have had access.

Because they *were* known, Snow talked easily of being a priest — even of his particular Order — but quickly insisted on his contentment at currently teaching English.

'How can you be content, having abandoned your calling?'

'I believe the need for what I am doing now is as much a calling,' said Snow, wishing he had a stronger answer.

Li missed the opportunity to press the point, instead trying to hurry a comparison between Western theology and Mao's version of Marxist-Leninist philosophy. Snow agreed that religion was a philosophy sometimes obscured by complicated mysticism but asked in return if the two

101

thousand years of Western religion and the even longer Confucian, Buddhist and Taoist philosophies in China hadn't proved more durable than the communism now abandoned in the Soviet Union and its former satellites. From someone so clearly — so proudly — a Party zealot, Snow expected the recorded-message response of Mao's interpretation being the pure creed to continue forever, not the corrupted doctrine of self-serving criminals in Moscow. Instead Li accepted that Christianity and Confucianism and Buddism and Taoism were formidable persuasions to be respected, pointing out that the three Asian philosophies were recognized in China, as was Catholicism. Snow considered making the point that Confucian and Buddhist and Taoist temples existed more as tourist attractions than as places of worship. He was glad of his restraint when Li asked, still in open-faced innocence, if Snow believed communism was a philosophy as doomed in China as everywhere else. Snow at once insisted he was apolitical. Li abandoned the conversation, as if it were of no importance, but tried to reintroduce it on four further occasions, each time phrasing differently the questions which, responded to wrongly, could have brought against Snow accusations of a counter-revolutionary attitude. Snow did not once respond wrongly.

By the second day of their travelling together Snow accepted that Li was assembling a file upon him. He confronted the awareness without undue concern: Father Robertson had openly warned of such a possibility, when Snow had talked of being officially escorted for more than half the journey. Snow believed he handled the personal questioning as smoothly as he had everything else, disclosing nothing he did not think the authorities already knew and had on record about him. Li expertly extracted the information by comparison, offering facts about himself to get responses from Snow, and although the priest was not sure Li would ever become someone of sufficient importance he mentally created a matching file on the Chinese, in the event of his emerging at any level in the Gong An Ju security service, to which he was convinced the man aspired if he was not an already overly enthusiastic member.

It transpired that they were the same age. Li volunteered an education at Shanghai University, identifying himself as the only son of parents who dutifully obeyed the government edict on the correct size of the family unit. Snow ignored the invitation to criticize the penalty-enforced method of Chinese birth-control, saying that he, too, was an only child. He avoided disclosing that his now dead father had been a general whose career culminated as NATO second-in-command of land-based forces in Europe, knowing that would elevate the importance of whatever information Li was gathering upon him. Li said he was married, with a son of three: it would, of course, be the only child he and his wife would consider having. When Snow said priests in his Order did not marry, the Chinese nodded and remarked that celibacy was a Buddhist tenet as well. It was after that particular exchange that Li made one of his other attempts to get an ill-considered response from Snow about the future of Chinese communism. Snow completed his file on the other man by manipulating a typical vacation photograph session, posing the escort in three different settings in Anqing, around the middle of the tour. Li responded at once, producing from a rucksack a camera of which Snow had, until that moment, been unaware. The Chinese seemed to have a problem getting someone of Snow's height into the frame, bending and twisting for a final elevation.

Snow had given the authorities in Beijing a vacation as the reason for his travelling throughout the country, and although it would also have been listed on the paperwork held by Li the Chinese still asked, in more than one way and on more than one occasion, why Snow was making such an extensive tour. Snow said that he saw it as essential to his teaching work in China to travel as widely as possible, to increase his understanding and perfect his command of the language. It was the cue for another entrapment attempt. Li asked openly — his first crude demand — if Snow saw his work as converting people to his faith. Snow insisted he did not live and work in China to practise as a priest but as a teacher of English. His faith was his own: he did not seek to preach it to others. What did he do if someone asked about his religion? Explain it. To convert? To reply to a question. How many people had asked for an explanation during his current journey? None. Was he disappointed? He felt nothing to be disappointed about: the purpose of his journey was to see and better understand the country and this he was doing. He was not a practising priest. Li industriously cleaned his spectacles, a gesture which over the course of several days Snow had come to recognize as a mark of frustration at having failed in whatever he was trying to achieve.

And Snow won, succeeding — although not to the degree of detail he would have wanted, such as developing another source like Zhang Su Lin — in his information-gathering mission. He had not expected to, in the first two days of their meeting in Zhengzhou. During those early days he had, in fact, been despondent at the control he was now under, refusing to weigh the undeniable successes before he'd met Li against the futility of achieving anything worthwhile afterwards.

And then he realized Li would identify for him anything he wanted to isolate as officially restricted, in any of the closed areas through which they moved.

All he had to do was ask.

If Li agreed, then where Snow wanted to go did *not* have anything the authorities wanted to keep hidden. If Li refused, it *was* a specifically designated high-security area, the best possible map coordinates of which were memorized or actually written down, in confused or apparently meaningless fashion, in the journal Snow was officially keeping of his travels, to be passed on to Walter Foster on his return to Beijing, possibly for some satellite aerial reconnaissance if the information was considered sufficiently interesting to be pursued further.

It was nevertheless exhausting, particularly with a companion who never relaxed the intrusive personal interrogation or the ambiguous, incriminating-reply questions. Snow visited copy-book communes epitomizing the Beijing government's successful marriage of communism to the private enterprise system which gave the country its economic strength, visits which Snow judged not to be an entire waste of time, hopeful of their being of some interest in London. He visited another private enterprise pottery and three agricultural centres boasting self-sufficient rice harvest for a vast area. He politely admired two bicycle manufacturing plants, and was properly respectful in four Buddhist temples the only occupants of which, besides themselves, were monks who seemed surprised to see any visitors, one mosque and an archeological site which Li claimed to be the remains of one of the first Confusian meditation centres in China. Someone had chipped 'J. W. Iowa. 1987' in one of the larger stones. Snow wondered how the graffiti carver had been able to finish his meaningless memorial before being arrested.

But at the same time Snow collected his information from the unsuspecting official escort.

There was an area to the south-east of Wuhan, in the direction of Echeng, that Li said was impossible to visit, using a hastily concocted excuse of transport difficulties. The man went to extraordinary trouble ensuring they took a night train to Tongling, from which Snow inferred there to be something of interest that could be seen from the line: the first hour of the journey was in fading daylight, narrowing the location, and Li became agitated near Huangmei, as they were passing what appeared to be a large factory complex brightly illuminated by its own lights. At Tongling Snow suggested a Sunday cruise on the Yangtze. Li was adamant they take a boat northwards down the river. From the timetable Snow calculated the southerly boats sailed for a total of two hours, before returning, from which he estimated whatever it was Li did not want him to see was between Tongling and Huaining. Shanghai, where Snow planned to remain for three days, was not officially restricted and he was initially intrigued that Li did not leave him there. On their first full day Li pressed for a trip inland, which Snow refused. In the afternoon, on a walk along the Bund, the historic road bordering the Huanpu River, Snow counted a flotilla of warships, three with what appeared to be extremely sophisticated radar and electronic equipment visible on their superstructures. Snow managed four photographs. Again he was matched by the rapidly snapping Li.

Throughout the trip Li had steadfastly insisted

upon a precise division of every expenditure, but on their last night together Snow demanded to be the host for dinner. As always, Li sat them at a table that could only be occupied by two.

'It has been a successful tour?' asked Li.

'Extremely interesting.' Snow was curious at the report the man would submit. He had little doubt by now that Li was a member of the Public Security Bureau: if he was, he had to be one of their best informers. The closeness with which his movements had been monitored was something he should also report upon, to Foster, although he was personally sure he had avoided all suspicion. He'd try to make contact with the embassy man as soon as he got back: he was excited by what he had to pass on. 'You are returning to Beijing?'

'I am meeting a party of American tourists here in Shanghai. They are going south, as far as Tunxi.'

The reason for Li remaining with him, accepted Snow. Quickly he realized a possible benefit. 'So many rail journeys,' he suggested, hopefully.

'We are travelling by car,' disclosed Li.

Something else to pass on. Car hire was only possible for foreign visitors in China with a driver and a guide to determine the route. What was there on the road to Tunxi that had to be avoided? 'You must miss your family?'

'I will see them again in ten days.'

Snow determined to put the limit into his account as well: the driving time to Tunxi could be estimated, so the length of any detour might be possible to calculate. 'Perhaps we will meet again, if I make another vacation tour?'

'You intend travelling again?' demanded Li, alertly.

Snow regretted the careless remark. 'I am always anxious to extend my understanding of China.'

'You see your life being here?'

It was a personally intriguing question, conceded Snow. China was his first posting and he hadn't ever imagined another. Father Robertson had to be in his sixties and should be withdrawn, although Snow suspected the old man wanted to die in the country in which he had served all his life. 'I will remain as long as I think I can help China,' said Snow.

'Are you happy here?'

Another intriguing question. Snow did not honestly know if he was happy or not: spiritually he was content, but to himself he admitted there was still sometimes a tug of apprehension about his other activities. 'Very much so.'

'Isn't the philosophy of China in direct contradiction to your beliefs?'

Persistently trying until the very end, thought Snow. 'My beliefs sustain me, as yours sustain you. I do not make a comparison. My vocation here now is as a teacher, as I have already made clear.'

'I detect some satisfaction in your attitude at the collapse of communism in the Soviet Union?'

This was verging upon desperation, decided Snow. And was pleased: it had to confirm that he had not committed any indiscretion with which Li felt he could colour his report. 'Then I have expressed myself wrongly. I have no satisfaction about that. The population of the Soviet Union have chosen a different method of government. That is their decision.'

'No opinion at all of your own?'

'My opinion is that people are free to make their own choice on how and under what authority they choose to live.'

'Some counter-revolutionaries claim the people of China are *not* free to choose how they live.'

Snow decided he could be straying into a conversational minefield if he allowed himself to become ensnared in such a direct debate. 'Do they?' he said. And stopped.

Li stared across the restaurant table, waiting for Snow to continue. The priest busied himself with his rice bowl and when that was empty made much of refilling his teacup. Li had refused wine.

'Do you?' pressed Li, finally.

'Do I what?' questioned Snow, not finding it difficult to convey the false misunderstanding.

'Consider that the population of China is not free to choose how it lives?'

Snow fixed the frown. 'To believe such a thing would surely make *me* a counter-revolutionary! Which we both know I am not.' For the first time, in any of their fencing conversations, Snow thought he detected an angry tightening of the other man's face. The spectacles came off once again, for a disgruntled polish.

'From someone trained as a priest I would have expected judgements.'

'A priest who is now a teacher.'

'Have you abandoned your God?'

'Of course not. It is not my function here to be a priest.'

'You live in the temple of your faith.'

'Church,' corrected Snow. 'By the instructions of the Chinese government, who wish us to act as caretakers. It is no longer used for religious purposes.'

'I would be interested to see your temple.'

Suspecting a reason for Li's remark, Snow said: 'I do not, of course, conduct my classes in the church. They're in a quite separate building.'

'Do you pray with your class?' demanded the man, confirming Snow's suspicion.

'Never,' replied Snow. 'They only come to learn English.' There had only ever been one Zhang Su Lin.

'No one has ever asked about your religion, knowing you are a priest? Able to see you live in a temple, like other priests do?'

If he answered honestly — that some had — Snow guessed he would be asked their names, if not now then later in Beijing. 'Never,' he insisted, strong-voiced.

Li regarded him with open disbelief. 'Maybe I will come one day.'

Snow answered the look, unflinchingly. Father

Robertson would regard any visit as hostile interest from the authorities — which it might well be — and be thrown into panic. With no alternative, Snow repeated: 'You will be very welcome.'

'So we will probably meet again,' said Li, increasing Snow's discomfort.

'It would be my pleasure,' lied the priest.

Natalia finally gave way to her conscience, which she'd always known she would, and when she made the decision she became irritated at herself for needlessly delaying it. With so much authority at her unquestioned disposal, it only took two days to discover Eduard's complete military record. After Baku — the last posting she had known about — her son had served briefly in Latvia and after that had been assigned to East Germany. It was there he had been promoted to lieutenant. His had been one of the last units to be withdrawn, after the reunification of Germany. His final posting, before the premature discharge brought about by the reduction in the armed forces, had been in Novomoskovsk. Eduard's record listed one commendation and four convictions for drunkenness. His character was assessed as superior, an average classification. His Moscow address was given as the Mytninskaya apartment Natalia no longer occupied. The new occupants had been there for over a year: no one resembling Eduard whose photograph they were shown, had come there during that time believing it to be her home.

Natalia got up from her desk after receiving the report of the Mytninskaya enquiry, going to the window to gaze out in the direction of the city, wondering where her lost son was now. She'd tried, Natalia told herself. But Eduard hadn't made any attempt to find her. So there was nothing more she could do. Or wanted to do. About Eduard at least.

How difficult would it be to find someone else: someone she wanted to see more than anyone else in the world?

Eleven

Gower was adamant they spend the weekend in Paris, calling it an anniversary of the time they had been living together. Both privately felt varying degrees of relief at how happy they were, although accepting it was ridiculously too soon to judge. Marcia still had to surrender the lease of her apartment.

Gower booked the George V, a room with an avenue view, and announced they were tourists. So they watched the promenade along the Champs-Elysées from a pavement table at Fouquet's, cruised in a *bateau mouche* along the floodlit Seine on the Saturday evening and later ate at L'Archistrate. Marcia said she didn't think they had that much to celebrate. Gower said they did. He was hopeful the excitement of the trip would provide the opportunity he wanted.

'You've changed,' she declared, suddenly. They'd finished the meal but were lingering over brandy bowls, with their coffee.

'It's just because you're getting to know me properly.'

'There's a definite change.'

Gower shifted, disconcerted, using one of the many tricks he'd so recently been taught to avoid the impression of guilt, gazing directly at her but with a mocking frown, remembering to answer any accusation with a question. 'Changed how?'

Marcia shrugged, disturbing the flowing blonde hair she was that night wearing loose to her shoulders: Gower thought she looked magnificent. 'I can't put it in words. It's . . .' The girl came to a halt. 'Your clothes, for a start. It's as if you're dressing down. *Are* you dressing down, for some reason?'

'You're imagining it!' Confronting uncertain points with ridicule was another dictum. Gower didn't feel any difficulty, practising the lessons upon Marcia. It wasn't cheating or misusing her: it followed the most repeated instruction, always to behave as if he were on duty until the denying innocence became instinctive.

'Why aren't you wearing the ring your father gave you?'

'No reason,' shrugged Gower.

'And I liked the moustache.'

'I didn't.'

Marcia swirled the brandy in her glass. 'And there's an attitude. It's like . . .' There was another pause. 'Like you're more confident . . . you seem to do things now with more self-assurance. I know that sounds silly, but that's the only way I can explain it.'

Hadn't he been warned about the danger of overconfidence? In an operational situation, Gower reminded himself: he was sure, after so much lecturing and so many practical demonstrations from the man who still remained nameless, that he wouldn't make the mistake on an assignment. He wasn't really surprised by what Marcia had said. He *did* feel more confident: surer than he had been before about the profession he had chosen, despite the warnings about loneliness and boredom and sometimes fear. 'It's because we're together all the time now. What's wrong with being confident, anyway?'

'Nothing,' she agreed. 'I like it. Makes me feel comfortable.'

This had to be the opportunity he'd sought by coming to Paris, hopefully to satisfy Marcia about the abrupt absences that were inevitable in the future. The hotel was superb and they'd already made love twice that day: she'd be lulled now, relaxed by being in such a restaurant, part of the romance of Paris. Embarking cautiously, Gower said: 'I think this last training course will be over soon.'

'You haven't talked much about it.'

'It's been interesting,' he said, generally. 'Ironing out the final points, really. Could be that administration won't be as boring as we thought it might be.'

Marcia finished her brandy, looking curiously across the table at him. 'Like what?'

She was responding exactly as he'd hoped. 'Seems I'm in line for the section that deals with embassies abroad: I might have to travel a bit, from time to time.'

'I always thought overseas embassies were autonomous?'

'They are, most of the time. It would be ir-regular.'

'How long would you be away? Weeks? Months?'

Gower didn't want to get involved in too many specifics: her acceptance had to be gradual. 'It would vary.' He hesitated, deciding against suggesting there could even be a permanent attachment. There was time for that later: there was the far more important point to establish in her mind.

'I hope it isn't too often.' She smiled. 'Or too long. I'm getting to like having you around.'

Gower recognized the invitation in her final remark but he ignored it. 'So I guess I'll be going through the big ceremony in the next week or so.'

'What big ceremony?'

'Swearing and signing the Official Secrets Act.'

'Secrets!' She frowned, head to one side, half-smiling as if anticipating a joke.

'I'm joining the Foreign Office, darling! It's routine to have to sign the Act.' Which was quite true, so there was no lie upon which he could be caught out. Another lesson: a good liar only ever lies to the barest minimum.

'It all sounds very dramatic.'

'It's not really.' He gestured for the bill. It was larger than he'd calculated but the setting had turned out to be perfect for the hurdle he believed he was crossing easily, so it had been worth it.

'Why is it necessary to swear to an Act?'

'I'll come into contact with information and facts that are classified: things I can't talk about.'

'Not even to me?' she demanded, in mock offence.

'I can hardly imagine you'd be interested in any case. It'll probably be dull statistics.' He paid, smiling his thanks to the head waiter. It had all gone exceptionally well: she'd accepted without as much questioning as he'd anticipated the thought of his unexpectedly going abroad, and with the truthful explanation of the Official Secrets Act he had a shield behind which he could hide if ever she became persistently curious.

'So you're going to keep things from me!' she said as they reached the vestibule leading out into the rue de Varenne, pretending still to be offended.

'Nothing important that will ever affect you and me,' promised Gower, taking her opening.

They set out walking unhurriedly towards the Dôme des Invalides, the Eiffel Tower illuminated in the far distance. Marcia clung to his arm, pulling herself close to him. Not thinking any longer of the talk he had orchestrated between them or of how successful it had been, Gower said: 'Nothing is going to stop it being like this always.'

Marcia stopped, bringing Gower to a halt beside her, determined in her slight drunkenness to emphasize what she was going to say. 'I'm never, ever, going to keep a secret from you! I love you so much I want you to know everything.'

At last Gower felt a flicker of unease at deceiving her, trying quickly to erase it. He'd *had* to do it, he tried to convince himself. Nothing he would have to keep from her would affect their personal relationship anyway. Better for her to know virtually nothing than everything and go through hell every time he went off on an assignment. Hadn't that been another lecture?

Snow knew that with so much information to pass on and even more to discuss it was essential for there to be a personal meeting between himself and Foster, although there was no close enough event on the British embassy calendar to use to cover the encounter. So it had to be governed by the system for emergency contact established by Foster.

The marker point was the Taoist temple to the west of the Forbidden City, a run-down area of lean-to food stalls and skeletal flower booths. It was because of the flower-sellers that Foster had selected the spot. The day after his arrival back in Beijing Snow went there to purchase a spray of meagre chrysanthemums, carefully selecting only four orange blooms in the bunch. He arranged the flowers on the far left of the travellers' shrine outside the temple. He had to pass the shrine on three consecutive days before he saw Foster's agreement signal, a replacement bouquet in which there were four white chrysanthemums, two already shedding their petals.

Back at the mission that night Father Robertson

said: 'Nothing happened during the journey that might have upset the authorities?'

Snow suppressed the exasperation. 'Nothing. My escort even talked of coming here, to see our work.'

'Why?' demanded the older man, in immediate concern. 'There must be a reason!' By this time in the afternoon the smell of whisky was always strong, the words slipping.

'I don't expect he will come.'

'We won't make any more travel applications for a while,' decided the mission head. 'It upsets them.'

Snow released the sigh at last. There was so much more he could achieve, on every level, if this doddering old man were withdrawn.

Twelve

The rendezvous was prearranged in the Purple Bamboo Park, triggered by Snow leaving the flower signal at the Taoist temple. Snow went through what he considered the totally unnecessary and ridiculous routine, impatient for Walter Foster to arrive. It was possible the man wouldn't make the meet at all. Foster only completed an encounter after satisfying himself it was safe to do so. If there was no approach, it would mean Foster was *not* satisfied: the attempt would have to be tried the following day at a different location.

Outwardly he was sure he appeared a foreigner relaxing in one of the city's most attractive public places. To Snow's right, in the park, there were several pockets of kite-flyers: closer, near the pagoda by a stream, a group of people, all elderly, were going through the *tai ji quan* dance of meditation, like choreographed, slow-motion boxers. Snow looked from one to the other with apparent interest, in reality seeking Foster, who had to be already there, somewhere, making sure.

Snow decided he couldn't go on like this. He had to endure the twitching existence with Father Robertson, because there was no alternative: the Jesuit Curia were prepared to accept the Chinese government retaining the elderly priest as their tame totem, which in turn enabled Snow to take up residence in the city, even though he was not officially recognized as a Jesuit priest, nor at the moment officially permitted to perform or instruct any of their teachings. But he was no longer prepared to endure this arm's-length existence with Walter Foster. If the man wasn't agreeable to any improvement, he'd complain directly to London. Snow smiled to himself, the irritation and impatience lessening at a sudden awareness. The ultimate resolve lay entirely with him: if a change wasn't agreed, he'd refuse to go on. Snow knew he was too good — too useful — for them to lose him like that. Christian or unchristian considerations about Foster's career didn't come into it: Foster had made the unacceptable rules.

And then he saw the man.

The supposed diplomat was hurrying from the direction of the pagoda, head lowered, eyes to the ground, as if he were trying physically to diminish himself. Getting nearer the bench upon which Snow sat, Foster lifted his head to make a last-minute check before lowering himself on to the adjoining seat. The entire charade had looked absurdly furtive.

'We're quite clear,' announced Foster. He was a small man, red hair awry from his hurried walk, red-faced as well from the exertion. The redness accentuated the freckles. The three jacket buttons of his tight, blue-striped suit were all secured: he didn't undo them when he sat down, straining into tight ridges the cloth around his slightly bulged body. In his lap his hands moved constantly one over the other, as if he were washing them.

'Of course we are!' said Snow. 'We could have set up something far more sensible if you'd agreed to see me before I left.'

'It wasn't possible.'

'It could have been *made* possible. I'm not prepared to go on like this. If you want me to continue — if London wants me to continue — there must be regular meetings.'

'I could talk with London. They make the rules.'

Snow sighed, wondering if the man had ever made an independent decision in his life. 'If there's no improvement, I want to take it up with London myself.'

There was another sideways look. 'Is that a threat?'

'I do not want to do anything to endanger your position here. Or your career. I will show you any letter I wish to be sent on to London.'

Foster was silent for several moments. 'You're being very honest.'

'Priests are supposed to be honest.' It was not, Snow accepted, a dictum he practised with Father Robertson. He considered the deceit justified. There was a concentrated movement far away to their right, a few people running, and Snow realized that the wind was dropping and the kites with it: two or three seemed to have collided, snarling their lines.

'I was told very specifically in London that there never had to be any official difficulty: since the changes in Moscow, this is the most sensitive posting in the world.'

Snow sighed again, realizing there was no purpose in taking this up at a local level. 'Talk to London,' he urged, but patiently at last. 'Say — and I really *want* you to say — that I can't continue working under this present arrangement.'

'That *is* a threat!' insisted the man.

'It's a choice. Your choice. London's choice.' Snow was surprised he didn't feel more uncomfortable, talking so aggressively: actually browbeating the other man. But was he? Wasn't he, rather, trying to restore a situation to the proper footing, the way he'd operated with all Foster's predecessors?

There was another silence between them, longer this time. Across the park, all the birdlike kites had come home to roost: men were huddled in head-bent intensity, untangling strings. At last Foster said: 'Tell me about the trip.'

Well rehearsed, Snow went chronologically through the journey, setting out the successes before reaching Zhengzhou and the less easily documented findings afterwards. He finished by edging along the seat to the other man a brown paper carton containing canisters of all the film he had exposed, his journal of the map coordinates he believed important and his full written account of everything that had happened. Foster became more and more agitated during the narrative, finally twisting directly to face the priest.

'You were suspected!' declared Foster, at once.

'For being what? Nothing happened to me — no conversation was ever begun with me — that doesn't happen every day to every *waiguoren* in every major city in China.'

'No!' refused Foster. 'You were under surveillance! Oh my God!'

'Stop it!' ordered Snow, curtly, unhappy at the other man's panicked reaction. 'I'm not under surveillance now. You personally checked it, before making the meeting. So you know you're safe: that I'm safe.'

'From what you've said Li seems far more than an escort. You were targeted.' He straightened further, looking apprehensively around the grassed area.

'If I *was* targeted, it failed, didn't it? I saw every ploy for what it was and refused to respond. Not even Li — for all the effort he put into trying to make me say or do something indiscreet — could make the slightest accusation in any report that I couldn't refute on every level.'

'I don't like it,' complained Foster. 'I'll have to give a full account to London.' Again he looked nervously around him.

'I've already done that, in my own report.'

'They'll need my opinion, too.'

Coloured to maintain the arm's-length meetings, guessed Snow. 'We'll need to meet again for me to get their decision how we're going to meet in the future.'

Foster attempted to back off immediately. 'We could use a normal drop.'

'I want a personal meeting.'

'The same as today,' insisted Foster. 'If I am not happy, I won't make the contact.'

Something *had* to be done! 'Don't run out on me.'

'What are you accusing me of?'

'I know how sensitive everything is here,' avoided Snow. 'Nothing has been endangered. Nor will it be. There's no reason for anyone to lose their heads.'

'London's got to decide about all this,' said Foster. 'There has been a lot of government-inspired comment in the *People's Daily* about foreign intervention and counter-revolution. Something is building up.'

Snow decided that instead of being his link with London this man was a positive barrier. 'But not connected with me. So there's nothing for London *to* decide: they just have to be told about what happened.'

'You've got to take care!' said the embassy man.

'I *always* take care,' sighed Snow, bored with the need for repetition. He'd have to complain, irrespective of any effect it had upon Foster's career.

'*Extra* care.'

Snow felt his chest begin to tighten. He always carried a relieving inhaler, but he was strangely reluctant to ease the asthma by using it in front of the other man. Foster might construe it as being brought on by matching nervousness when in fact it was caused by his angry impotence, at this fool and this meeting.

'You leave first,' ordered Foster. 'I'll watch you out: make sure you're clear.'

'A week from now. Here,' repeated Snow. 'No flower signal nonsense.'

'All right,' said Foster, uncertainly.

Snow *did* feel some apprehension, walking from the park, and his anger at the other man increased for creating the totally unnecessary tension. His discomfort grew, banding tighter, and he began to strain for breath. But still he denied himself the relief until he knew he was well beyond Foster's view. By which time he had left it too late. The seat was actually filming before his eyes when he reached it, slumping down to fumble the inhaler finally to his mouth. It took a long time for the muscles to relax: even then there was a rasping wheeze which Snow knew would take maybe an hour completely to leave him.

It was the worst attack he could remember for months and it disturbed him. Foster *was* a fool, to have caused it: a frightened, stupid fool who was making life intolerable, physically now as in every other way. Snow didn't see any reason to worry about the man's career: clearly Foster loathed it and would positively welcome a chance of escape.

'He really is unusual,' admitted Gower. 'Not

at all what you'd imagine anyone attached to the Foreign Office to be like.' Very nominally attached, Gower qualified, to himself.

'So what *is* he like?' demanded Marcia, sharing the dinner wine evenly between them.

'He complains all the time about bad feet: wears things that look more like snowshoes than proper footwear. I suppose the first impression is that he's scruffy but he's really not: that's the trick. It's difficult to get a proper picture of him at all, even when you've been with him as constantly as I have.'

'I want to meet him!' declared the girl, at once. 'Invite him for dinner. That would be all right, wouldn't it? My meeting your instructor, I mean.'

'I'm not sure,' said Gower, doubtfully. He'd been reluctant to engage in the conversation with Marcia in the first place: now he regretted it even more.

'Invite him!' she insisted. 'I must meet this mystery man!'

He *was* a mystery man, accepted Gower. There wasn't even a name to introduce to Marcia, if the invitation were accepted.

Fyodor Tudin was a dedicated career officer, an asexual bachelor whose only indulgence was sometimes to drink himself into a stupor in the secure solitude of his Sytinskij Prospekt apartment. The drinking had become more frequent since the changes, which still frustrated and angered him. It was not enough to have survived

128

the KGB restructuring. He should have got the chairmanship of the Directorate, not that icy bitch of a robot Natalia Nikandrova. He'd earned it, for all he'd done in the past: would get it, despite her trying to bury him under the organization of the republic networks.

He just had to find a way.

Discovering personal failings — or best of all, personal, discrediting secrets — was the way. Which was why, within a week of his humiliating appointment as her deputy, he had searched her personal file in the archives. He'd been disappointed by the sparseness of what was there, hinting at an existence here in Moscow as empty as his own. A baby had been an intriguing hope, but the record of a woman who lived alone showed the death of a naval officer husband eighteen months earlier, so there had been nothing useful there. He had been equally hopeful of an odd involvement with an Englishman, until he saw it had been considered an operational success, contributing to her promotion.

Determined to find something, Tudin had initiated a discreet monitor on everything Natalia did, and was therefore curious when he discovered her necessarily recorded official enquiry about the son, Eduard, linked to an apartment at Mytninskaya.

So curious, in fact, that he extended it with additional enquiries of his own. And kept hoping.

Thirteen

Having taught Gower as well as he believed he was able, Charlie set the graduation tests, never once giving the man the slightest warning, even ordering some checks when he was not personally present, the obvious times for Gower to expect something. Others he staged when Gower would have considered himself to be off duty.

Gower only failed to locate one displaced object in a room-entry check. He picked out every shadowing car, on motorways and minor roads. Without being told, he took to hiring cars on credit cards and driving licences held under false, department-supplied legend names, and by so doing destroyed any paper trail from which it would have been possible to discover his true identity. He extended the hire-car precaution, detecting surveillance during one of the planned observations and lulling the professional department Watchers by constantly using the vehicle to embed his connection with it in their minds before evading them completely by abandoning the car in the most prominent place for them to continue watching while he disappeared. His basic tradecraft proved to be impeccable. Three times he beat professional observers on a ground pursuit by dodging in and out of department stores with front, side and back entrances. On two subsequent occasions, he defeated the same increasingly angry department observers passing in a brush contact an unseen package to another person — a woman — going in the opposite direction on a crowded street. He emptied and filled dead-letter drops faultlessly. He carried out his own surveillance on trained men instructed to lose him, which they did only twice in six different situations, never once establishing identifying eye-contact which would in turn have marked him out to an intelligence professional. There were three separate efforts to photograph him, using a team to appear as holidaymakers posing for a vacation souvenir in such a way as to have put him in the background. These he avoided every time. Under simulated interrogation by department specialists, he obeyed Charlie's constantly repeated instruction by lying as little as possible — and by always being able to remember the lies he'd told — and withstood four hours of questioning before being caught out, and then in such a minor mistake that he was able to recover in what Charlie considered a sufficiently convincing way.

And on every one of those concluding days Charlie stressed it was all building up to an ultimate approval which Gower had to discover and announce, before the end of the session.

The session that Charlie intended to be their last — although he didn't declare it as such, still wanting to be satisfied — took place in Charlie's cramped office where they'd first met. It seemed to Charlie to have been a long time ago. 'Think you're ready?' he demanded.

'Your decision, not mine,' Gower retorted. He'd weeks before lost the best-boy-in-the-class need.

So what *was* his decision, Charlie asked himself. Gower was inestimably improved from the day he'd entered this same office and called him sir, which he didn't do any longer. But sufficiently? Charlie didn't know. He'd never had to make this decision about another officer: only about himself, of whom he was supremely confident. Honestly he admitted: 'I can't think of anything else to teach you.'

'Now it comes down to my instinct?'

'If it's possible to instil instinct.'

'Is that the ultimate approval?'

'You have to tell me,' reminded Charlie.

'I don't think that's it.'

'What then?'

'What you were trying to make me?' suggested Gower.

'Go on,' encouraged Charlie.

'Aware, all the time. Of all and everything around me. That was it, wasn't it?'

Charlie nodded hopefully. 'So! Do *you* think you are ready?'

'I hope so.'

'There's no such thing as hope in an operational situation,' lectured Charlie. 'Or luck. It's just down to you: how good you are.'

'Yes,' said the corrected Gower. 'I've learned. I'm ready.'

'You sure?' Charlie feared he was going to be disappointed.

'Our flat was entered four nights ago, while Marcia and I were at the theatre,' said Gower, evenly. 'The cupboard beneath the sink in the kitchen was open when we got back. It hadn't been, when we left. My clothes drawers had been gone through, papers in the bureau put back in a different order. The night before last there was another entry: there were even slight score marks where the lock had been picked. We've got a rack, for unanswered mail: it's dreadful but Marcia keeps it because it was a present from her mother. The letters were replaced in the wrong sequence.'

'I was worried,' admitted Charlie, finally relieved.

'I was waiting, in case you'd tried something else. I couldn't think of anything, apart from that.'

'The people who went in weren't told to be obvious. It was supposed to be completely professional.'

'Will you file a critical report?'

'Yes,' said Charlie. 'And you were quite right, after our first meeting, to put in a memorandum criticizing as bad security my advice about naming instructors and the deputy Director-General.'

Gower shook his head, in mock weariness. 'So that was another test!'

'You can never relax,' insisted Charlie.

'Your name isn't James Harrison, is it?' challenged Gower, enjoying the chance to prove himself.

'No,' said Charlie. 'I didn't see you check the register of the safe house in Berkshire: that was good.'

'You knew I'd try to read it?'

'I would have been unhappy if you hadn't.' Charlie spread his hands before him, satisfied. 'I think we've finished.'

'How did I do?'

'Well enough.'

'But not one hundred per cent?' Gower sounded hopeful.

'No one ever gets one hundred per cent,' said Charlie. 'Two final pieces of advice, as important as always securing an escape route. Never trust anybody. Not me, not this department, not even Marcia. Just trust yourself.'

'That sounds bloody cynical! How can I not trust people I work for here? Marcia! We'll probably get married, for Christ's sake!'

'You find your own definition,' said Charlie. 'The other rule is don't ever follow rule or regulation. Not what you were told before we met, or what you'll find in all the manuals, and not even what you think you've learned from me. And I'm not talking insubordination. It's mixed up with not trusting. Adapt any instruction: go very slightly off course, so that you can't be anticipated.'

The two men sat without speaking for several moments, neither sure how to end the encounter.

Eventually Gower said: 'I *have* learned.' He hesitated, then blurted: 'I've told Marcia about you. She wants you to come to dinner. I do, too. I reckon I owe you dinner, for these last few weeks.'

How pleasant that would be, thought Charlie: a civilized dinner with civilized people. 'No,' he said, bluntly.

'Oh.' Gower looked nonplussed.

'And it is personal,' said Charlie. 'I have refused to let myself think of you in any terms of liking or disliking. Of forming any personal opinion, apart from a strictly professional one. I *don't* want to become your friend. To meet and like Marcia . . .'

Gower's face creased in confusion. '. . . What the hell . . . ?'

'This way there will only ever be the minimal professional regret if I hear, later, that something's gone wrong,' finished Charlie, even more bluntly.

'Jesus!' protested Gower.

'Didn't I also tell you once this wasn't a game?'

'Not as clearly as you just have.'

'So it's a third thing always to remember.'

There was a further silence. Gower stood awkwardly, not appearing to know what to do. Then he thrust his hand forward. Charlie scuffed to his stockinged feet to respond.

'I'm still nervous,' said Gower.

'Don't ever be otherwise,' advised Charlie.

'We could have made it to fit in any time with his schedule,' Marcia pointed out.

'He said he was sorry,' repeated Gower. 'His diary was tight as hell, for weeks. And there was some course or other he was committed to attend.'

'I wanted to compare,' she disclosed.

'Compare?'

'How close you'd come to making yourself like him: all those outward changes.'

Gower moved to make the denial but didn't. 'I don't think I'm even close,' he admitted.

Liu Yin was acknowledged in the West to be one of the strongest critics of the Beijing government, one of the protesters in Tiananmen Square who survived the massacre and who ever since had lived underground, refusing to leave China. Her escape into Hong Kong therefore received widespread publicity. She had had to flee, she insisted, at an arrival press conference. The Public Security Bureau was moving throughout the country, making widespread but totally unpublicized arrests of people they regarded as dissidents. According to her understanding, at least fifty were already under detention. She believed there might even be show trials, sometime in the future.

Snow heard scraps of the conference on the BBC World Service, recognizing the name and the person. She had been a friend of Zhang Su Lin. It had never been admitted openly, but Snow had guessed the couple lived together during the time Zhang had been his student.

Fourteen

Natalia had never drawn Charlie Muffin's complete target file from the KGB archives.

Immediately after her return from London, the Directorate had been undergoing external transfer changes because of the political upheaval. Internally it was in turmoil from what Alexei Berenkov had attempted for absurdly private reasons. At that time it seemed more likely that she would be purged, along with Berenkov, not promoted as she eventually was. So to have provably called for the records of the man who had been at the centre of the entire fiasco would have been personally and dangerously impolitic.

After her complete exoneration and quick all-powerful promotion she could, of course, have demanded the file whenever she'd wanted, without any question or challenge. But by then her feelings about Charlie had gone through several phases, becoming confused and intermingled. Natalia Nikandrova Fedova, someone always able without any prevarication instantly to make a professional decision, in this, the most private part of her private life, found herself helplessly lost, unable to decide *how* she felt.

In the initial weeks and months of her promotion Natalia *had* hated Charlie. Or believed she had. There had been times when she'd physically wept, with aching frustration, at what she'd lost forever by his not keeping the meeting at which she had finally been prepared to turn her back forever upon the Soviet Union and the KGB — and Eduard — just to be with him. Mentally she had raged against him, thinking of him as a coward, not allowing herself to find any excuse for him.

Realizing she was pregnant could have hardened the contempt, but ironically it lessened the feeling: not, in the beginning, into complete forgiveness but tempered at least with some understanding of why Charlie had held back — professional judgement always having to be more important than personal emotions — and certainly no longer thinking him a coward.

In a country where termination is quite casually used as a method of birth-control, it would have been extremely easy for Natalia to have had an abortion. She had scarcely considered it. It was just as easy, at the echelon she now occupied, to have and to keep a baby: not that there would have been any stigma attached — and with so few friends, even acquaintances, that hardly mattered anyway — but she had still been officially a married woman within a satisfactory time-frame of the birth, with no cause to justify or explain.

It was during her confinement, with the opportunity to think of little else, that she confronted the impossibility of hating Charlie: of *ever* hating him. Alone in the privileged private ward of the privileged security agency hospital, the perfectly born, beautifully formed Alexandra beside her, Natalia finally tried to come to terms with how she truly felt. Huge sadness, the most obvious. Bitter disappointment that would always be there. But most of all, *above* all, the love: a love that overwhelmed everything, consumed everything.

Which gave her the strongest reason possible for not going to the archives. Having acknowledged her true feelings, Natalia equally recognized that she had to find some way of compartmenting the emotion, locking it securely inside her, like a miser hoarding the most precious treasure. Because unlike a gloating miser, she could never retrieve that lost treasure: never again know the pleasure or the beauty. It was difficult, but Natalia grew to think she could make the sadness and the disappointment bearable, as the weeks went into months and Alexandra became the focus of her entire existence: someone upon whom Natalia could lavish the love she could give to no one else, someone who would always be her unbreakable link to the man she would never see again.

In the final analysis there was no useful, sensible reason to recover Charlie's private records, to disturb from the securely locked emotional compartments all the heartache Natalia hoped she now had under unshakeable control.

Or was there?

The reflective question — after the other reflective question when she'd failed to discover the whereabouts of Eduard — did not come simply or without contradiction, because nothing came simply or without contradiction when she thought about Charlie Muffin. But Natalia knew she *did* now have her feelings locked, bolted and barred forever.

It wouldn't be trying to find him, wherever he was, whatever he was doing. That would have been preposterous. It would be finding out as much as she could about the father of her child. One day, inevitably, Alexandra would want to know. Natalia was not sure, at this stage, how or whether she would be able to tell their daughter the truth. Almost certainly not. But at least she owed it to the child to be *able* to answer the questions that might be asked.

The red-starred, Top Priority designation on the bulky, concertina-sectioned folder was over-stamped with a discarding 'Erase — Grade IV' marking, indicating minimal remaining importance. Only important to me, thought Natalia. She realized, with surprise, that she was frightened, without knowing what to be apprehensive about.

The moment she opened the file Natalia was aware her emotions were *not* that tightly controlled and that the mere sight of him, even in snatched and grainily blurred photographs, was enough to jar her composure. It was the standard assembly, with photographs in the first section. There was a total of five, arranged in dated sequence, the final two far better quality than the others: she didn't need the dates to know they had been taken when they had been reunited in

London, when she had become unknowingly pregnant. In one of the other, earlier pictures Charlie was actually bending, soothing fingers inside the heel of a sagging left shoe. Natalia began to hurry the photographs back into their pocket, not needing any physical reminder of how he'd looked. But then stopped, expertise taking over from emotion. The pictures were unquestionably of Charlie Muffin, whom she believed she would have known and recognized anywhere. Unquestionably identified, in addition, by their being in an officially created file designated by the man's name and description. Yet none, not even the later ones, were by themselves sufficient definitely to identify him: simply by the way he was standing or holding himself or half-concealing his face in a head-twisted posture, two could arguably and easily have been of quite a different man.

The first written material was almost twenty years old, paper already yellowed and brittle at the edges.

Charlie had told her of this first episode, but not in detail: the Cold War at its most frigid, Alexei Berenkov already suspected as the London-based Control for one of the most successful Soviet cells in Europe in the late 1960s. Now here, before her, *were* the details. All of them, chronologically set out, easy to comprehend. It had been a Berlin Wall crossing by Charlie and two other SIS officers, to collect the proof legally to bring Berenkov to trial: proof they'd got, because there was a full transcript of the interrogation of the later discovered East German double who'd passed it all over. The next documents in the bundle were the flimsy paper cables, setting out the time — even the vehicle — in which the then unknown Charlie would be making the return, a return that British intelligence and the American CIA had sacrificially leaked to distract from the coordinated crossing back of his two colleagues, with the evidential proof. But it hadn't been the always cautious, always self-protective Charlie who'd driven the car: it had blown up in the Border Guard crossfire, destroying the identity of whoever the driver had been, providing the diversion for Charlie also safely to cross back to the West by U-Bahn. According to the archive, Charlie had been asked, subsequently, but always refused to supply the name of who he had duped to protect himself.

There was a gap here in the chronology: an actual notation, attested by a signature Natalia could not read, conceding that the interception had been a failure and that the London cell had been wrapped up, Alexei Berenkov with it. The sparse details of Berenkov's incamera trial was just a single page concluding with the forty-year sentence.

And then more cable flimsies, from the Soviet embassies in London and Vienna, at first highly suspect but anonymous approaches finally confirmed to be from a man called Charlie Muffin who wasn't offering secrets or defection. Just a way to wreak retribution upon those prepared to let him be captured or killed, a scheme that eventually enabled Berenkov to be swapped in exchange for the SIS and CIA Directors held in humiliating Soviet detention.

It had meant personal contact, between Charlie and the then head of the First Chief Directorate, General Valery Kalenin, someone else whom she had known but who had long since disappeared into oblivion through KGB changes. Natalia was caught by the assessments that Kalenin had recorded about Charlie. *Absolute professional* was a frequent phrase. Twice the exchange scheme was qualified as being in no way a defection by the Englishman. Kalenin had written: *This is a man believing himself betrayed and vindictively intent upon creating the maximum embarrassment for men who planned to abandon him. I consider it extremely unlikely this man could ever be turned: throughout our meetings he has — although illogically — consistently presented himself as a loyal British intelligence officer. It is a morality difficult to understand but obviously a situation of which we have to take the utmost advantage.*

There was another gap in the timetable, but here again Natalia was able to fill it in for herself, from what Charlie had told her. Of months stretching into more than a year of endless running, dragging the hapless Edith from country to country while he was hunted by the British and American agencies: of his wife's death, intentionally putting herself in the path of a bullet meant for him: an even greater retribution, against her murderer: of eventual capture, treason trial and British imprisonment with a believed KGB agent, and the phoney jailbreak and defection, to Moscow.

The moment of their meeting, reflected Natalia, enveloped now in smothering recollection. She hardly needed any reminders from the file but she read on, actually studying after the gap of almost six years her own reports of debriefing Charlie Muffin. He'd deceived her, Natalia conceded: just as he'd deceived the repatriated Berenkov and even Valery Kalenin, the man who had earlier decided Charlie would never become a traitor. At once Natalia found the personal contradiction. He'd deceived her professionally, convincing her his defection was genuine, so that she never once suspected the entire exercise to be a discrediting operation against Berenkov. But he'd never deceived her personally. Theirs had been a genuine love — still was on her part — and when, finally, he'd triggered the trap for Berenkov he'd done it in a way that kept her beyond any danger from their intimate relationship.

Now, before her on the desk in black and white, she finally had the confirmation of how successfully he had shielded her. General Kalenin had conducted the inquiry, extending to the absolute limit the friendship that existed between the two men to minimize the harm to Berenkov's career. And exonerating her completely.

Comrade Colonel Natalia Nikandrova Fedova at

all times conducted herself in an exemplary manner, the General had recorded. *It was she who finally alerted senior officers that the Englishman's defection was, after all, a false one. The failure to affect an arrest was that of counter-intelligence not reacting quickly enough upon information supplied by Comrade Fedova.*

Natalia stretched up from the dossier, needing a moment's break from the jumble of words, passingly amused now at being referred to as 'Comrade', which seemed so archaic after all the changes. She remained scarcely conscious of her official surroundings, still wrapped in long-ago memories. She'd believed she would never see Charlie again, after his escape back to England. But the hurt had not been so bad that time. She'd been more easily able to accept the division between their personal, impossible dilemma and what he had to do operationally.

Natalia hunched over the file again, reaching the second inquiry upon Alexei Berenkov, the one from which the man had *not* escaped. Nor deserved to escape. It was not difficult, even in the stilted official language of what virtually amounted to a trial without judge or jury, to gauge Berenkov's megalomania: the man's unshakeable belief, even under interrogation, that he was justified to carry on a personal vendetta operation to discredit Charlie Muffin as Charlie Muffin had — minimally because of Kalenin's intervention — discredited him. It was, she supposed, the dread of every organization such as theirs: that someone with enormous power would become mentally unstable and start abusing it to satisfy private ambitions.

Natalia closed the file, trying to form judgements on the necessarily separate levels, as always finding one overlapping on to the other.

By staying away from the final London rendezvous — the meeting she'd kept, finally deciding to abandon everything and everybody — Charlie had avoided being discredited as a Soviet sympathizer, to prove which Berenkov had created a miasma of additional disinformation material. So yet again — as always — Charlie had proved himself the ultimate survivor.

And by doing so destroyed whatever there could have been between them, personally.

Natalia believed she could have settled with Charlie, in England: certainly now, with the baby. It would have been difficult at first, of course: horrendously so, because she would never have been a defector, never prepared to disclose any secrets from her organization, any more than Charlie had ever been prepared — truthfully — to disclose anything from his side. So the official pressure upon her — upon both of them — would have been staggering. But *with* Charlie she could have endured it, eventually for them to have been together.

In the solitude of her Yasenevo office, Natalia shook her head, as if trying physically to throw off the reminiscence. What might have been could never be: so why had she bothered to go through the charade she had for so long denied herself?

Having at last posed herself the question, Natalia forced herself to answer it, properly for the first time. Because she hadn't embarked upon it as a meaningless routine, unnecessarily stirring old memories better left undisturbed. She'd studied the dossier with a very determined objective, and the disappointment she felt now was not that of lost chances in the past but of not finding what she had been looking for, in the future.

She'd been seeking the slightest clue from which she might have been able once more to find Charlie. But hadn't found it.

Within twenty-four hours, in another part of the same building, Fyodor Tudin wondered if he had found the indication he had been seeking, when he learned from her signature against the withdrawal authority that Natalia had studied the file on the Englishman with whom she was linked, in her own personal files.

Was there a weak spot there after all, he wondered.

They'd considered all of Jeremy Snow's material, working on Miller's side of the desk with their chairs familiarly together but without any physical contact or even conversation as they went through each report and each photograph. Finally the Director-General said: 'He did well: damn well.'

'It's unfortunate it has to turn out like this,' agreed Patricia Elder.

147

Fifteen

'Their separate accounts contradict each other, to a large degree, but it's fairly obvious there is *some* suspicion.' As he talked Peter Miller, who was concerned with neatness and order in all things, assembled in edge-to-edge stacks on his desk what had arrived overnight from Beijing. Snow's information and opinion formed the larger pile, then the photographs, and finally Walter Foster's account. The Director-General did so with his head habitually to the right, to benefit his better vision from that side.

Patricia Elder nodded, in agreement. 'But just how much? We can't get a single thing wrong, not now.'

Miller finished his assembly, finally reaching across for her hand. 'Foster is clearly over-re-acting, even this early.'

'What's the greater risk? Leaving Foster in place? Or bringing him out right away?'

'If we bring him out, there can't be any official accusation from the Chinese.'

'The speed of it all is what surprises me,' admitted the deputy. 'I would have thought it would be much more gradual.'

Miller shook his head, in a warning gesture. 'He was moving through closed areas. And maybe he hasn't picked up the observation until now. Or not thought it important enough to report it, putting it down to the normal attention paid to Westerners permanently resident in China. Let's not forget it's Foster who is using phrases like "heightened surveillance" and marking everything urgent.'

'Snow does concede that Li is probably a member of the Public Security Bureau,' the woman pointed out. She rose from beside Miller, taking her chair with her.

'Every official escort acts as an informer.' The man paused. 'I wish we could go back for more definite guidance.'

'We can't risk that,' she said at once. 'We've got to go blind: make the decisions from here.'

There was an interruption on the intercom, closed from Miller's end from the frequent open communication. The Director ordered the promised tea in five minutes: by the time Julia Robb entered, the second chair was returned to its normal position on the other side of his desk and Patricia Elder was already sitting there. Neither spoke until the girl left the room. As Miller served he said: 'The suddenness *is* surprising.'

The woman took the offered cup. 'I'm not arguing against myself, but let's remember just how little we've got to guide us on how and when the Chinese will react about *anything*. This isn't any longer the Soviet Union and the KGB, which we spent all those years studying and thought we *could* anticipate.' She gestured towards Miller's tidily arranged piles. 'No matter how well placed we might have thought ourselves, we're still just scratching the surface as far as Chinese intelligence goes.'

'I don't think we panic, because of what Foster says,' mused the Director. 'Or stay complacent, which Snow appears to be.'

From their ten years of professionally working together, apart from their deeper relationship, Patricia recognized the move towards a decision. 'We don't bring Foster out at once?'

'Not quite yet,' decided Miller. 'But we can't have him keeping the meeting Snow's demanded. That's a stupid risk. We'll send Snow a message, for a drop delivery. They will have to wait for an embassy excuse personally to talk. There's the *People's Daily* warnings. And what Liu Yin claimed, at the press conference.'

'What about an emergency?'

The Director considered the demand. 'We'll tell Snow to wait, for our signal. But make it clear to Foster that he can take an on-ground decision personally if there's no time to consult. He's to warn Snow to be ready to get out, of course. And say so, in a message here.'

Miller began rearranging the Beijing information, like someone playing with worry beads. 'As it is, we've got a tremendous amount to follow up . . .' He hesitated, halted by an abrupt thought. 'We must congratulate Snow. A personal cable, separate from the fresh instructions.'

'I'll get it all away tonight,' promised Patricia.

She remained looking pointedly at the man. 'What *about* tonight?'

Miller smiled back at her across the table. 'Ann's taken two horses up to Newmarket. She'll be there for at least three days, for the major part of the sale.'

'Good,' said Patricia. Jeremy Snow wasn't the only one not prepared to tolerate an existing situation, she thought. She'd been very patient — stupidly and regrettably so — but Peter had to make a decision soon. He couldn't go on evading things.

Charlie managed three contrived encounters — two in the lift, the other when she was heading for the basement dining-hall for lunch — but each time Julia Robb refused the persistent invitation. She agreed finally on his fourth attempt, surprising him: he'd been about to give up. They agreed on the Spaniards, on Hampstead Heath. He got there considerately early and had almost finished his first Islay malt before Julia arrived. She wore jeans and a sweater big enough to reach to mid-thigh, like a short coat, and she was shiny-faced, with only the vaguest suggestion of lipline. She chose beer, further surprising him. There were no vacant tables and Charlie was glad. Proper drinkers stood in pubs, they didn't sit: one of Charlie's few affectations was to consider himself a proper drinker. They found space near the corner of the bar.

'This your local?' He recognized the first-meet-

152

ing uneasiness. It wasn't work — not *proper* work, where deceit was all part of the business — and Charlie always felt a vague regret at cheating the innocent. A man's gotta do what a man's gotta do, he reassured himself. He liked John Wayne movies, looking out for reruns on television.

'I come here occasionally.'

'A long way from the office.'

'That was a factor, too.'

'Frightened of gossip?'

'Misunderstandings.'

Charlie touched his glass to hers. 'By two people in particular?' Charlie didn't want to go too fast but he didn't want to waste time, either. This might be his only chance.

The woman looked steadily at him. 'No shop talk, OK?'

'Just talking generally.'

'They probably wouldn't like it,' she conceded.

She was suspiciously cautious: he needed to ease back. 'Why did you say yes, at last?'

There was a grin lurking at the corners of her mouth, but she was trying to control it. 'You'll be offended.'

'Try me.'

'Buy me another drink: if you storm off there'll be something for me to stand here with in my hand.'

Charlie grinned back, beginning to like the encounter. He was lucky: there was a barmaid at their end of the bar. He handed Julia the refill and said: 'So?'

'You're so bloody *odd!*' she blurted. 'I mean
. . .' Julia's shoulders humped up and down.
'That's the only words for it: just bloody odd.'
She paused. 'And there's something else that
doesn't matter . . .'

Charlie was unsure how to pick up on that.
He said: 'Like going out with a man with one
leg, an act of Christian charity?'

'What a load of self-pitying bollocks!' Julia
erupted, laughing openly at him. 'I can't really
believe you said that!'

That hadn't gone the way it should have done.
'I can't either.'

'I knew you'd be offended.'

'I'm not.' Charlie sought a different way forward. 'I'm glad you accepted, anyway.'

'Why?'

Shit! thought Charlie, off-balanced again. 'It's
fun.'

'Too soon to know whether it's fun or not,'
she insisted.

This was turning out to be a bloody sight more
difficult than he'd expected. 'We'll postpone the
verdict, until another time.'

'Who said there's going to be another time?'

'You're right. I might not ask you again.'

'I might not accept, if you do.'

'You should be considerate to those forcibly
retired.'

Julia frowned. 'You're not retired.'

'Fact of life. You can't argue with it.'

'They seemed impressed with what you've just

finished,' she offered.

Now we're getting there, decided Charlie, happily. 'You must find it bloody difficult, acting for both of them: worked off your feet?' He kept the remark as casual as he could, not even looking at her in the end, turning to motion for more drinks.

'They created the system, where they were before.' She smiled again. 'They work incredibly closely all the time: it's obviously more efficient that I know what's going on with both of them. There's a whole battery of secretaries to do the heavy stuff.'

He handed her the fresh glass. 'You actually telling me it's easy?'

'I'm not telling you anything,' Julia said, pointedly. 'You forgotten what I told you the first day? I don't — ever — talk about the job.'

Keep it light, determined Charlie, quickly. 'Or get too familiar with the staff.'

'That, too. That most of all.'

'I wasn't asking you to do either.'

'You were coming close.'

'I'm not going to try to persuade you to sleep with me,' said Charlie.

'Good. I won't.'

'Or talk about the job.'

'Good. I won't do that, either.'

Don't you believe it, thought Charlie, seeing the evening as a challenge. 'The system might have worked at counter-intelligence. Often things don't transfer so well.'

'I try not to make too many mistakes,' she snapped.

Charlie realized he had hurt her pride and couldn't quite understand why. He wondered how much further he could lead her on. 'I'm glad they were happy with what I've done. It was a pretty odd experience. You know how I felt, all the time?' Come on, my darling, Charlie thought: come on!

'How?' she asked, precisely on cue.

'Jealous,' said Charlie, briefly honest. 'I kept thinking he was going to go out and do things that they don't believe I'm any longer capable of doing . . .' Julia moved to speak, but Charlie hurried on: 'All that's not more self-pity. That's being objective, confronting the reality of being taken off the active operational roster.'

Julia hesitated. 'You're still at Westminster Bridge Road, aren't you?'

'That's a consolation, I suppose,' Charlie agreed, not wanting her to know he'd understood the significance of her remark, which he had, angry it hadn't occurred to him before, which it should have done. How the hell could he lecture young entrants like John Gower about the importance of recognizing everything when he'd overlooked a fact as obvious as the one she'd just pointed out to him?

'So you're not going to like it?'

Charlie shrugged, seeking another avenue: chauvinism, he decided. Julia just might be the type to rise to what could seem to her a sexist remark. 'It's a case of *having* to like it, isn't it? But it's not just getting used to a new role: always in the past I've had a different relationship with those on the ninth floor.'

Julia stood looking at him quizzically, head slightly to one side. 'Ha, hah!'

He thought she'd got it. Hopefully he said: 'Ha, hah what?'

'Do I infer that Mr Muffin doesn't like the person to whom he's responsible being a member of the female sex?'

'Don't be ridiculous!' said Charlie, trying not to overstress the phoney outrage of the denial.

'You are!' she insisted, pleased with her imagined insight.

'I'm not,' he denied again. It was important to keep the momentum going. 'It's just unusual for me, that's all.' He allowed another grin, thinking he'd spent practically the entire evening with his mouth stretched apart, like a fool. 'Maybe I should invite *her* out, even though she's the boss.'

'Forget it,' advised Julia, with curt but amused finality.

'Why not?' demanded Charlie, able to make the outrage open mockery this time. 'She's not married. There's no ring.' It wasn't always an indicator, but Julia would have to respond one way or the other.

'She doesn't have to be.'

'I don't understand what you've just said,' protested Charlie, who believed he did. Bingo! he thought.

'I haven't said anything.'

Careful, Charlie warned himself: very, very careful. 'So she's out of bounds?'

'This conversation is.'

The moment for retreat, judged Charlie: the moment to scuttle away with the prize, like a dog with a juicy bone to be buried. 'On my way here, coming up the hill, I saw what looked like a few good restaurants.'

'I thought it was only supposed to be a drink?'

'What's wrong with dinner, as well?'

'I imposed two rules,' reminded the woman. 'You tried to break one.'

'Not intentionally,' evaded Charlie. 'I promise no hands on knees under the table.'

They ate at an American-style bar-restaurant called Kenny's. Having achieved all he wanted, Charlie fully relaxed, genuinely enjoying the quickness with which Julia came back at him, telling invented anecdotes against himself and making her laugh a lot.

'I've had a good time,' she said. She'd refused his offer to escort her home: her taxi was waiting outside.

'We could do it again sometime, if you'd like.'

Once again there was a moment of indecision. 'I don't know. I might. Same rules?'

'Guaranteed.'

'There's a reason.'

'There's always a reason.'

'This is special.' She was very serious.

'Do you want to talk about it?'

'No.' She positively ended the conversation by walking away towards the waiting taxi.

Charlie stood politely, watching her leave. In no hurry himself, he ordered another cognac, wanting to evaluate the evening. Extremely productive, he decided: more so than he might have expected. A most important discovery — which he shouldn't have needed her to point out to him — was that he had *not* been taken off active operational duties, like all the other instructors and stiff-backed men on duty at safe houses.

If he had been reduced in status, he would have been assigned to some building or place other than Westminster Bridge Road, every occupant of which was only *ever* on active duty. There was, of course, a counter-balance to that reassurance: that it was about to happen but delayed by departmental bureaucracy. Which in turn could be argued against, in his favour. Julia Robb wouldn't have made the point if the transfer instruction had been issued but still blocked on its way through the pipeline, because she would have known about it. Charlie, always the optimist until the first falling slate warned him that the roof was caving in, decided it *was* in his favour. He hadn't yet been officially dumped, so there was still a chance of his being restored to his old function. Maybe.

What else?

The hint about Patricia Elder was the most

fascinating: and not just about the deputy Director-General, if he was reading the runes correctly. *They work incredibly closely all the time,* Julia had said. And then — despite the verbal gymnastics — had made it crystal clear that the lady was very much out of bounds. Which she would have been anyway to someone as lowly as him, but he didn't think that had been the point of Julia's remark. Still just a hint, Charlie cautioned himself again. But he did not think he was stretching it too far to wonder if Peter Miller, the very proper and upright Director-General, wasn't unfastening those pin-striped trousers to throw a leg over the very proper but perhaps not always upright deputy Director-General.

It was very definitely a possibility to be looked at extremely closely: always a useful thing, to know as much as you could about potential enemies. Not that he regarded either of them as enemies, not yet.

He didn't consider them friends, either. So it was well worth a little further enquiry.

Behind the locked doors of his Yasenevo office, further protected by the bright red 'no entry' light, Colonel Fyodor Tudin spread out for convenience the bulky file that he knew Natalia had already studied on the intriguing Englishman.

As Natalia Fedova's immediate deputy, Tudin was aware of most ongoing operations, and there had been no indication, in any discussion or internal memorandum, of any official activity involving someone called Charles Edward Muffin: no indication of anything ongoing concerning England at all. Which left the possible conjecture that the woman was interested in someone with whom she had once been connected. And *retained* an interest.

Only a conjecture, Tudin warned himself. But wasn't conjecture one of the central threads of basic intelligence? Unquestionably. It was definitely worth pursuing. But how? He couldn't initiate any enquiry to London. It would be traceable, to him by name. And officially Western targets weren't his responsibility anyway, so he had no explainable reason. The only obviously safe way would be to continue discreetly monitoring everything the bitch did. And be ready to move when she made a mistake.

Tudin felt the excitement warm through him at the thought of at last finding what he had been looking for.

Sixteen

Jeremy Snow's initial reaction was a reason-blurring, breath-robbing anger which diminished only gradually, never completely leaving him. Neither did the asthma. He rejected outright the congratulatory cable and the warning messages as any sort of praise or concern for his safety. Instead he saw them — and the refusal for the second meeting he'd insisted upon — as London accepting Walter Foster's bowel-opening hysteria rather than his own properly balanced assessment.

He'd come inches close to making the open accusation — actually considering calling Foster a coward — in the first few irrational hours, after waiting fruitlessly in the park and later collecting the London communications from the dead-letter drop. In his drop-delivered reply he accused both Foster and London of blatant over-reaction. He appreciated their congratulations and their evaluation of his worth. He was not, however, any longer prepared to operate under the conditions now being imposed. He wanted an entirely revised operational procedure and most particularly to work through someone different at the embassy. He had no intention, therefore, of doing anything further until he heard direct from London. Until the changes were agreed, he was temporarily terminating their relationship.

It was the letter he'd wanted and planned to write about Foster for a long time — even before the latest panic had brought everything to a head — but there still remained more frustration than satisfaction after he sent it.

In the days following the threat to quit, Snow's anger subsided further and he had time to consider what it would mean. And concluded, with some concern, that it would mean a great deal to him not to go on.

He rationalized that his feelings did not in any way conflict with his more important vocation as a Jesuit. Rather, they were closely related. It was impossible, in any sense of the word, for him properly to function in his true vocation. It was a sham, lecturing on basic English to a varying handful of Chinese: as much a sham as Father Robertson remaining as caretaker of an echoing, dead church in which only the two of them could practise their faith and that — because of the old man's fear — surreptitiously, afraid the simple act of praying might offend some unknown official into some unanticipated gesture of correction or punishment. So he'd come to see his second role as the only way he could operate as a soldier priest. At his theological college, his Jesuit tutor had frequently preached Busenbaum's creed of the end justifying the means. Snow could relate to that: get something like spiritual comfort from it, in the sterile religious situation in which he was forced to exist.

Until now, the secret work had justified his continuing there, with no one able to forecast what the end might be. But now Snow realized that by quitting he had precipitated that end. It was too late to change his mind — he didn't *want* to change his mind, about working with Foster — but he didn't want to stop an activity he believed gave some purpose to his being in Beijing.

His concern kept the anger bubbling, particularly with his conviction that London had already come down on Foster's side.

Having demanded a decision direct from London, Snow daily visited the four use-at-random message drops in and around the Forbidden City for their reply. Each day they remained empty. He considered trying to prompt a response by leaving a message for Foster to collect and transmit to London, before accepting he'd already told them he would not any longer communicate through the man, who therefore probably wasn't maintaining any checks upon the drops anyway. After a week Snow came close to eroding his threat against Foster by activating the emergency meeting procedure at the Taoist temple, but in the end he didn't do that either: the warning cancellation of the second park meeting had prohibited any further public place encounters, so Foster would not have turned up, even if he'd monitored the demand.

Snow recognized that effectively he had, for the moment, been abandoned, as much by his own decision as by London's. Nevertheless he

164

knew when there would be a meeting. Only a week away there was a reception at the embassy for visiting British industrialists to which both he and Father Robertson had been invited.

It became a period of permanent impatience which Snow thought, however, he kept from becoming obvious. Despite their being thrown together in such a self-enclosed environment, from which a mutually dependent friendship might have been expected, Snow's relationship with the head of mission had always been distantly formal, so Father Robertson did not notice the younger man drawing even further within himself. And the association with the current English students was even more formal: only twice did Snow come close to snapping at irritating mistakes and both times stopped himself.

He was glad of the restraint on the second occasion, because that was the day Mr Li made his unexpected visit.

Snow was not initially aware of the man's presence, so he did not know how long he had been standing in the half-lit rear of the room. It was only after he'd almost shouted at a boy he'd taught for six months and who therefore should not have repeatedly confused the verb with an adjective in a practice sentence that Snow detected movement at the back. It had started off as a small class, and Snow thought it might have been a late arrival, momentarily holding back from interrupting the session. Or someone temporarily sheltering: there had been two Gobi storms, although the wind outside hadn't seemed too strong that day.

Snow stopped the lesson and said: '*Jin-lai*', waiting for the newcomer to enter further, never quite sure if he kept the surprise from showing when he finally recognized his cloying escort from the information-gathering journey.

'I am sorry,' said Li, speaking in English. 'I do not wish to intrude.'

There were five men and three girls forming that day's class. Each turned, at the interruption. The instinctive recognition of Li as an official was immediate and the stir of unease rippled discernibly among them.

'I am glad you accepted my invitation,' said Snow. Conscious of the need to reassure his students, he repeated in Mandarin the circumstances of his meeting with Li.

'We became friends,' exaggerated Li, expanding the explanation after Snow finished, in Chinese himself this time.

None of the students looked reassured. To Li, Snow said: 'Please join us.'

The Chinese shook his head. 'Please go ahead: I will just observe.' He finished the sentence already withdrawing into the gloom: the scant light was such that Snow's view was of a pair of disembodied legs, the upper part of the man lost in darkness.

Snow made a determined effort but it wasn't a success, more from his students' apprehension than from any uncertainty of his. Two of the men repeatedly twisted in their seats, trying to see what Li was doing, and all of them made so many stumbling mistakes in the conversational exchanges that finally Snow abandoned that part of the lesson. He ended the session early, setting revision to be done in their own time before the next lesson.

Throughout Li remained apparently unmoving at the back, not coming forward until after everyone apart from Snow had left: all the class did so hurriedly, three with their heads averted from the man.

'It was obviously a beginners' class,' said Li pointedly. As always, he wore a buttoned-to-the-neck tunic suit.

'I am surprised to see you,' admitted Snow. He wished the session that Li had witnessed had not been such a shambles. 'I did not think you were serious, about coming here.'

'I'm usually serious.'

There was no doubt about that: Snow found it difficult to imagine the man ever laughing. He gestured around the now empty room. 'Sometimes the classes are much better attended: the students more mature.'

'And not held in your temple?'

'I told you they were not,' reminded Snow. Li's visit *did* surprise him but he still refused to be alarmed. Father Robertson would be, though. And doubtlessly London, if they learned about it. Snow decided not to tell either.

'Of course you did.'

'How was your visit to Tunxi?'

'You have an excellent memory.'

'Not really,' denied Snow. He decided some Chinese played ping-pong with a ball, others with words.

'They were from Texas. The man smoked cigars that smelled like perfume. They invited me to visit them if I ever go to America.'

'The Americans are hospitable people: you will enjoy it.'

'I have no wish to visit America.'

'Yet you have learned the language.'

'For the benefit of China.'

Imagining an opening, Snow said: 'How, exactly?'

Li smiled again, as if pleased at some success. 'Showing its greatness to others.'

'Which you do very well.'

Li looked around the sparse room. 'So this is where you teach?'

'Always,' insisted Snow, believing the man was pressing the obvious suspicion about meetings in the adjacent church.

'Three times a week?'

Snow couldn't remember telling Li the extent of the curriculum. 'I fit in with the other demands upon my students' time.'

'Which must leave you a lot unfilled, for yourself?'

Snow wished he had anticipated the pitfall. 'There are quite a lot of extra-curricular duties: work out of school hours to be marked and commented upon. And administration.'

'I suppose there must be.'

Snow felt the beginnings of breathlessness, the familiar insidious closing around his chest. 'I could offer you tea?' Whereabouts would Father Robertson be? Although he went out every day, the mission chief seemed to spend most of his time around the complex.

'No thank you. I wondered if you had managed yet to get your photographs developed. I would like to see them.'

The oversight hit Snow like a blow. There was no danger from those he'd taken at Anqing, but the Shanghai shots were incriminating. There would be a delay but he could retrieve the Anqing prints from London. But Li was too astute to forget the others. Stalling — unable to think of anything better — Snow said: 'I didn't consider getting anything developed here. I sent all the negative rolls home to my family, in England.'

'But they will be returned to you here, after they are printed?'

'Not necessarily,' said Snow, anxious now.

'You took six of me,' said Li, definitely. 'I would be extremely grateful if you could let me have copies as a memento of our trip. The Shanghai pictures, against the river, should be particularly good. I would like to see them, as well.'

Snow was well aware of the yawning hole into which he was about to fall but couldn't think of a way to avoid it. His chest was constricting even more tightly. 'It would be a pleasure.' He would have to tell London of this visit from Li: and be forced to maintain contact with the Chinese.

'Are you not well?' demanded Li, perceptively.

'I suffer from asthma. Sometimes the weather affects me.' The chain reaction began, Snow's breathing worsening because of Li's awareness of it. He forced himself on: 'I shall need an address: somewhere to deliver the photographs when they arrive.'

'I will not put you to such inconvenience. I will come to you, here.'

'I don't know when I will get them back. You could have many wasted journeys.'

'It will not be a problem.'

Snow could not think of any better, stronger objections. 'As you wish,' he conceded. Finally he hurried the inhaler to his mouth, sucking in deeply. Almost at once the relief started.

Snow expected the man to make some comment. Instead Li said: 'I have another request.'

Snow regarded the other man nervously, trying to anticipate what was to come. 'If I can help in *any* way.'

'I would like to see your temple. As you saw ours.'

Why? wondered Snow, not believing that anything this man said or asked was casual, without some hidden reason. 'Of course.'

'When?'

'Why not now?'

'You don't need notice?'

'Why should I need notice?'

'I just thought . . .'

'. . . What?'

The smile was like a camera shutter, something missed if a person blinked. 'Nothing. I did not want to impose.'

'You won't be,' assured Snow. He led ahead through the interlinking closed-in passages and open paths. As he approached, Snow thought the church looked like a medieval boat, beached to get it clear to rot: it had to be a visual distortion, because of how he was squinting against the wind, but it even appeared to be tilting slightly sideways as if it were collapsing.

Father Robertson was turning away from the altar before which he had apparently been bowed in prayer when they entered: Snow felt another snatch of breathlessness. The head of mission came to an immediate halt, a frightened man immediately expecting disaster: his head moved between Snow and Li, like a spectator at a tennis tournament.

'You must be Father Robertson?' said Li.

'That is so.' Only at the very end of the short sentence did the confirmation become a throat-clearing cough.

Hurrying to cover the awkwardness, Snow made the formal introductions, identifying the Chinese as his recent travel companion. 'Mr Li asked if he could see our church.'

'And the photographs?' said Li, at once.

'Photographs?' The question rasped from the

older priest. The whisky intake was discernible.

'Souvenir photographs,' elaborated Snow. 'Reminders of the trip.'

Father Robertson remained where he had stopped, appearing lost in a church in which he should have felt most at home. Li gazed around at everything, tilting his head to look up into the organ loft, then closely examining the altar area. The day had faded even more now, much of the main church already dark, the two side chapels blacked out from view. The spiked stand for votive candles was empty, showing no sign of use, beside a confessional in which Snow occasionally went through the charade with Father Robertson, never once making a proper confession, satisfied the avoidance would not lead to eternal damnation because of the necessity of what he was secretly doing. Father Robertson must have extinguished the two larger, thicker altar candles before they entered: both still sent a tangled thread of smoke upwards, quickly to be lost in the expanse of the place. Li returned up the aisle from the altar, dragging his finger over the pew backs to make arrow trails in the dust. Snow realized the Chinese was looking for indications that the church was used for regular group worship, happy the man was going to be disappointed.

Li halted, beside them, and said: 'It is a large building. This could be a home for many people.'

'It was, in the past,' scored Snow, immediately, careless of the tremor that visibly passed through Father Robertson.

'That was a use of words that I don't quite understand,' complained Li.

Snow didn't believe the protest. Before Snow could respond, however, Father Robertson said: 'It is no longer used for worship! The government has agreed it can remain as it is, though.'

'Yes,' said Li, as if already aware. Looking directly at Snow, he said: 'You worship here?'

'I do,' confirmed Snow, at once. 'There is no official restriction upon our doing that.'

'Quite so,' agreed Li, again as if he already knew.

'Is there anything else you would like to see?' invited Snow.

'Is there anything else I *should* see?'

Snow gestured around the vaulted building. 'This is what there is. All there is.'

'Thank you, for giving me so much of your time.'

'You gave me so much of yours,' said Snow, conscious of Father Robertson's head swivelling worriedly back and forth again.

'You won't forget the photographs?'

'I would not expect to hear back very quickly.'

'It is not difficult for me to call.' To Father Robertson, Li said: 'I will probably see you again then?'

'Yes.' The quaver was scarcely noticeable.

Pointedly Snow said: 'The front door of the church is permanently locked. I will guide you out the way we came in.'

Li fell into step with the priest without any

attempt at conversation: at a turning, Snow saw Father Robertson at a hesitating distance. The chief of mission was hovering in the office corridor when Snow came back from the street exit, one hand clasped over the other.

'What photographs?' the white-haired man demanded once more.

'Ordinary tourist photographs.' Snow was not alarmed by Li's visit, but for the first time he was prepared to admit, to himself, that the man's interest was going beyond that of a normal tour escort: he didn't want an additional inquisition from his superior.

'Your trip has offended them! We're under scrutiny.'

'Which will discover what?'

'I don't want the mission closed down!'

'The mission *is* closed down!' said Snow, in renewed annoyance.

'We're permitted to remain here.'

'As what? It's surprising we're not officially part of group tours, as another aspect of Chinese history.'

'A Jesuit mission exists as long as we are a presence here!'

'We're a joke!' insisted Snow, utterly careless of letting the anger show. Careless, too, of upsetting the old man: welcoming, in fact, a target at which to direct some of the pent-up frustration.

Father Robertson winced, as if there had been a physical blow. 'God's work is not a joke.'

'We are not *doing* God's work!' persisted Snow.

'We are doing what we are told to do, by the Curia.'

What was the point of any discussion with this man? 'There is nothing here that can cause any official difficulty. We both know that. The man is a busybody: that is all. I will get him his photographs. And that will be the end of it.'

'I have personal experience of how they think!'

'The Cultural Revolution is over!'

'The official mentality is the same. I shall have to make an official report, to Rome. We should advise the embassy, as well.'

And Snow supposed he would after all have to tell Walter Foster: it was becoming difficult any more even to think of the journey through the southern and eastern provinces as a success.

'We were sorry you didn't manage to come last month.'

Charlie didn't doubt the matron, whose name was Hewlett, had positioned herself at the door of her office to intercept his arrival. 'Pressure of business, I'm afraid.'

'She does so much look forward to personal visits, you know? Particularly now she is maintaining this improvement.'

'I'll come as often as I can.'

'As long as you do,' said the matron, bossily.

On his way back to London Charlie realized he hadn't tried to confirm his inference of what

Julia Robb had conveyed about Miller and Patricia Elder. Perhaps he would have time before he was assigned a new apprentice.

Seventeen

Patricia Elder used Miller's discarded shirt as a dressing-gown to make the breakfast coffee, naked beneath. The apartment, the entire top floor of a period mansion on the edge of Regent's Park, was owned by Miller's wife and she used it when she came up from the country, so Patricia never kept any of her clothes there. The programme and ticket stubs for the previous night's opera at Covent Garden were on the hall table, ready to be taken and disposed of when they left. So was the after-theatre dinner bill for two.

The breakfast alcove was in the bay of the window overlooking the park. Miller was already at the table, dressed apart from his jacket, when Patricia came in from the kitchen. 'Do you want anything to eat?'

The Director-General looked up from his newspaper, shaking his head. 'Last night's got a bad review. I've certainly seen better performances. Glyndebourne, for instance.'

'I wasn't with you at Glyndebourne,' reminded Patricia, pointedly. As with everything else, they took great care where to be together in public. It was at Miller's insistence, not hers.

'Believe me, it was better,' he insisted, looking directly at her, guessing the mood in which she had awoken. His impression was that they had lately become more frequent. He hoped she wasn't going to become difficult.

Patricia poured the coffee and said: 'These are the good times, when we can spend two or three nights consecutively together.'

Miller suppressed the sigh. 'I like it, too. But don't, darling. Please!'

'Don't what?' she demanded sharply. 'I didn't say anything!'

'You don't have to,' he said, wearily. He wondered if he could cut the conversation off by returning to the newspaper but decided against it. She'd become even more resentful.

'You don't love her. She doesn't love you.'

Instead of immediately answering — because he could not quickly think of an answer he knew would satisfy her — Miller gazed fleetingly around the sprawling, antique-cluttered flat. That was a mistake.

'I can't believe it!' exclaimed Patricia, seeing the look. 'I can't believe you stay just because she's got money!'

'I didn't say that,' Miller defended, weakly.

'You didn't have to,' she said, using his words against him.

'It's not the money.'

'So why then?'

'I want to get the boys settled. We've talked it through enough times.'

'*You've* talked about it enough times, as an excuse! They're grown up, for Christ's sake!' She hadn't argued this forcefully before. She wanted to but at the same time she was frightened, not anxious to push him too much.

'They're still both at university. I don't want to create a family crisis that could affect that.'

'You know how long we've been together, you and I?'

'Of course I do.'

'Five years!' said Patricia. 'Five years of unkept promises. I even transferred from counter-intelligence because you said you didn't want us to be apart!'

'I don't!' insisted the man. 'But the transfer was as much professional as personal.' He was desperate for something to deflect the attack, surprised by her determination. Patricia *had* made all the concessions and all the sacrifices since the affair started. So why didn't he divorce Ann? There *was* no feeling between them now: he wasn't sure much had ever existed. It had practically been an arranged match, both minor aristocrat families — his impoverished, Ann's securely wealthy — knowing each other for years, expecting their respective children to marry. Which they'd done, having the same expectation without quite knowing why.

It *wasn't* the money, Miller told himself, although he liked the security of having it always available. So what was it? A mixture of things, he decided, answering the repeated question. There was the impact a divorce might have upon his career, which he despised himself for thinking.

179

It wasn't a fear directed towards Ann, who he didn't think would give a damn. The risk came from her impeccable family being offended by the minimal slur a divorce might cause: a family whose influence had carried him through his official career so far. Ann's was a lineage traditionally involved for almost a hundred years through Permanent Secretaries and ministry mandarins in the perpetually enduring government of the country, irrespective of which political party imagined itself in power. And those influences and panelled-club connections extended particularly through the Foreign Office, to which he was now attached. What other element was there in the mixture? Selfishness, he conceded. He didn't *want* the upheaval, the absolute disruption, that a divorce would even temporarily bring to his comfortably arranged, comfortably convenient life. Which could only surely mean that he didn't love Patricia sufficiently? He was sure — or fairly sure — he did.

'I'm not prepared to go on for ever,' warned the woman. She was, she recognized at once. She didn't have any alternative, apart from lonely, solitary spinsterhood.

'I'm not asking you to.' He was becoming irritable at her persistence.

In her confused anxiety it was Patricia who backed off, changing the subject with the abruptness of a switch being thrown. 'Are we leaving separately this morning?'

Sometimes they staggered their departure from

the Regent's Park mansion, from which the penthouse apartment had its own discreet exit, so as to produce an acceptably different time to arrive at the office.

'The diplomatic pouch from Beijing should have arrived overnight,' said Miller, seizing the escape. 'I want to get to it first thing: I'll précis it, before you get in.'

'I'm more interested in what we get *after* the embassy encounter.'

Miller realized, relieved, that Patricia had turned completely to professional considerations. 'I'm not sure how objective Foster's evaluation will be any longer, when they finally *do* meet. And Snow has made his position clear, refusing any further liaison contact.'

'Snow will be expecting our response, to his demand for a new controller.'

Miller leaned forward over the table, looking reflectively downwards. 'That's got to be balanced by a hair: one mistake on our part and it'll all end in disaster.'

'So what's the guidance we give Foster?'

'We'll have to wait to see if there is anything new in the pouch this morning,' pointed out the Director-General, logically. 'If there *isn't,* I don't see we give Foster any fresh instructions at all.'

'You don't want the withdrawal orders from us?'

Miller screwed his face up quizzically, at the same time shaking his head. 'I'd rather it be his decision. It would ultimately look better.'

181

'Something else that hangs by a hair,' mused the woman.

'Foster's got to be out first. The sequence has to be right.'

'The sequence has *always* had to be right,' reminded the woman.

After he'd left, Patricia hand-washed the breakfast things, dried them and restored them all to their respective cupboards so no evidence remained of two people having used the flat. Before finally leaving she checked carefully through every room — particularly the bedroom — to ensure she'd left nothing behind that shouldn't be there. As she was passing the hall table, she saw Miller had left the theatre programme, ticket stubs and restaurant bill for her to throw away. She hesitated for several moments before gathering everything up and stuffing it into her handbag. She waited until she had crossed the river and was several miles from Regent's Park before tossing the things into a waste basket. Even then she found a separate bin for the programme than for the tickets. She went directly into Miller's suite when she arrived.

'Just as it was,' reported Miller at once. 'Foster wants guidance, for the embassy meeting, that's all.'

'Good,' said the deputy Director.

Every building with any sort of vantage point directly overlooking the headquarters of Britain's external intelligence service is government-owned and occupied, to prevent a hostile service gaining access — or worse, permanent occupancy — to carry out surveillance of people entering or leaving. The monitoring that is attempted is, therefore, haphazard and virtually unproductive, snatched from passing vehicles or briefly parked cars and vans or temporarily halting pedestrians. Any effort positively to identify SIS operatives is additionally hampered by the building itself on some floors being occupied by government offices totally unconnected with any intelligence activity.

Natalia still tried, because it was the most obvious way and she couldn't think of anything else. She demanded every surveillance report and photograph obtained in the previous three months and spent every spare moment for four days looking through them all, straining for the slightest indication or sight of Charlie. And found nothing.

She even thought, briefly, of ordering a positive surveillance operation until she realized she was considering precisely what Berenkov had done and by so doing brought about his own downfall. Charlie had to be found another way, Natalia accepted.

But which way? Dear God she wished she knew.

Eighteen

The underlying tension that had always existed between Snow and Father Robertson came even closer to the surface in the days following Li's visit, frequently erupting into open argument. Both priests were stretched in opposite directions by conflicting emotions, Father Robertson seemingly racked with even greater fear than ever, Snow even angrier than before at his frustrating isolation from any contact with London. They even ceased, without discussion, taking each other's confession: for his part Snow was relieved, spared the hypocrisy.

The dissent between them was exacerbated by Father Robertson's constant insistence — usually in the evening, after he'd been drinking — that both the embassy and the Vatican Curia of the Jesuits had to be warned, until finally Snow's patience snapped with his demanding why the older man didn't just do something instead of talking about it.

So Father Robertson did. Three days after their uneasy encounter with the Chinese, he broke his daily schedule of always being around the complex in the morning by announcing he was going out — without saying where — and being absent for three hours. When he returned the head of mission made the further announcement that he'd sent to Italy through the diplomatic mail a full account of what had happened and had an hour-long discussion at the embassy with the political officer, Peter Samuels.

'He agreed with me that there's a potential difficulty,' concluded Father Robertson.

'I should talk with him as well,' insisted Snow.

'I suggested that. Samuels said for you to visit, so closely after me, would be a mistake.' His words were slightly slurred.

'Why?' demanded Snow.

'The embassy is watched. If I go, then you follow almost immediately after, it could suggest that we have something to be frightened about: that we *are* conducting services — preaching religion — from the mission.'

'But we're *not!* If the Chinese suspect that we are, they will have been watching us here, as well. And we know they won't have found anything because there's nothing to find!'

'You're being insubordinate.'

'I'm being truthful and factual and objective. You're building this into something far greater and far more important than it is!'

'That is not for you to decide. Or me.'

'It's an opinion that will be reached from how the facts are presented. Yours have been. Mine haven't. I want the opportunity to put my assessment forward.'

'You'll be given it, if it's thought necessary.'

'*I* think it's necessary.'

'You serve. You don't demand.'

Snow's breathing started to become difficult. 'What have you told the Curia?'

'Precisely what happened.'

'With what recommendation?'

'None. I also serve, not demand. Any decision has to be theirs, uninfluenced by any opinion of mine.'

'What will you recommend, if you are asked?'

'That you are withdrawn. This mission *can't* be endangered.'

'How is it any less endangered with only you here? You can conduct religious services just as easily as me.'

'Before your appointment, when I worked here by myself there was never any official interest.'

Because you're their hollow totem, thought Snow, contemptuously. Just as quickly he confronted the reality. His primary function, as a Jesuit, *was* to serve: so he would have to leave, permitted no opposing argument, if he were ordered out of the country by the Vatican. So why did the prospect make him so unsettled? Surely his unofficial activities had not assumed greater importance than his avowed vocation? Of course not, he assured himself: a ridiculous doubt. Snow said: 'When do you expect to hear back from Rome?'

'I don't impose time-limits,' avoided the older man.

Snow sighed, but shallowly because his chest was still tight. With strained patience he said:

'In normal circumstances how long does it take to get a reply from Rome?'

'There is no formula,' said the mission chief, almost as if determined to be difficult. 'Sometimes weeks. Sometimes months.'

In fairness he *should* be allowed to give his calmly reasoned side of the issue, despite Father Robertson's pedantic reminder of humility. If he were allowed to state his case, Snow wondered if it would not be the most opportune time to suggest that Father Robertson be the one to be withdrawn, a burned out man obsessed by imagined demons, doing little if any good remaining here on station, too prone always to sound alarms where none were justified. He said, with minimal sincerity: 'I am sorry you don't think this a happy ministry.'

Father Robertson moved at once towards conciliation. 'It hasn't been easy for either of us. Me, from what happened before: you, from it being your first posting. Because circumstances here — and I don't mean this current situation — *aren't* normal. God knows when they ever will be.'

Snow realized, surprised, that Father Robertson was no longer prevaricating but arguing forcefully and positively expressing an opinion. Moving towards conciliation himself, he said: 'Possibly more difficult for you than me, because of what happened in the past.'

Father Robertson physically shuddered. 'Now *in* the past, thank God.'

Gentle-voiced, no longer having any anger, he

said: 'Have you ever thought of leaving China? Going home, perhaps?'

Father Robertson frowned across his desk, a look of total bewilderment on his face. 'This is my home. Here.'

'This is your *posting*,' insisted Snow, but gently now.

'Home,' said Father Robertson, even more insistent, although his voice was oddly remote. 'There is nowhere else. It's important work, being here.'

Snow judged, at that moment, that the older man was completely lost, his mind full of confused images. Which Snow decided gave even more reason for suggesting the transfer, if he got the opportunity. And for no other reason than simple Christianity: Father Robertson had served and suffered dreadfully during a devoted lifetime in their special priesthood. Now he deserved peace and contentment and hopefully relief from the terrors that constantly gripped him. There were caring Retreats throughout the world — in Rome particularly — where the old man could live out the rest of his life in prayer and meditation. 'Don't you feel you have done enough?' Snow asked, still gentle.

'No one has ever done enough,' smiled Father Robertson. 'There's always so much more to be done.'

And finally the day came.

In the early morning, before setting off, Snow

and Father Robertson prayed separately, which they often did anyway, and afterwards Snow wondered if the head of mission had sought guidance as fervently as he had. He took the older man's meaningless, mumbled confession but declined to make one himself, pleading lack of time that day. Father Robertson didn't argue.

It was an extensively planned schedule, a reception for the visiting British businessmen in the forenoon, a lunch culminating with an introductory speech from the junior British trade minister accompanying the delegation, and in the afternoon a seminar for discussions with Chinese government representatives and officials. Snow didn't know how long it would take him to manoeuvre the encounter with the despised but still necessary Foster.

In his anxiety to get at last to the embassy Snow suggested they take a taxi to Jian Guo Men Wai, but Father Robertson dismissed the unnecessary expense. The old man had pressed his usually concertinaed trousers, donned what Snow knew to be his best jacket and put on a tie. His hair, as always, looked like a wind-blasted wheat field. The nervousness was obvious, shaking through the man: increasingly, as the time approached for them to leave the mission, his sentences became gabbled, most ending unfinished and none of any consequence. Twice, as they talked, Snow smelled whisky.

Snow himself made a greater effort than usual, wearing his one good suit, surprised when he put it on at the tightness of the trouser band, unaware he had been gaining weight. He wasn't, however, surprised at the snatch of asthma, well aware how tense he was. He used his inhaler and considered wearing the pollution mask but decided against it. As a precaution he slipped it into his pocket.

The head of mission walked slowly, but Snow still found himself breathing heavily; towards the end he wished he had argued more strongly for a taxi. Twice they were intercepted by money-changers. It was Snow who rejected both, ahead of the older man. There was a lot of activity around the embassy compound, a scattering of soldiers as well as militia. In a city where bicycles are the accepted mode of transport, so many official black limousines had attracted a curious group of onlookers at the perimeter fence. There was a polite parting of those closest to the gates, for them to enter.

The room in which the pre-lunch reception was being held was immediately to the left of the vestibule, overlooking a checkerboard garden. There was a small receiving line just inside the door. Names were announced in both English and Mandarin by a diplomat comparing the invitations with an official list. Snow courteously fell behind Father Robertson as they were greeted by the principal guests, further introduced by the ambassador to the junior minister and trade officials beyond.

Snow accepted orange juice from a statued

waiter holding a tray of drinks: Father Robertson took Scotch. The elderly man nodded across the room and said: 'There's Samuels.'

Snow was already searching the room, looking for Walter Foster. He followed Father Robertson's direction. Peter Samuels was a dark-haired, saturnine man whom Snow guessed to be almost as tall as himself. At that moment Samuels looked in their direction: there was no recognition or acknowledgement. As quickly as he had focused on them, the political officer turned away. Still unable to find the man he really wanted, Snow indicated Samuels and said: 'I'm going to talk to him: put my side of the case.'

'It'll look too obvious, approaching him so quickly.'

'It won't look like anything of the sort!' dismissed Snow, moving off through the crowd, glad to separate himself from the other priest.

Samuels saw him coming. This time there was a facial reaction, and Snow got the impression that had the diplomat not been involved in a discussion with three other Westerners he would have tried to avoid the encounter. Instead Samuels remained where he was, managing a thin smile when Snow reached the group. He made the introductions with cold politeness: all three strangers were from the British Department of Trade and Industry. There was the customary cocktail party small-talk of how interesting it must be permanently to live in such an unusual society, how long it had taken Snow to perfect the language, how much they hoped to get to the Great Wall and see the Terracotta Army, and how exciting they considered the trade potential to be. Snow kept up his side of the conversations, thinking as he did so how rehearsed and practised all the talk sounded. Samuels, the professional diplomat, made his contribution, but seemed at the same time constantly to be surveying the room.

Samuels expertly broke up the gathering, suggesting to the trade officials that the minister might want them close to him as he mingled throughout the room, which he was now doing.

When they were alone, Samuels said at once: 'Father Robertson appears worried at some official interest.' The man had a slow, word-tasting manner of speaking. Like Snow, he was drinking orange juice.

'*Overly* worried,' insisted Snow, at once. 'I really do not think there is any cause for concern.'

'Father Robertson told me the escort for your recent trip actually inspected the church?'

'He came to the English class that I take,' qualified Snow, determined upon absolute accuracy. 'While he was there he asked to *see* the church, which of course I showed him. Just as he'd shown me various temples, when we were travelling. It was *not* an inspection, in any sense of the word.'

'Why *did* you make the journey?'

'A holiday. I obviously want to see and get to know as much of the country as possible.' Snow wondered what Samuels' reaction would have been to knowing the truth: probably the same sort of hand-wringing that Father Robertson engaged in. Snow could see the mission chief in distracted conversation with one of the British officials with whom he had spoken earlier: the old man was looking directly across at where he was, with Samuels. As Snow watched he saw Father Robertson take another Scotch from the tray of a passing waiter and wondered how many there had been since the day had begun. Quite a few by now, he guessed.

'Don't you think it odd for the man to make such a visit?'

Snow hesitated. 'I virtually invited him.'

'Do you think he is attached to the Security Bureau?'

'It would not surprise me if he were.'

Samuels paused, smiling and imperceptibly shaking his head to a man and a woman who were approaching. The couple veered away. Samuels covered the refusal by gesturing around the reception area. 'There's a great deal of importance attached to visits like these. It might have sounded trite, but those remarks about the enormous trade potential *are* true.'

'I understand that,' said Snow, expectantly.

'We do not want any local difficulties interfering with the better links that have been established between our two countries. It's taken a very great deal of time and effort to get to this stage.'

Snow disliked the other man's unctuous manner and thought he talked like the other officials, earlier, as if everything had been rehearsed and pre-pared, well in advance. 'What possible difficulty could be created by Li's coming to the church?'

'We're talking generally.'

'I don't think we are,' rejected Snow. 'I have done nothing — nothing *whatsoever* — to cause you any official concern. But we are not allowed to preach or engage in any sort of religious ob-servance involving the Chinese. So we do not. As Li discovered when he came to the class. When he went into the church, it would have been ob-vious to him it was unused. We don't *preach:* do anything to offend the authorities. So there is absolutely nothing for you to worry about: noth-ing that *can* be worried about.' He wasn't sure the diplomat was accepting anything of what he was saying.

'Father Robertson seems to think otherwise,' reminded Samuels, in virtual confirmation of Snow's doubt.

Snow sighed, carelessly. 'You know what hap-pened to him, during the Cultural Revolution. It effectively broke him. I think it's a mistake for the Curia to let him remain here: I know it's at his own request but I think it is putting too much strain upon a man who has already suffered enough.'

'I felt it necessary officially to advise London,' announced Samuels.

'I would have welcomed the opportunity to give my version of the episode.'

'I really must be circulating,' said Samuels, gazing enquiringly around the room again.

'It would be unfortunate if a biased account misled London,' said Snow, unwilling to be put off like some minor irritant.

Samuels came fully back to Snow, frowning at the remark. 'I made my report completely factual: I did not give a biased account.'

'If it was based entirely upon what Father Robertson told you it must have been biased.'

Samuels mouth tightened, giving his long face a pinched look. 'I did not overstress the matter.'

Would whatever Samuels had written percolate through to the department to which he reported? Before Snow had time to consider his own question, he at last saw Walter Foster. The embassy liaison man was at the extreme end of the large room, with a mixed group of English and Chinese businessmen: from the way his head was moving back and forth Snow inferred the man was helping with a translation difficulty. 'I would like to think you'd add to your report, giving my version of events.'

'What *is* your version of events?'

'That I was assigned an over-zealous escort for part of a journey through southern and eastern provinces of the country. During that journey I did nothing to cause any official offence. Towards the end of the trip, there was some discussion about my being a priest and I invited the man to visit the mission when he returned to Beijing. This he did. Again there was nothing to cause any official offence.'

'I see,' said Samuels, stiffly.

'Will you add that?' pressed the priest.

'If London seek further clarification,' promised the diplomat, unconvincingly.

'Not otherwise?'

'Wouldn't there be a risk of indicating an importance you insist does not exist if I send an additional report?' said Samuels. Once more the room was examined. 'I really must start moving around.'

Snow thought Samuels' response showed the typical convoluted thinking of the diplomat milieu. 'Perhaps if there is any further exchange, we could talk again before you report back? It's very easy for me to come up from the mission at any time.'

'Perhaps,' said Samuels, distantly noncommittal. 'And be a good chap, don't keep openly referring to it as a "mission" as you are doing: gives the impression that it really might be used for religious services, don't you think?'

Snow eased his way through the crush of the now full room, beyond anger, gripped by helpless impotence at what he considered to be a pointless conversation. The one reassurance he kept repeating to himself was that it did not matter how irreversibly slanted Samuels' memorandum had been: in no way could it affect his remaining in China. It would still have been better to have had his say, to counter the hysteria of Father Robertson.

Foster, whose official embassy description was

that of a cultural attaché, *was* translating. Snow approached from the rear of the cluster of men, behind Foster, able to hear quite a lot before the man became aware of his closeness. He detected several words where the vital nuance in the Mandarin pronunciation came close to giving a completely wrong interpretation of what Foster was trying to convey. Foster's concentration faltered when he finally saw Snow and he had to ask one of the British businessmen to repeat himself, to complete the bilingual exchange. It was a further ten minutes before an official Chinese translator rejoined the group, but even then Foster lingered, clearly reluctant to break away until Snow very obviously started forward to make the contact on his terms.

Foster intercepted him but said, vehemently: 'Not now!'

'Now!' demanded Snow.

'It'll be easier after the lunch.'

'Walk with me towards the canapés table,' ordered Snow. 'There is more you have to know.'

'More!' Instead of walking casually, the man actually stopped, staring directly at the priest. Snow kept going, making Foster hurry to catch up. 'How much more?'

'You haven't talked with Samuels?'

'No!' said Foster, anguished.

Having reached the canapés table, both had to go through the pretence of selecting hors-d'oeuvres. Snow picked up another glass of orange juice.

Snow waited until they moved away before re-counting Li's visit, aware of Foster visibly flushing: the man's face became redder and therefore seemingly more freckled than normal by the time Snow finished.

'Dear God!' exclaimed Foster. 'There can't be any doubt, not now!' As always at times of stress the man began darting looks around him, as if fearing he would be seized at any moment.

'There's no proof, of anything.'

'There doesn't have to be, not in China. You know that. And how the hell are you going to explain why you can't produce the Shanghai photographs? You've got to get out. Like I'm going to. I'm empowered to make the decision myself. So I'm making it for you, as well. I'm ordering you to leave with me.'

Snow regarded the other man evenly. 'You can't. I only officially obey the Curia, at the Vatican.' People were gathering near the main door, preparing to file through into the banqueting room. Snow saw that Father Robertson was beside Samuels, although they did not appear to be talking very much.

Foster was momentarily open-mouthed at the obvious truth of Snow's statement. 'But that's ridiculous!'

'It's the unarguable fact,' said Snow, calmly. 'And I don't in any case see the need to panic: even if I had the freedom to leave I would not.'

'You're being absolutely foolish.'

'It's rational, sensible thinking.' Snow was surprised — and glad — at how easily he was breathing. He felt no tension at all now.

Foster was briefly silent. 'I read what you told London: about not working any longer with me.'

'I gave the undertaking that you could,' reminded Snow.

'None of this is my fault,' insisted Foster. 'You brought investigation upon yourself.'

'There *is* no investigation!' said Snow, brusquely. 'At the moment you are my only link with London. I'm asking you fully to advise London of Li's visit. But *don't* make it any more sinister than it is: which is hardly sinister at all. The one thing I *do* need, however, are copies of the photographs.' Abandoning an earlier unease, he went on: 'It must be scientifically possible to treat them to take out what I got in the background in Shanghai. The ones that can't be altered I will say spoiled in the developing.'

'He won't believe that,' said Foster. 'No one would.'

'Ask London to come up with a better excuse then,' said Snow. 'The photographs will provide an obvious first meeting, with whoever it is I am to liaise with in the future.'

'London won't continue with anything, not after this!' predicted Foster, adamantly. 'It would be madness!'

'Wouldn't it be greater madness for them *not* to continue? Surely if I don't at least provide *some* photographs it'll be confirmation of whatever suspicion you think Li has about me.'

'What a mess!' moaned Foster. 'A complete and utter bloody mess!'

'It'll only become a mess if it's mishandled.' Did he really think that? Yes, Snow decided, positively. Li's unexpected visit was unnerving, but that was all, at its worst. And only then to someone who allowed his nerve to go at the first uncertainty. Foster was wrong, as he was wrong about most things, in saying the Chinese did not need proof before taking action against Westerners. That might have been true during the Cultural Revolution: Father Robertson was a prime example of what things had been like then. And they still behaved as they thought fit against their own people, in the name of stability against counter-revolution, as they had in Tiananmen Square. But he was sure the ruling hierarchy were now, if belatedly, too conscious of outside world opinion to move arbitrarily against a foreigner.

'You're a fool!' said Foster, quiet-voiced in final resignation. The initial redness had gone but a nerve was pulling beneath his left eye, making his face twitch.

'You'll tell London all I've said?' There was no reason to let things degenerate into acrimony.

'Of course I will.'

'Exactly *as* I've said it?'

'Of course,' repeated Foster. The looks about him now were practically those of embarrassment, as if he were anxious to break off contact with someone with whom he was socially ill-at-ease.

'I don't want any new arrangement maintained

at a distance. Emphasize that to London. I want *meetings.*'

The encounter was broken by the summons to lunch. The seating was at round tables, variously set either for groups of eight or ten. He and Father Robertson were at separate places, with a mixture of Chinese and English, obviously for the communication bridge both could provide, beyond the top-table interpreters for the official speeches. The purpose for his being at the embassy already fulfilled, Snow relaxed, although still unsure how accurately Foster — and to a lesser extent the annoyingly supercilious Samuels — would pass on what he had said.

The official speeches were predictably boring, made more so by the slowness of the simultaneous translation between the two languages. Frequently Snow had to correct misunderstandings on his immediate table and he wondered just how much was really being comprehended by the audience. Both Samuels and Father Robertson were seated directly to face him, from their respective tables. Throughout the meal and the speeches, both men studiously ignored him. Foster was on the far side of the room, with his back towards him.

Snow broke away from his table group at the end of the meal, not wanting to become inveigled as an unofficial interpreter in the afternoon seminar. Five tables away, Father Robertson was standing in what looked to be confused aimlessness, people swirling around him. Snow hurried to the man and said: 'I think we should go now.'

The smell of alcohol was very strong from the old man. He allowed himself to be led towards the exit, not the door leading deeper into the embassy for the business conference.

As they crossed the courtyard, towards the Guang Hua Road, Snow dropped the guiding hand and said: 'I spoke to Samuels.'

Father Robertson rallied, stiffening himself as he walked. 'He told me you don't think it is serious.'

'It isn't,' insisted Snow, practically automatically now.

'He said he hopes you're right.'

'So do I,' said Snow, wishing at once that he hadn't: it made it seem as if he were unsure and he wasn't, not at all.

Nineteen

They met again at The Spaniards, so Charlie Muffin guessed she lived somewhere in the Swiss Cottage or Hampstead area. As before he got there first, managing one drink ahead of her arrival. She was shiny-faced again. The top, over the same jeans, was all-enveloping but a different colour, tonight a subdued brown. Charlie hadn't ordered for her, in case she wanted something different, but again she chose beer. He waited until the second drink before suggesting dinner again. She accepted after a token hesitation.

Charlie let the conversation drift for a while before saying: 'Surprised I haven't heard by now from the stony Miss Elder.' He decided, too late, that it was a clumsy effort but the other toss-and-catch conversation was becoming a pain in the ass.

Her reply was interesting. 'Do you think she's stony?'

'Rocklike,' he insisted. Exaggerating, he said: 'She frightens the shit out of me.'

'I don't believe you.'

'It's true,' persisted Charlie. 'Miss Elder is the original ball-breaker. No humanity. No feeling.'

'You're wrong.'

What the hell did that mean? 'I don't think

I am,' he said, inviting the contradiction.

'Professionally, maybe. She can be very kind, otherwise.'

That hadn't come out as well as he'd wanted. 'Well hidden,' he said, still encouraging a contrary argument.

'She's definitely very controlled,' agreed the girl.

Still not good enough, judged Charlie, signalling for more drinks. 'She was hard-assed towards me. Take it or leave it ultimatum: except that I couldn't leave it. The other choice was to be a caretaker.'

The idea amused Julia. She sniggered and said: 'I don't really see you as a caretaker.'

'Neither do I,' said Charlie. 'So here I am, stuck.'

'Maybe things will change, in time.'

A pointer, from some inner-circle knowledge! seized Charlie. Or a casual, meaningless remark? Pressing the exchange, he said: 'I'd certainly like to think so.'

'What's so important, about being actively operational?'

'It's what I know how to do.'

'You seem to have adjusted well enough to the new role.'

That *had* to be an indication. But then she'd already intimated he'd done well with John Gower. Very briefly — contravening his own prohibitions on personal involvement — Charlie thought of the young and eager entrant, hoping that whatever assignment Gower was given would work out all right. Charlie was the first, with his Teflon-edged cynicism, to acknowledge it was impossible to generalize, but he tried to convince himself that it should do: Gower had learned a lot, even if everything he'd tried to teach the man hadn't been absorbed to the point of it being reflexive. He said: 'It might be nice, to be told.'

'Come on!' erupted Julia, in mock sneer. 'Ten out of ten for Mr Muffin!'

Too clumsy again, conceded Charlie, irritated. 'It *will* be necessary for me to be officially told by her, or by Miller, that it's going as they want.'

'That will only come from the practical successes of people you train. Or lack of success,' the girl pointed out. 'And if it doesn't work out as she wants, you'll know about it soon enough!'

Back on track, decided Charlie, relieved. 'Hard taskmaster, even though you think she's got a lot of hidden feelings?'

'The hardest, professionally.'

The opening beckoned, a chasm of opportunity. 'That why Miller brought her across with him? Sure of her professional ability?'

Julia Robb stood looking directly at him in the crowded bar. Pointedly refusing the response, she said: 'I liked the place where we ate last time.'

Intentionally Charlie did not speak until they reached the restaurant in Heath Street. Julia didn't try to break the silence, either. Charlie ordered a bottle of wine rather than an aperitif, and deep fried eggplant to pick at, while they decided what properly to eat. Without looking at her, he said finally: 'You didn't answer my question, in the pub.'

'No, I didn't,' she agreed.

'She's not married,' insisted Charlie. 'He is, though. Wife's got an hereditary title. And a stud-farm and racing stables. Lives out of London.'

'Really?' Julia sounded indifferent, the menu before her.

'It's all listed in *Who's Who*.' So was a Regent's Park address he intended to visit.

Julia put the menu down on to the table: the plastic covering made a slapping sound. 'Maybe I shouldn't have come here tonight after all. Thanks anyway . . .'

'Don't go!' said Charlie, urgently.

'I think I should.'

'I'm sorry. Really. I mean it.'

'I thought we had an understanding.'

'We have.'

'You seem to have forgotten it. Again.'

'I'm sorry,' he repeated.

'I don't want it always to be an interrogation. We're *not* at the department now, not that it would make any difference anyway. I won't answer your questions. Not any of them.'

'I don't think you have to,' said Charlie, meaning it.

'I didn't say anything!' Her reaction unsettled him. Her face broke and momentarily he thought she was going to cry.

'You didn't!' Lying, he said: 'I haven't inferred anything.'

'It's their business. No one else's.'

'Sure.' So obvious was her distress that although he'd spent so much of the evening trying to guide the conversation in this direction Charlie now wanted to get away from it. 'I didn't mean to upset you. Honestly. It won't happen again. I promise.'

Julia smiled, faintly and with difficulty. 'Who said there's going to be an again?'

'I deserved that,' accepted Charlie. A blown situation, he decided. He supposed he'd learned what he set out to discover, but he really hadn't intended to bring her close to tears. Her near breakdown intrigued him. He definitely couldn't pursue it now.

'Maybe you deserve something more,' she said.

Charlie frowned, confused. 'You're losing me.'

'I don't think I'm being very fair. In fact I know I'm not being fair.'

'I'm still lost.'

'I'm married,' blurted Julia. At once she corrected herself. '*Was* married. Not any more.'

'So?' queried Charlie. If she wanted to unburden herself, it was all right with him.

Julia stared down into her glass, appearing unable to meet his look. 'I enjoyed the last time. And tonight . . .' She looked up briefly, smiling. 'Most of it, that is. But I don't want it to go beyond . . . get difficult . . . lead to your expecting something that can't happen . . .' She stopped,

207

the smile hopeful now. 'Do you know what I'm saying?'

Forced to speak finally, Charlie said: 'Some of it. Not all.'

'His name was . . .' She smiled, apologetically. '. . . is, Andrew: I still can't get the tenses right. Andrew . . .' Babbling now, wanting to get the explanation out of the way, she said: 'He's a finance lawyer: specializes in international tax affairs, always on aeroplanes to Europe and America and those tiny islands with special arrangements for those who can afford them. Absolutely brilliant. Directorship promised before he's forty, eventual chairmanship of the group a foregone conclusion. We had a hell of a life: the whole yuppie bit . . .' She gulped at her wine, further steeling herself. Flat-voiced, Julia went on: 'I thought everything was wonderful: I suppose it was. But do you know what? All the time it was wonderful for him with someone else, too.' Julia stared directly at Charlie. 'And can you guess who that was?'

She seemed to expect a reply, so Charlie said: 'No, I can't.'

'My own sister!' declared Julia. 'How about that? My own sister! One night, eighteen months ago, he came home and we went to bed and made love and then he announced it was over. I actually laughed, thinking there was some joke . . .'

'Are you sure . . . ?' started Charlie, but she interrupted him back. 'Yes! Let me, please! I want to talk about it!'

'OK,' accepted Charlie, waiting.

'He told me who it was, too. While we were lying there, side by side. Not just wrecking my marriage. Wrecking the family, too. I didn't know what to do . . . still don't, I suppose. That's what I meant about using you. Wanted to see what it would be like, going out with some-one again. I hadn't, you see. Not for years. No one apart from Andrew. Didn't know if I could still do it properly . . .' She smiled, wanly. 'Classic Agony Aunt stuff. Destroyed wife, destroyed con-fidence.'

'I didn't guess. It was a great performance,' said Charlie.

'I don't want anything!' she said, in another of her blurted announcements. 'Not someone else . . . romance . . . sex. I really don't. I'm not going to become a manhater or anything ridiculous like that. I'm just more comfortable — happier — by myself. Trusting myself.'

It *was* a classic case history of a dumped wife, decided Charlie. 'I can understand that.' Particu-larly the bit about only trusting oneself. He re-membered lecturing Gower about it.

She looked at him uncertainly. 'Can you?'

'It's kind of a personal philosophy of mine.'

'But I get so damned lonely,' Julia admitted. 'I go out and do things by myself and just some-times — very occasionally — I forget where I am and what I am doing but mostly I am as lonely as hell.'

'I can understand that, too,' said Charlie.

There'd been aching loneliness, after Edith had been killed. That brief, wonderful, impossible period in Moscow with Natalia had probably been the only time since that he hadn't lived permanently with the feeling.

'I mean what I said,' insisted the girl. 'I really don't want sex. I don't want a lover or any sort of complication that is going to end up hurting more: I've had enough of that. You know what I want?'

'What?'

'A friend. Someone I can trust: feel safe with.'

Charlie didn't speak for several moments, like Julia drinking his wine to cover his hesitation. Finally he said: 'Can I apply?' What about trust, after the way he'd used her?

'It wouldn't be fair,' she said, positively. 'That's why I've told you. Didn't want you to think there was anything . . . you know.'

'And now I do,' said Charlie. 'So why not?'

'Platonic relationship?' Julia queried, doubtfully.

'That's what it's called,' agreed Charlie.

'I'm not sure,' she said, uncertainly.

'We won't be, until we give it a shot.'

'You mean it?'

'Sure.' Did he? wondered Charlie.

Natalia discovered Fyodor Tudin was spying on her from routine bureaucracy.

It was an inviolable rule, dating from the KGB period, that archives were registered against the name of whoever requested them, with the file cover itself dated with all previous withdrawals. When she called for Charlie's records for yet another search, in the hope she might have missed something the first time, she found a date immediately following her initial examination. A simple cross-reference to the main register revealed Tudin's name, which was also recorded against her own personal records, which the man had consulted soon after their respective appointments.

What else had he already done, in the hope of undermining her? And how, she wondered, could she protect herself? She'd have to find a way. It wasn't just danger to her: it was danger to Sasha.

Twenty

Walter Foster's emergency cable was coded for the Director-General's 'Eyes Only' attention. Miller handed it to Patricia Elder as she responded to his summons and said: 'It's a bastard.'

Patricia looked up from the message and said: 'We didn't anticipate this, did we?'

'We couldn't, not until it was too late: after the photographs had already been taken.' Miller nodded to the cable slip on the desk between them. 'There's no reason to wait until Foster gets here personally with a fuller account.'

'What about Snow's suggestion?' asked the woman, doubtfully.

Miller shook his head. 'Claiming some got damaged during processing or didn't come out is as phoney as hell.'

'It wouldn't provide evidence for an actual seizure, though, would it? Snow is not one of their own people, where proper evidence doesn't really matter. And it would give us time: everything has got to be in sequence.'

Miller shook his head again. 'A time-frame we'd have no way of controlling: maybe cause more moves we couldn't anticipate. You forget another problem, maybe as big as any other — the obvious determination of this bloody man Li. He won't be stalled for long, not from the way he's behaved so far.'

'There'd still be no positive evidence to justify an arrest,' persisted the woman.

'We can't rely on delay that goes on too long.'

Patricia got up, moving aimlessly about the office. 'We don't know how sophisticated their photographic analysis is: what scientific techniques they have. The only thing we can be sure about is that there *will* be technical analysis.'

'Talk it through with our own Analysis here,' ordered Miller. 'They will have examined every one by now. Some photographs will be easier to treat than others. Get a list, in order of priority. What has to be erased or covered. How easy and undetectable it will be. Explain the problem fully to Technical. Have them make prints first, so they can suggest to us what is feasible before they actually do anything to the negatives.'

'It's possible the Chinese examination will *only* be a physical one, by eye: obviously by Li himself,' suggested Patricia. 'Maybe they won't go to any laboratory.'

'We've got to work from the opposite assumption,' refused Miller.

'We've got something!' declared the deputy Director suddenly, stopping her perambulation. 'In his account of the journey Snow referred to Li taking his *own* photographs. What if what Li took were copy sheets of everything Snow photographed, for comparison? That could be *why* Li wants to see Snow's pictures: because the Chinese know already from examining Li's stuff that they show things in the background that shouldn't be there.'

'It's a possibility,' conceded Miller, reluctantly.

'More than a possibility,' argued Patricia, increasingly convinced she was right. 'Certainly one we *have* to consider.'

'Definitely a question to put to Snow, to see if he can remember.'

Patricia Elder sat down again. 'An additional reason for the direct contact he's demanding.'

'If there are true copy prints — and we alter ours here so the two don't compare — it will provide whatever espionage proof the Chinese need: unquestionably be sufficient for an arrest.'

'It's all unravelling too quickly,' complained the woman.

'So we have to adjust just as quickly!' said Miller. 'I'm not worried. Merely trying to recognize the pitfalls before they open up ahead of us, as this has done.'

'Shall I brief Gower?'

'Both of us,' determined the intelligence chief. For several moments he remained looking down at his desk, immersed in thought. 'The speed of things is restricting our manoeuvrability.'

'Which is being further restricted by his refusal to accept any authority other than that of his Order in Rome,' added the woman.

'It will still be all right,' said Miller.

'So what *about* the authority of the Order?'

demanded Patricia. 'That could become a very real problem.'

'Have you forgotten any Vatican exchange with their mission in Beijing comes through our embassy channels, Father Robertson *and* Father Snow being British nationals?'

The woman *had* briefly overlooked the ease of interception. She nodded, wishing she hadn't. 'Yes,' she agreed, slowly. 'We can monitor every exchange. That could be useful.'

'So we can control him *very* effectively,' said Miller, confidently.

'Sure we don't need to see Foster, before we go on?' queried the deputy.

'No,' said the Director. 'We've got to catch up.'

John Gower entered the Director-General's office with polite deference, but no lack of confidence.

'Your first assignment,' announced Miller.

Gower smiled. 'I was hoping it would be that.'

'You're going to Beijing,' said Patricia Elder, taking up the briefing. 'An emergency has arisen: something that has to be resolved from here.'

Gower felt the beginning of excitement: the likelihood of his going to China had never entered his mind, during any private speculation as to where in the world he might go. 'What?'

'We think an agent is about to be exposed,' said Miller. 'You're to get him out. We can't risk an arrest: any political or diplomatic embarrassment.'

Political embarrassments had been covered in his most recent, unusual instruction, Gower remembered. 'When do I go?'

'We'll begin the travel and visa arrangements today,' said Patricia.

'Who is it I have to get out?'

There was no immediate reply. Then Miller said: 'You'll get that later.'

Now the silence was from Gower. Then he said: 'Why don't you simply order the man to leave?'

'He doesn't accept the situation is as serious as we believe it is,' said the woman. 'He's freelance, not officially attached to the department.'

'Could there be an official attempt to stop us getting out?'

'Not if we move quickly enough.'

'But it's a possibility?' pressed Gower. How was he expected to handle official obstruction in perhaps the most ordered and restricted country on earth?

'A possibility,' agreed the Director-General.

'I'm to travel with him?'

'Yes.'

'*How* do I get him out?'

'The quickest and most practical way: that'll have to be your decision, according to the circumstances you find when you get there,' said Miller.

'He's already been warned? There's been an

216

attempt to get him to leave?'

'Yes.'

'What if he refuses to come with me?'

'There was a personality clash with our resident officer, who is being withdrawn,' said the Director-General. 'There mustn't be, with you. You've *got* to get him out.'

'I'm to work through the embassy?' He was already wondering how to tell Marcia.

'Officially you'll be a representative from Foreign Office Personnel, making a ground tour of existing embassy facilities: that cover puts you *in* the embassy, but only as long as you need: we won't have to claim you're filling a diplomatic vacancy.'

'Who in the embassy will know my real function?'

'The ambassador, obviously,' replied Miller. 'Possibly his most senior attaché. You'll work quite alone.'

At that moment, at either extreme of the world, two things that were very much to affect John Gower occurred simultaneously.

At London's Heathrow airport, Walter Foster disembarked from the Beijing flight. He paused just inside the terminal building, allowing himself the theatricality of breathing deeply, feeling free, which was a sensation he had not known for months.

And in the church complex in Beijing, Jeremy Snow looked up at Li's unexpected appearance, again at the back of a class in progress.

217

'I thought you might have received the photographs from England,' said the Chinese, when the class had once more hurried away, frightened by another official intrusion.

'Not yet,' apologized Snow.

The London apartment address listed in *Who's Who* for Lady Ann Miller — an entry which recorded in one line the occupation of her husband as a civil servant — formed part of one of the most spectacular Regency mansions built by Nash at the very edge of the park. It was a penthouse and therefore far too high for Charlie to gain an impression of its interior, but he was able to see into other lower flats on the nights when their occupants didn't draw their curtains. This wasn't simply wealth, Charlie decided: people who lived here wouldn't know how much they were worth because money — the need for it and most certainly never the lack of it — would never have intruded into their lives.

He alternated between morning and night, an observation he accepted from the beginning was inadequate if attempted irregularly by only one man upon a house with possible exits not only on to the park but into Albany Street as well.

After several unproductive days and nights, Charlie began to wonder if his inference from Julia's remark might not, after all, have been wrong. Or if this wasn't the love-nest in any case.

Twenty-one

Father Robertson collapsed forty-eight hours after Li's second visit. It was not until the middle of the morning, after the older priest had failed to appear for early prayers, that Snow went to Father Robertson's personal quarters and found him. The man — and his bedding — was soaked in sweat, but at that stage he was still rational, talking with reasonable coherence although his teeth chattered from the helter-skelter fever.

Snow changed both the man and the bed, shocked when he blanket-bathed the old priest to see how emaciated he was. There were scars, too. A lot, on the back, were evenly spaced and in the same direction, as they would have been if Father Robertson's skin had split under repeated beatings. Another, to the right of his chest, high on a bony, skin-stretched ribcage, was indented like a stab wound. It had healed in a large, uneven white circle, as if it had not been properly, medically, treated.

Within an hour of the first change and bath, Father Robertson and his bed were as soaked as before.

'I have to get the embassy doctor.'

'No!' His irrational agitation had Father Robertson virtually on the point of tears. 'It's nothing. A small fever.'

On his way to the kitchen with the newly fouled bedclothes, Snow decided to ignore Father Robertson's refusal, picking up the telephone to call the embassy. The line was not dead but inoperable, which it frequently was, emitting a familiar high-pitched whine through which it was impossible to dial.

There was a temporary calm — even an apparent respite in the fluctuating temperature — when the two men said the rosary together. Snow led the observance, anxious against tiring someone clearly on the edge of exhaustion. Before lapsing into a shuddering, tossing and turning sleep, Father Robertson several times apologized.

Snow remained constantly by the bedside throughout that day and into the night. Sweat had constantly to be sponged from the man's face and body. In between doing that, Snow soaked two towels into cold compresses, rotating one after the other on the priest's forehead.

The telephone continued to whine, unusably, at him.

Towards dawn on the fourth day the older priest's sleep became more settled, although the fever remained high, and for the first time Snow allowed himself briefly to snatch moments of half-aware rest.

The ugly, rasping sound of Father Robertson's unconsciousness brought Snow abruptly and fully awake, frightened how long he had abandoned the man. Father Robertson was on his back, mouth wide open, dragging the breath into his frail body, which still vibrated with the fever. Ridiculously, close to panic, Snow physically shook the other man, shouting for him to open his eyes. *No more sleep. Don't want you to sleep any more. You've got to wake up! Come on! Wake up!* The head rolled out of time with the movement of the priest's body, but the eyes remained closed. Snow thought Father Robertson looked on the point of death.

When he tried the telephone once more it was completely dead.

It had been idiotic, delaying so long. Reluctant as he was to leave Father Robertson alone, he had to go to the embassy for proper help. But he couldn't do that in the middle of the night: if he tried to enter the compound now he'd be prevented by the permanent Chinese guards, running the risk of even further delay. Snow timed his move with the beginning of proper light.

Wanting to leave Father Robertson as comfortable as possible, he washed and changed the man yet again: throughout, the snoring rasped on, the perspiration bubbling up the moment it was wiped away.

The streets swarmed with bicycles, and this early smoke-belching delivery trucks added to the congestion. The nightsoil collection was beginning, fouling the air. Snow hurried at a trot, head in perpetual movement in search of a taxi or a pedicab, seeing neither. The exasperation welled up inside him, contributing to the inevitable tightening in his chest. He refused to reduce his pace until a throbbing ache threatened to bring him to a complete halt. He still continued faster than was good for him, so that he was gasping for breath when he arrived at the embassy.

Snow was surprised that it was the serious-faced Peter Samuels who came from deeper inside the legation. The political officer immediately summoned the resident doctor, an overly fat man named Pickering whose spectacles were too large for his features, giving him an owlish look heightened by the infrequent way he blinked, otherwise staring open-eyed at anyone to whom he talked. Pickering pedantically checked everything Snow told him: when the priest protested they could talk on their way to the mission the doctor, more controlled, asked the point of setting out without medication he might possibly need when he got there. 'Why are you so convinced it's as serious as you say?'

'He's an old man!' said Snow. 'He was a prisoner of the Chinese for years: any resistance to illness would have been undermined!'

'Why didn't you call me before now?'

'He wouldn't let me,' said Snow, inadequately.

'Wouldn't *let* you?' demanded the doctor, incredulous.

'The idea of a doctor distressed him too much. Then for a while, he seemed to improve.'

'You're a fool!'

'Yes,' accepted Snow.

'You say his health is undermined by imprisonment?'

'I don't mean he suffers permanent ill health,' apologized Snow. 'I just wanted you to know what he's been through, in the past.' Was there some guilt, at so constantly and so easily disparaging Father Robertson, in how he felt and was reacting? Honestly, although reluctantly, Snow conceded to himself that there was: that in fact a lot of the panic was a belated attempt to compensate for his failings towards the old man.

'He's usually fit, despite what happened to him in the past?'

'Yes.' Snow hesitated, momentarily uncertain. 'And he drinks a little.'

The doctor's head came up, enquiringly. 'What's a little?'

'Every night. Quite soon after lunch, really.'

Samuels drove them in an embassy car back to the mission where they found that Father Robertson had fouled the room and himself: he'd been sick again and there'd been a bowel movement. Pickering was professionally unoffended, actually collecting specimens from the mess before helping Snow clean everything up. Samuels remained by the door, doing nothing, face tight with disgust.

The doctor's examination was extremely thorough. After questioning Snow about the number of times he'd had to change the sweat-soaked man, Pickering erected a saline drip to replace the lost body fluids. He also administered an injection to stabilize the man's temperature.

'What's wrong with him?' said Samuels, towards the end of the examination.

Pickering frowned at the question. 'I haven't got the faintest idea. He's got a fever, obviously. And he's unconscious. His blood-pressure is too high. All or any of which could indicate one of a hundred things.'

Snow withdrew near to the door, close to the diplomat, to give the doctor more room. Without looking in Snow's direction, Samuels said: 'He didn't complain about feeling unwell, before you found him and saw he quite obviously was ill?'

'No.'

'What *did* he say, in the time that he remained rational?'

Snow shook his head. 'Nothing, not really. He just kept repeating how sorry he was. He said that over and over again.'

Speaking louder, to the doctor, Samuels said: 'I think we should move him, to the embassy infirmary, don't you?'

The doctor looked sourly over his shoulder. 'You making diagnoses now?'

There was the faintest flare of colour to Samuels' face. 'It just seemed obvious.'

'Not to me it doesn't. Not until I've found out what's wrong with the man. The embassy facility is not an isolation unit.'

'It could be infectious?'

'Of course it could be infectious! You forgotten that all the major infectious diseases of the world are still considered endemic in China!' Pickering looked directly at Snow. 'I'm not for a moment saying it's as serious as that. Or that you're in any danger. I need to get back to the embassy, to make some tests on these samples.'

Snow didn't feel the slightest apprehension: perhaps, he thought, nursing the old man through an illness — infectious or otherwise — would continue to assuage his finally self-admitted guilt.

'You can drive the car back, can't you?' Samuels said, to the doctor.

'Why?' frowned Pickering. The doctor was collecting his medical equipment, replacing each piece carefully into its grooved and socketed place in the bags he'd brought with him.

'I thought I might stay here.'

'What for?' asked Snow.

'When was the last time you slept?' asked Samuels.

'I . . .' started Snow and stopped. 'The night before last, I suppose. I can't really remember.'

'You won't be able properly to look after anyone if you're totally deprived of sleep,' pointed out the diplomat, realistically. He looked at the doctor. 'Are you coming back today?'

'Of course I am,' said the man. 'He's on a drip, isn't he?'

Samuels nodded, positively, returning to the younger priest. 'You can get some rest: try at least. Maybe by the time Pickering gets back he'll have a better idea what the medical problem is: see if we can get Father Robertson into the infirmary. If not, you'll be better able to carry on.'

'Suits me,' shrugged the doctor, packed and ready to leave.

Snow didn't think he would be able to sleep but he did, dreamlessly. He awakened suddenly and was surprised to be in bed during the day and not instantly able to remember why. Then he did, hurrying up. Samuels was in the main living-room, but with the connecting doors open to see into Father Robertson's bedroom. The saturnine man smiled at Snow's entry and said: 'He's much easier.'

Snow had been aware of that, before the diplomat spoke. Father Robertson appeared to be sleeping properly, no longer emitting the growl of unconsciousness.

'He isn't sweating so much, either,' added Samuels.

'Let's hope it's all ending as quickly as it all began.'

'You'll be telling Rome?' asked the diplomat.

The need to inform the Curia hadn't occurred to Snow until then, although it was obvious that he had to. Awareness tumbled upon awareness. Would this breakdown, whatever its cause, finally bring about the long-overdue retirement and withdrawal of Father Robertson? Leaving Snow blessedly alone at the mission? Not a wrong or unfair reflection, he told himself: no conflict, with his most recent remorse at the tension between himself and the older priest. His sole concern was for a worn out, overstrained old man who needed rest, not perpetual apprehension. He said: 'It's necessary that I do.'

'Will they retire him?' asked Samuels.

'I don't know.'

'I've come to realize he's extraordinarily attached to China,' said Samuels. 'Which, considering what happened to him, is difficult to understand.'

'Not, perhaps, to a priest.'

'You can't properly practise as priests,' contradicted Samuels, at once.

'It's his dream that one day things will change: that he *will* be able to.'

'Do you believe that?'

Snow thought before answering. 'I don't think there can be any doubt that communism will crumble here, as it's crumbled everywhere else. But I'm not sure how long it will take . . .' He paused, glancing through the open doors towards where the old man lay. '. . . I certainly don't think it's going to be in his lifetime. So he's going to die disappointed.'

'Father Robertson came to see me, two or three days ago. Told me that your escort had visited again.'

'He wants copies of some photographs I took when we were travelling.' Snow had wondered how long it would take the subject to be raised.

Samuels came forward in his chair, and when he spoke the words were spaced even more than usual in the odd way he talked. 'What photographs? You haven't done anything insensitive, have you?'

'He was an official escort!' reminded Snow, pleased as the explanation came to him. 'I wouldn't have been *allowed* to photograph anything I wasn't supposed to, even by accident, would I?'

Samuels continued to look at him doubtfully. 'Offence is very easily given here. Even by doing something that would not cause a problem anywhere else in the world.'

'I have undergone a great many lectures on the political realities of living here,' reminded Snow.

'With Father Robertson incapacitated — we don't know for how long — I would like you to let me know if this man keeps turning up here,' said the diplomat. 'I don't want us — at the embassy, I mean — caught out by not being prepared.'

'I'll keep you in touch,' promised Snow. There was an irony here: Father Robertson's illness would provide a valid excuse to visit the embassy whenever he liked in the immediate future, but there was no contact any more with whom he could liaise. Quickly, seeing the opportunity, he said: 'When I was at the trade reception Foster told me he was leaving. Is there a replacement yet?'

Samuels frowned and Snow feared he had been too direct. The diplomat said: 'Not yet. There will be. Always essential to maintain the personnel quota we're allowed.'

'Quite soon then?' said Snow, risking the persistence. If the new liaison man arrived in a week or two the opportunity might still be there for them to have safe embassy encounters to plan the new system for the future.

Instead of replying Samuels' face creased at an overlooked question of his own. 'Where *are* the photographs this man wants?'

'I sent them to England, to my family, for developing. I've asked for the prints to be sent back.' Snow decided the moment was lost and that it would be wrong to try to get back to it.

'So he'll be returning?'

'Obviously.'

'I'm not happy with this.'

'Really!' said Snow, stressing the weariness at a repeated conversation. 'We talked this through very fully at the reception. There isn't *anything* to worry about.'

'I think I should advise London, of this second visit.'

'Good!' seized Snow at once. 'It'll give you an opportunity to include my full explanation this time.'

'I'll put your views,' promised Samuels.

The exchange did not amount to a dispute but an atmosphere developed between them. With his mind occupied by his unexpected access to the embassy, Snow decided to alert the Curia as quickly as possible of Father Robertson's condition.

But alone, in his own quarters, Snow did not start to write at once, instead gazing uncertainly at the blank paper in the ancient, uneven-keyed typewriter. This was his first chance to communicate direct, without having to go through the censorious Father Robertson, with those in Rome who ordered and dictated their lives and whose instructions had to be unquestioningly obeyed. Written in a certain way — and not an unfair or untrue way — Snow knew he could manipulate Father Robertson's enforced retirement. He could remind the Curia of the old man's past suffering and honestly recount the constant apprehension and set out the apparent seriousness of the sudden illness.

There was the sound of movement along the corridor and Snow looked up in time to see Samuels coming out of Father Robertson's room. The diplomat turned, sensing Snow's attention, and shook his head to indicate there was no change.

He couldn't do it, Snow determined. Father Robertson was being medically cared for, as safe as he could possibly be at this time and in this place. That was all he was entitled to tell Rome. To do anything more — to try to use the illness for his own selfish, personal benefit — would be monstrously wrong, betraying any and every principle with which he had been indoctrinated as a priest: principles which, if he were brutally honest, he might already have put into doubt by his secondary activities which, at times like this, almost seemed more important than his first and proper calling. It had been agonizing trying to salve his conscience over the confessional: he couldn't, at the moment, sacrifice any more of his unsteady integrity.

Snow began to write at last, keeping the account absolutely factual and strictly limited to the collapse. He made a carbon copy, for Father Robertson to know everything Rome had been told. And having completed the letter Snow left the envelope open for the doctor's return, hoping to add a suggested diagnosis, reluctant for Rome to regard the illness as a mystery.

It was not, however, properly resolved when the doctor *did* return.

It was mid-afternoon before Pickering came back, initially shouldering past them with the briefest nod of greeting, interested only in the now peacefully sleeping priest. While the other two men watched, Pickering went progressively through the earlier temperature, blood pressure, somnolent eye reaction and nerve sensitivity tests before removing the saline drip from Father Robertson's arm. He gently dressed the induced puncture wound — which showed no tendency to bleed — and as he dismantled the drip frame finally said: 'He's a lot better. Certainly won't need this. Everything seems to be stabilizing nicely.' At last he turned to them, smiling proudly.

'What is it?' demanded Samuels, again.

The smile faded into the familiar irritable scowl. 'I don't know *what* it is. But I know what it's *not*. Definitely not infectious.'

Snow said: 'I want to give an indication to my Order in Rome.'

'I don't know,' repeated Pickering. 'It could be a virus: maybe we'll never scientifically know.'

'What about the seriousness?' persisted Samuels.

'He's an old man and he's quite frail,' declared the doctor, unnecessarily. 'At his age and in his condition, a virus has got to be regarded seriously. But the improvement is quite remarkable in the last few hours: almost dramatically so. Which is encouraging. His temperature is practically normal, and for his age I regard his blood pressure as practically normal, too.'

'Is there any risk . . . I mean, could he die?' stumbled Snow.

'Good God, no!' erupted the man, who appeared permanently on the point of exasperation. 'He'll need care, certainly. But I don't think he's in any danger.'

'What's the treatment?' asked Samuels.

'Simple antibiotics, as far as I can see. He's no longer unconscious: this is just a sleep of exhaustion, nothing more.'

'So we'll move him to the infirmary,' declared the diplomat.

'Why?' demanded Pickering, querulously.

'Why not?' said Samuels, equally forcefully. 'He's not infectious. But he needs care. It's obvious he should be moved where he is closer to you.'

'There's no reason why he shouldn't stay here,' refused Pickering. 'In fact, it's far better than trying to move him, which we'd have to do by car, because to wait for days for the Chinese to provide ambulance facilities would be ridiculous . . .' He nodded towards Snow. 'He's more than capable of doing what's necessary, which is just seeing the medication is administered at the proper time. And I can make all the daily visits that are necessary . . .' Again Snow was indicated with a nod. 'I can give him my home as well as official number, for when the telephone gets fixed, so he can call me at any time if there's any relapse. Which I don't believe there will be.'

'I think he should be moved,' said Samuels, doggedly.

'It's not your decision to make!' rejected Pickering. 'I am responsible here for the medical care of British nationals.'

'And I am responsible for that and every other care,' yelled Samuels, in a surprisingly un-diplomatic outburst. Striving at once for control Samuels said: 'I can't see any reason why Father Robertson can't be taken somewhere better medically equipped than this place.'

Snow thought the diplomat sounded like someone offering a defence to a later accusation, which perhaps he considered he was. Concerned himself with Father Robertson's well-being, Snow said to the doctor: 'Wouldn't it be better to take him into a hospital?'

'If I thought it would be I'd do it!' said Pickering. 'At the moment this man is medically better here, where . . .'

The sentence was never finished. Behind the doctor Father Robertson gave a snuffling sigh, shifted uncomfortably and finally opened his eyes, staring without focus for several moments at the cracked and dirt-rimmed ceiling directly above his bed. The blank face and the blank eyes cleared at last. He turned his head sideways and saw them. 'What?' he said, in a vague, one-word demand.

It was Pickering who conducted everything, without ever offering Father Robertson an answer to his question. With the elderly priest able at last minimally to communicate sensibly, Pickering took the man through a series of verbal examinations, greatly extending the neurological tests. He expanded the medical in step with Father Robertson's recovery. Within fifteen minutes the mission head was taking by mouth the antibiotics the doctor produced from his bag. Over his shoulder, generally to both of them, Pickering said: 'An even greater recovery!' This time the pride was in the voice, not in a smile.

Samuels and Snow approached the bed together. Father Robertson was fully conscious. Again, repeatedly, he begged their forgiveness for whatever trouble he had caused, at one stage reaching out imploringly, which unintentionally revealed to them both the sticklike fragility of his arms.

'You feel better?' pressed Samuels.

'Tired. That's all. Just tired. I am so sorry.'

'I was worried,' came in Snow.

'Forgive me. So stupid.'

'He'll need rest, for several days,' bustled Pickering. 'I will prescribe a mild sedative, to go with the antibiotics. And come every day: as often as I consider necessary . . .' The look to Samuels was dismissive. 'Everything will be done that needs to be done.'

Ignoring the doctor, Samuels said to the sick man: 'I feel you should come to the embassy: that would be best, wouldn't it?'

'I really think . . .' began the indignant Pickering, behind them, but Father Robertson cut in over the doctor. 'I really feel much better. It's here I should be. I will be all right here: quite all right.'

'Thank God that's settled!' declared Pickering. Careless of the small audience, the doctor said to Samuels: 'I resent your interference.'

Snow didn't think further examination was necessary, but was instead a gesture physically to relegate Samuels, and guessed from the colour of the diplomat's face that Samuels thought the same.

Snow listened intently to the doctor's instructions about the dosages and medication and accepted the offered telephone numbers, making a mental note to check whether the already reported fault had been corrected.

Throughout there was no conversation between the doctor and the diplomat. Both men remained unspeaking when they left the mission.

The sedative had taken effect and Father Robertson slept for another three hours before stirring again. He was heavy-eyed.

'I'm getting old,' he said, sadly.

'You'll be fine,' assured Snow.

'Did I cause much trouble?'

'Nothing,' dismissed Snow.

Father Robertson's eyes began to close. 'Old,' he said, indistinctly.

'So this is a farewell feast!' Marcia had been for more than a week at an exhibition in Birmingham, so they'd only talked by telephone of his going to Beijing.

'Hardly farewell,' said Gower, smiling across the restaurant table. 'I've yet to get a visa.'

'And I thought you were just some lowly clerk: would be for years!'

'I was surprised, too,' admitted Gower. He accepted that formalities had to be completed — visas particularly — but he was impatient at the delay. He had expected to leave practically at once after the promised final briefing: every day that passed surely increased the danger if their source had been exposed.

'How long will you be away?'

'It's an on-the-spot survey of embassy facilities,' said Gower. 'I shan't really know until I get there.'

'It's odd they have to send someone from London.'

'They seem to think it's necessary.'

The girl offered her glass, for more wine. With

innocent prescience, she said: 'This could be a big chance for you, though, couldn't it?'

'If I get everything right.' I hope, thought Gower.

Marcia looked away, nodding agreement for the waiter to clear her plate. When the man left, she said: 'It's worked well, these last few weeks, hasn't it? You and me, I mean.'

'Very well,' agreed Gower. The Beijing assignment *was* obviously important. So for him to have been given it must indicate he was highly regarded: maybe even one of a selected few. He could make all sorts of plans and commitments if he were that well established.

'The lease to my place is due for renewal right away. I've had a letter asking what I want to do.'

'I remembered the dates.' He'd been expecting her to raise it.

'There doesn't seem much point in my going on with it. Unless you want me to, that is.'

Gower reached across for her hand, making her look at him. 'I don't want you to go on with it,' he said, decisively. 'I want you to give notice and move all your stuff in with me and I want us to start thinking of getting married.'

Marcia's face opened into more than a smile, practically laughing in her excitement. 'I accept!'

'Everything's going to be perfect,' he said.

'I'll sort it out while you're away,' promised Marcia. 'Can I tell the family?'

Gower nodded, enjoying her excitement. 'I'll tell mother, before I go.'

Charlie Muffin looked up curiously at the tentative knock, smiling when Gower pushed his cubicle door.

'Hoped I'd catch you,' said Gower, smiling back. 'Wanted you to know I've got an assignment.'

Charlie regarded the younger man seriously across the desk, not speaking.

Gower's smile widened. 'Don't worry! I'm not going to say what it is! Don't properly know myself, not completely. Just that I'm soon to be operational.'

Charlie remained serious. 'Get it right,' he said. 'There's usually only one chance.'

'I'll get it right,' assured Gower. 'You taught me how, didn't you?'

Had he? wondered Charlie. He'd sometimes found it difficult to look after himself: he didn't like the responsibility of having to do it for somebody else. The more he thought about it, the more he hated this bloody job. Jealousy, he acknowledged, honestly. It should have been him going operational, not this young, inexperienced kid.

Was he so inexperienced? He'd passed all the tests much better than Charlie had expected. Which wasn't the point, rejected Charlie, determinedly. The point was that Charlie wanted whatever it was Gower was being assigned. Christ, how he hated being a teacher.

Twenty-two

There was a lot of slow-moving traffic on the country roads and Charlie was glad to loop up on to the motorway at last, settling in the cruising lane at just five miles over the speed limit, fast enough to get him back to London on time without seriously risking police interference. One of life's elementary precautions was to obey the obvious civil laws: all part of never drawing unnecessary attention to himself. He was unsure whether he'd given John Gower that advice. He should have done. Too late now. On his own, about to become operational. From now on Gower had to learn for himself, develop his instincts. It wouldn't be easy because operational assignments never were: sometimes boring, too often abject failures, but never easy. Charlie hoped this would not be as difficult as some could be. Always useful to have a fairly simple ride the first time, to build up just the right amount of confidence.

Enough reflection, Charlie cautioned himself. Wrong to let himself get personally involved, as he'd told the man himself. Lied, too, saying he'd refused to think in terms of liking or disliking. He hadn't intended to, but he *had* liked John Gower. Have to guard against it happening with the next one. He'd thought there would already have been someone to follow Gower: expected his still unfamiliar, thoroughly unwanted role to be ongoing, one apprentice approved, another waiting to follow. Something else he hadn't properly understood about the job. He hoped there'd be someone soon: the boredom factor was creeping up on him, although he hadn't yet started playing with paper darts.

Charlie checked the dashboard clock, contentedly ahead of the evening traffic build-up. He wanted to go back to Primrose Hill before meeting Julia: shower if he had time. He'd considered suggesting she come with him this time, not to the nursing home but just for the ride: there were enough antique shops in Stockbridge to browse around while he was seeing his mother. Then they could have spent the rest of the day in the country. Then again, perhaps it wouldn't have been a good idea. He wouldn't have wanted her to think he was suggesting a night as well as a day in the country, because he wouldn't have been.

Charlie was enjoying the friendship with Julia. It had practically been a reflex to offer it that night in the Hampstead restaurant, and for some time afterwards he hadn't been sure what either of them had agreed upon. So far it was fine. She'd accepted the cinema invitation, laughing in disbelief when he admitted it was his first visit for over a year, and having decided against inviting her to the country he'd bought theatre seats that night for a play she'd said she wanted to see. He'd been tempted to make it a surprise, but decided against it as he'd decided against asking her to drive down to Hampshire. Hopeful lovers created surprises: friends discussed things in advance, ensuring outings were mutually convenient, with no need to impress.

Charlie *was* comfortable with Julia, just as she seemed comfortable with him, neither having to try too hard. Best of all, there was no sexual tension, which would have made everything difficult. After the restaurant confession she'd spoken once or twice about the divorce and the double despair she'd felt at the betrayal, but as a catharsis, not in any way as an invitation. Never once had she asked a direct question about himself. Cynically Charlie had wondered if Julia might have known all there was about him from the red boxes and manila envelopes for which the deputy Director-General had shown such contempt on the day of his reassignment. Just as quickly he dismissed the suspicion. When he had talked of Edith, briefly and only then to let her know he was familiar with loneliness too, Julia had given no indication of being aware of Edith's death or of its circumstances, and he didn't think she was a good enough actress — or liar — to have done that.

No one would learn everything about him from the archival records, of course. Remarkably little, in fact. And definitely not about Natalia, who had been the most important part of his life after Edith.

Perhaps confusingly, although not to himself, Charlie believed the forever lost Natalia had made it easy for the friendship with Julia. The way he felt — and would always feel — about Natalia meant he didn't want, romantically or sexually or on any other level, an involvement with anyone. Any more than Julia did, for her part. Charlie supposed he and Julia qualified as the perfect platonic couple. A marriage, almost, without the difficult, messy parts. He didn't imagine it an analogy easy for anyone else to follow.

The word — marriage — stayed with Charlie. What about the involvement of the beneficially married Peter Miller with the unmarried Ms Patricia Elder? Charlie had maintained his occasional and therefore inadequate observation of the Regent's Park mansion. And confirmed that Peter Miller used it as a London base. But so far always alone. The woman who had also used the private penthouse door — but only on two occasions — had not been Patricia Elder, so he assumed her to be Lady Ann: she'd certainly looked a lot like the horses she was said to breed. Remembering his earlier doubts, Charlie thought again that maybe Miller didn't use the place for his affair with his deputy: even wondered, indeed, if they were *having* an affair. Another earlier doubt, like the possibility that Patricia Elder's apartment or house could much more safely be the love-nest. And as she wasn't listed in any of the biographical reference books — and there was no way he could search department records without the request becoming known — he didn't have any idea where she lived.

All of which made it a fairly good bet that he was wasting his time, playing at nothing more than amateur surveillance, like playing with paper darts. But then time seemed to be something he had a lot of to waste. And he did, after all, have practically to go past Miller's London home to his own flat in Primrose Hill.

What would he do if he *did* confirm an affair? Strictly according to regulations, he had to report it as a security risk. But doing things according to regulations wasn't the point of Charlie's exercise: it rarely was. The point was personal protection, hoarding any ammunition available. And ammunition wasn't any good thrown away in advance of the battle: far better to wait until the shots were fired in his direction. Charlie accepted at once that with their power and authority, Miller and Patricia Elder outgunned him. But if they seriously moved to bring him down — permanently to get rid of him, for instance — he would, if he could, bring them down, too. So he'd go on hanging around outside the lavish mansion.

The warning proof from what he'd done all those years ago when he'd been offered up for sacrifice was clearly there in those red boxes and manila files, but Charlie doubted they fully understood that if he believed himself under attack he was an overwhelmingly vindictive bastard. And proud to be so. Sometimes he even practised.

Charlie followed motorways completely to reach

London, connecting with the M4 by the M25 orbital link, beginning, but quickly refusing the recollection, to think of the evasion technique he'd taught John Gower on part of the same route. Just as quickly, refusing the refusal, he forced himself — alarmed — to remember the routine, positively rising more fully in the driving seat, as if coming abruptly awake.

Which was about bloody right, Charlie decided, horrified. He *had* been asleep. Not once, since leaving the nursing home almost two hours before, had he once searched around him, which he'd patronizingly lectured Gower it was always essential — 'until it becomes instinctive' — to do.

So much for the conceit of considering himself a good and conscientious intelligence officer! The lapse did more than worry Charlie: it frightened him. It had *always* been automatic in the past: should still have been, something he never had consciously to think about! So why hadn't he done it this time? There was no excuse, no explanation. No matter how deeply he'd been preoccupied, part of his concentration should have remained on what was going on around him. It wasn't an argument — not to Charlie anyway — that it didn't matter because he was no longer operational. He didn't *want* to lose the constant alertness: *wouldn't* lose it. If he stopped being alert, aware at all times of what was going on about him, he would start to atrophy: start to sink into mumbling insensitivity, the dinosaur ready for retirement that Patricia Elder clearly considered him to be. Too late, a stupid effort at reassertiveness that didn't work, Charlie began checking, using all the mirrors, actually gazing around himself on the filled up, six-lane highway. What the fuck was he doing so late: *too* late? Playing with himself, without any satisfaction at the end of it. No, he rejected at once. He could have still recovered, if he'd found himself in a genuine situation: dodged and weaved, evaded a problem. There was still no satisfaction: failed mental masturbation.

Charlie remained unsettled after he got back, in good time, to his Primrose Hill apartment after returning the hire car. He confirmed the order in which he'd left the letters on the mat, before picking them up, and checked the traps he'd set in the bedroom and the kitchen by leaving the doors slightly ajar. There had not been any entry. There was still time to shower before meeting Julia.

In the bar, during the theatre interval, Charlie said: 'Gower came to see me: said he was going operational.'

Julia regarded him seriously. 'Still missing it?'

'Always will,' said Charlie, shortly.

'Let go!' she pleaded. 'Accept it's over!'

He couldn't, Charlie realized. Not yet, though maybe he should after that afternoon's fuck-up. 'I guess you're right.'

'Welcome back!' greeted the Director-General. Walter Foster smiled, although uncertainly, looking between the man and Patricia Elder, unsure what sort of meeting it was going to be. At once he blurted: 'I believe it was essential I leave: it wasn't panic or anything like that.'

'We're sure it wasn't,' soothed the woman.

'You said it had to be an on-the-ground decision,' continued the man, unconvinced by her assurance.

'It's officially recorded, on file,' said Miller. 'We're glad you're back. We need your impressions: everything. Far better than written reports.'

Foster relaxed, very slightly. 'Quite simple. Snow's blown: they're just waiting their time. Maybe waiting for something positively incriminating, although I'm not sure they'll bother.'

'And Snow himself?'

Foster, who was perched on the very edge of the visitor's chair in the Director-General's office, had finally to look away from their concentrated attention, disguising the avoidance as a moment of head-lowered contemplation, properly to answer the query. Tentatively he said, 'He is not an easy person. Never has been.'

'Go on,' urged Patricia Elder.

Foster hardly needed the prompting. 'He and I never hit it off: it was always particularly difficult.'

'His last complete report was a refusal to work with you any longer,' Miller pointed out.

Instantly Foster inferred criticism. 'I am extremely sorry about the breakdown. I did everything I believed proper and safe to correct it. Followed your orders from here to the letter. Nothing worked.'

'That becomes clear, from your side of the exchanges,' said the Director-General.

Foster relaxed again. 'He's extremely arrogant. Refuses to accept that he is under any sort of official scrutiny.'

'What do *you* think?' said Patricia Elder.

'He's unquestionably under suspicion.'

Miller waved a hand generally towards the folders in their neat order on his desk. 'There didn't seem to be any doubt, from what you already provided. So it's the arrogance that's preventing his coming out?'

'He insisted it's the Jesuit Curia that holds the power of withdrawal over him,' qualified the former liaison man. 'He won't accept that he's been compromised. He thinks there will always be an explanation to satisfy the authorities.'

'We're having trouble with the Technical Division, over the photographs,' disclosed Patricia, slightly changing the direction of the debriefing. 'Zhengzhou is no trouble: they were virtually tourist shots, apart from identifying Li for our records. It's the Shanghai prints we can't successfully alter.'

'Not at all?' queried Foster. He *had* been right, getting out when there was still the chance: he couldn't conceive what a Chinese detention centre or prison would be like. Whatever, Foster was sure he could not have survived any term of imprisonment without quickly losing his mind.

Miller took up the explanation. 'They can, intentionally, be poorly developed. With two that is very effective: reduces the background virtually to make what is technogically interesting on the warships meaningless . . .' He paused. 'But on two it doesn't work.'

'What about positively changing the Shanghai background?'

'He was photographing *away* from the city and the Bund, towards the river. It's impossible,' dismissed Miller.

Foster smiled, pleased as the idea came to him. 'Why worry about the real photographs at all? Why don't we send back four completely innocuous photographs of Shanghai that Snow *didn't* take?'

Miller and the woman swapped looks. Patricia said: 'According to Snow, Li took pictures too. They've got a comparison, to put against whatever we provide: every photograph was to be from exactly the same position, with exactly the same climatic conditions, even to the same cloud formations.'

Beneath his red hair Foster blushed slightly, bringing out the freckles. 'Can't we ask the Curia to bring him out?'

'How? And on what grounds?' demanded the Director-General. 'We couldn't explain the reason for our approaching them. Or even how we know a man named Jeremy Snow is a Jesuit priest, in Beijing. Believe me, if that had been a route to follow, we'd have done it weeks ago.'

Foster flushed further. 'What then?'

'More persuasion,' said Patricia Elder.

There was a brief silence in the room. Then Foster said: 'By somebody else?'

'Yes,' said Miller.

'I'm sorry,' said Foster, accepting the criticism without it having to be openly made by either of them.

'You were an accredited British diplomat attached to the embassy,' reminded the woman. 'You're out. We're saved *official* embarrassment, if Snow gets arrested. The government line will be to deny all knowledge of any Chinese accusation: dismiss the whole thing as nonsense.'

'Which means completely abandoning Snow,' said Foster.

'He was told to get out,' said Miller, with a hint of irritability. 'And we *are* making another attempt.'

'He won't come,' said the liaison man, flatly.

'Then his problems are his own, aren't they?' said the Director-General.

Neither spoke for several moments after Foster had left. Then Patricia said: 'He didn't ask what his next assignment was going to be.'

'Foster's a fool whose use is over,' dismissed Miller.

'What *are* we going to do with him?'

Miller shrugged. 'Something internal, I suppose. Nothing we need to decide in a hurry.

You ready for Gower?'

The woman nodded: 'Ten o'clock tomorrow. His flight leaves in the afternoon.'

'I wonder if it will work,' said Miller, unexpectedly reflective.

'I wish to Christ I knew,' said Patricia.

Twenty-three

Gower's final, eve-of-departure briefing was given by Patricia Elder alone. She provided two identifying photographs of Snow, explained he was a priest and described the need to get him out as an operational tragedy. She went carefully through the contact and meeting procedures, making Gower repeat them until she was satisfied he had completely memorized them.

'We couldn't risk a spy-cell accusation, involving Snow *and* Foster,' said the deputy Director. 'And we still can't. *Don't* set up any contact with Snow *outside* the embassy, where you're vulnerable and beyond diplomatic protection. Use the Taoist temple signal to get Snow to a letter drop of your choice. And use the drop to bring him to the embassy. Tell him it's his last chance. He either comes out, or we're severing all responsibility: disowning him.'

'What if he goes on refusing?'

Patricia produced the Shanghai pictures from the folder on her desk. 'He'll never even reach the airport unless he hands these over to the Chinese. The top four are quite innocent, but we've tricked them, to be slightly different from any copy prints his escort might have taken. It'll confuse them: occupy their time working that out.

The rest are the important ones: they told us a lot about Chinese naval technology. We've doctored them, too: as much as our technical people say is possible. But it'll show, under scientific examination. Make it absolutely clear to Snow that these pictures give him time to run. But that's all. If he doesn't come out with you, they'll be used against him to *prove* he's an agent. If he accuses us of blackmailing him, tell him he's damned right: that's exactly what we're doing.'

'You're showing a lot of loyalty,' admired Gower.

'Mutual protection,' said Patricia Elder.

Natalia Fedova was far too professional to be panicked by the discovery of Fyodor Tudin's surreptitious interest in her. She was forewarned: now she had to find some way of being forearmed. Which presented problems of differing urgency.

She had every right to consult her own records: so an explanation would be easy to provide, if one were officially sought. Not so if she were asked why, from among the thousands of still retained former KGB files on foreign intelligence officers, she had withdrawn the one upon a man with whom she had provable links in the past. She'd have to find a justification to protect herself there. Which still left the biggest problem of all: not knowing if consulting the files was *all* that Tudin was doing. And what she didn't know, she couldn't guard against.

Very quickly Natalia contradicted herself. That

252

wasn't the biggest problem. The biggest problem was that now she was aware of being spied upon, she would have to abandon any hope of locating Charlie Muffin to tell him he was a father.

Twenty-four

The apprehension settled deep within him during the long outward flight. Gower went through the pretence of trying to sleep but couldn't, lying cocooned in an airline blanket for hours in the darkened, droning aircraft, trying instead to exorcize the unformed ghosts: to put everything in order in his mind and anticipate what he was likely to encounter. Had he been told to do that, or *not* to do that, during the final, street-wise training sessions? He couldn't remember. At once fresh anxiety flared, because that had certainly been one of the edicts, *always* to remember, *always* to be aware. The scruffy man who'd refused to be identified had told him it was all right to feel nervous. But *how* nervous?

Nothing in the training had equipped him to work in Beijing. Apart from the two inadequate briefing sessions with the deputy Director-General and from what he'd learned from the equally inadequate file in the few days prior to his visa approval, there'd been no preparation or guidance whatsoever.

He had to take hold of himself: accept the nervousness but not the panic. It could, in fact, be an easy operation. Certainly one upon which, by specifically obeying London's instructions, he was always going to be protected, beyond the reach of Chinese seizure.

He wasn't bringing anything dangerous into China: the incriminating photographs of Shanghai and all the file material and the methods and locations for clandestine contact were arriving in the untouchable diplomatic bag.

And again following London's instructions, he was forbidden to make any contact with the Jesuit priest outside the diplomatically secure embassy compound. Safe again. So why the stomach-emptying fear? Twenty per cent first-time nerves, eighty per cent uncertainty at being in Beijing, Gower decided.

It *wasn't* going to be a difficult operation, he determined, positively. He would always have the protection of the embassy, literally all around him. And the awkward priest — confronted with the ultimatum of the photographs — had no alternative but finally to get out, as he should have done weeks earlier.

Beijing airport was a maelstrom of people and noise and confusions: Gower thought it was like being in the middle of a river full of debris constantly colliding and bruising into him. Only occasionally did the flow slacken, as people swirled off at the last moment, not to avoid bumping against him but to regard him curiously, as an oddity. As he queued through immigration and Customs control, Gower thought wryly back to another lecture in those final sessions, about awareness of people surrounding him. Recognizing the colonial cliché before it completely formed, he decided it was another lesson difficult to follow here: in a crowd in which there were perhaps only another twenty or thirty Westerners, everyone else *did* look identical to his unaccustomed eye, making it impossible to isolate one from another.

Gower had been told he would be met but not precisely how. He stopped and looked uncertainly around him directly outside the official arrival area. At once he saw an almost unnaturally tall, sharp-edged man moving easily through the crowd that still bewildered and jostled him.

'Peter Samuels,' introduced the man. 'Political officer. Your photograph's a good likeness. Good flight? Goes on forever, doesn't it? Car's outside. Come on.' The man was turning practically before the handshake was completed, uninterested in any reply: Samuels loped rather than walked and Gower had difficulty keeping up, constantly obstructed by people.

Gower was caught by the oddness of the other man's speech. It was as if the words were glued together and had to be prised apart at the moment of delivery.

The car, an English Ford, was parked almost directly outside. Samuels left Gower to open the boot himself to dump his suitcase, continuing on around to the driver's side. There were a reasonable number of cars in the immediate vicinity of the airport, but almost as soon as they got out upon the road they became immersed in bicycles, some engulfed in produce or wrapped bundles. Curiously Gower turned, to look behind them. Another gap in the training, he reflected, remembering the motorway avoidance trick: how was he supposed to identify a bicycle that looked the same as every other bicycle ridden by a man who looked the same as every other rider?

'According to what we've been told from London, you're not going to be here very long?' said Samuels.

'No,' agreed Gower, shortly, letting the other man lead.

'Meeting new arrivals *is* the usual custom,' announced Samuels. 'But normally by a chauffeur.'

Gower began to concentrate inside the car. 'Yes?'

Samuels jabbed his finger impatiently on the horn, staring directly ahead at the two-wheeled mêlée through which he was manoeuvring. 'Important to understand the way things are here.'

'I'd welcome any guidance,' said Gower, politely but still cautious.

'Probably the most difficult diplomatic posting in the world,' said Samuels. 'But it is opening up. Very slowly. There was a trade delegation here recently that could bring in orders to Britain well in excess of £300,000,000.'

'That's impressive,' agreed Gower. Despite his concentration on the other man, he found himself looking curiously at the wooden houses with their curled roof corners by which they were driving. He thought of fairy tales and gingerbread houses.

For the first time Samuels turned briefly but directly to Gower. 'Important nothing is done to upset relationships.'

Gower supposed the political officer would be one of the diplomats aware of his true function. *Trust no one*, he remembered. And then another edict: *In an unknown situation, you take, never give.* 'I understand the point.'

There was another snatched look. 'We don't want anything to sour relations.'

'I can understand that, too.' He wished he'd managed to sleep on the plane, to avoid the tiredness dragging at him. There was no sun getting through the low, sullen yellow clouds but it was very hot, his shirt already clinging.

'The ambassador wants to see you as soon as you've settled in.'

'Entirely at his convenience,' said Gower.

They drove carefully, slowed by the unrelieved congestion, for several moments in complete silence. Abruptly Samuels said: 'Your first overseas assignment?'

Gower considered lying, not wanting to concede his inexperience, but he didn't. 'Yes.'

Samuels nodded, an impression confirmed. 'Very necessary you know exactly how people feel.'

Gower had expected the distancing attitude — could recall the actual warning — but he hadn't anticipated being confronted by it literally within an hour of getting off the plane. He felt an edge of temper but quickly curbed it. There was still no reason for him to be cowed by the overbearing manner of a man who rolled words around in his mouth. Intentionally difficult, Gower said: 'Feel about what?'

Samuels' face creased into a confused frown. 'Thought that was obvious.'

'I would have thought it to be equally obvious that my function here is *not* to create problems, that I'm fully aware of that fact and that London would not have sent me to such a sensitive place as Beijing if they imagined for one moment there was the slightest danger of my doing so!' Towards the end Gower was running out of breath, only just finishing with his voice even. He'd spoken throughout turned directly to the diplomat, intent upon a reaction.

Samuels' already furrowed face coloured, but oddly, two sharply defined red patches appearing on his cheeks, like a clown's make-up. Stiffly he said: 'I think it is essential for you not to forget that I am a senior member of the legation here!'

'I won't,' promised Gower, just as stiffly. He believed he had made the necessary correction, but it was important for him not to become too cocky.

They were in the city now, and after the curly-tipped traditional houses on the way from the airport Gower was surprised at the row after row of modern concrete blocks, some almost sky-scraper-high. The streets were wider, too, enabling them to move slightly faster.

'You speak any Chinese languages?' demanded Samuels.

'No,' confessed Gower.

There was a grunt from the other man, as if the admission was confirmation of another undisclosed impression. 'There are English-language maps at the embassy, with places marked to show their positioning to the legation. Don't go wandering off without one. You'll get lost.'

Gower reckoned the other man found it difficult to be anything other than patronizing. 'I won't.'

'Do you intend moving around the city a lot?'

'Not a lot,' said Gower.

'Good.' There was another quick look across the car. 'Always remember the embassy is very closely monitored by the authorities.'

'I won't,' repeated Gower.

'Some material has arrived for you, in the pouch,' announced Samuels. 'It's in the safe, in the embassy vault.'

'I'd appreciate it remaining there, until I might need it.'

'Not for too long,' said Samuels.

'It's not causing any inconvenience, is it?'

Samuels didn't reply.

The residential compound was at the rear but separate from the legation itself, a range of low, barrack-type buildings. The quarters allocated to Gower were at the end of an apparently empty wing. It consisted of a living area furnished with a basic three-piece suite, very old-fashioned in style and hung in Paisley-patterned loose covers.

An unsteady-looking table with four chairs stood in a dining annex with one wall almost completely occupied by a dresser-type piece of furniture with drawers and cupboards below and a latticework of shelves and standing places above a long, flat display surface. There was a television, with compatible videoplaying equipment beneath, on a fitted television table. The carpet directly in front was oddly threadbare in one place, as if someone had intentionally rubbed away the weave. Everything was covered with a faint layer of dust. The dust continued in the bedroom, with just a bed, a bare dressing-table and fitted wardrobes along one wall and a strangely sized bed, wider than a single but not big enough to be considered a double. The kitchen was narrow, without any appliances on the Formica working tops. The kettle was an old metal type that had to be placed on heat to boil, and the refrigerator was small and bow-fronted, from the same era as the suite in the outside living-room. Gower thought it looked like a forgotten furniture repository rather than a place to be lived in.

'Temporary accommodation; that's all you'll need, after all,' said Samuels, defensively.

'It looks very comfortable,' lied Gower.

'Be pointless your trying to watch Chinese television,' said the political officer. 'Rubbish anyway. There's a video selection in the embassy library: pretty old stuff, though.'

'I'll remember that.'

'Ian Nicholson's the official housing and hospitality officer. Anything else you need to know, ask him.' He paused. 'An hour, for the ambassador?'

'I'll be waiting.'

The shower was hot, although the water came unevenly and in spurts, juddering loudly through the pipes: Gower forgot to wipe the dust from the bottom of the stall and initially, mixed with water, it formed a faint mud scum. As he dressed, Gower made a mental note to ask Ian Nicholson about clothes-washing facilities, which shouldn't be a problem in a country that had given the world the Chinese laundry. All the hangers in the wardrobe were metal wire. Remembering the instruction to trust no one, wherever he was, Gower set his traps. He put one jacket away in the wardrobe facing in the opposite direction to the other three, fastened the right clasp of his suitcase but not the left, and closed the bottom drawer of the dressing-table with just an inch protruding.

Samuels telephoned precisely on the hour.

The interior of the embassy was a marked contrast to the barely functional sparseness of the living accommodation. Everything gleamed from polish and attention: there were Chinese carpet wall hangings and a lot of Chinese carvings and sculptures in niches and on display pedestals. There were revolving fans in the ceilings of all the rooms and corridors through which Gower passed, but he guessed at additional air-conditioning from the coolness, which was practically chilling compared to the outside courtyard across which he had walked, with worsening perspiration, to reach the main building.

Peter Samuels was standing beside Sir Timothy Railton when Gower entered the ambassador's office. The man nodded to the formal introductions but offered no handshake. It was Samuels who gestured to an already positioned chair: the political officer remained standing.

The ambassador nodded sideways to the other diplomat and said: 'You've talked? So there's no misunderstandings? You know your position here?'

'I did, before I left England,' said Gower, surprised both by the staccato questioning and by the man himself. The ambassador was immaculately dressed, although the suit was light grey and discreetly checked, and with a waistcoat, despite the outside heat. The tie was Stowe, the shirt-collar hard and starched. Gower couldn't see but he guessed there was a monogram somewhere. There was a signet ring, although he was too far away to see if it carried a crest. Railton was a very smooth-faced, narrow-lipped man, his hair black but thinning and combed directly back from his forehead, flat against his skull. Although the ambassador was so much smaller in stature, Gower decided at once from their demeanour and attitude that he and his political officer were very much a matching pair. Gilbert and Sullivan could probably have written a convincing duet for them.

'Most ambassadors choose not to be aware of

you people in their embassies,' declared Railton. 'I'm not one of them.'

Gower couldn't think of a reply.

'I regard you as a questionable but not a necessary evil,' declared Railton. 'Don't want you thinking, no matter how little time you're here, that you're welcome. You're not. Don't want any nonsense, any difficulties, while you *are* here. Am I making myself clear?'

Gower hesitated. 'I have already assured Mr Samuels that I am fully aware of the sensitivity of this embassy.'

Railton gazed unconvinced across the heavy, inlaid desk. Decorative carpets hung from two of the walls and on a display stand to the left of the desk was a stampede of high-necked Chinese horses. Behind the man, through an expansive window, Gower could see three conical-hatted Chinese bent over ornately created, almost barbered lawns and flowerbeds. Railton said: 'I've no intention of having this embassy compromised. Any nonsense and I shall complain to London. And I want you to carry out your supposed function here: don't want staff gossip about what you're supposed to be doing. Certainly not gossip spreading outside the embassy.'

'I will do everything I have to do as discreetly as possible,' guaranteed Gower.

'The sooner you're gone, the better,' insisted Railton.

'I agree,' said Gower, sincerely. Whatever happened to diplomatic niceties?

'Nothing more to say,' dismissed Railton. He nodded sideways again. 'Anything you're not sure about, don't decide for yourself. Talk with Samuels.'

'Thank you,' said Gower, unsure precisely for what he was expressing gratitude. Taking his guidance from the political officer, who started forward, Gower stood to follow from the room.

In the corridor outside Samuels said: 'Sorry about that.'

Gower was intrigued by the sudden change of attitude and at once further confused when the political officer went on: 'Expressed what we all feel, of course: but I think he went much too far.'

'He was certainly very direct,' said Gower, curiously, hurrying as he'd had to at the airport to keep up with the striding diplomat.

'It's his first ambassadorial appointment. Father was an ambassador before him: four prestige embassies. So Railton sees himself having to keep up a family tradition. Makes him naturally nervous of any problems.'

They halted at a side entrance but still behind the closed doors, within the fan and air-conditioning coolness.

'I can't get involved in whatever you're going to do,' said Samuels. 'Know you wouldn't let me, even if I asked. But if there is anything I can do other than that, then of course I will. Just ask.'

'That's very good of you,' said Gower, at last

genuinely grateful. 'All I want to do at the moment is sleep.'

'Don't forget an orientation map, when you first go outside the compound. The city is like a maze: certainly if you haven't got the language. I'll ask Ian Nicholson to contact you in the morning.'

'I hardly need another diplomatic lecture,' said Gower.

For the first time since they'd met, Samuels smiled, a strained, difficult expression. 'Just to see if you need any help settling in.'

The air-conditioning was much less effective back in the residential section. Gower was aching with exhaustion but still did not fall immediately to sleep. He wasn't gripped by the nervousness he'd known throughout the flight, but supposed it would come back when he actually started working. The only feeling he had at the moment was disappointment. He hadn't expected friendship but he hadn't anticipated openly being denounced as a pariah, either. Which *did* make genuine his parting remark to Sir Timothy Railton: he was probably more anxious to get out than the ambassador was to see him go.

Marcia Leyton wanted everything about the wedding to be perfect and was determined to make it so: even though they hadn't fixed a date and it was clearly some months off she wanted to have most of the arrangements made by the time Gower got back from Beijing. On the day he left London, she surrendered the lease to her flat and that night drove to Bedfordshire, arriving with champagne to break the news to her parents. Her mother cried and her father said he'd begin a cost assessment that could be updated as the details were fixed. He insisted on making notes, although Marcia said it was far too early. Her mother wanted to know how many of John's titled relations would be attending. Marcia said she didn't know if any of his relations were titled.

The following day she visited the local vicar by whom she had been both christened and confirmed to learn the procedure for calling the banns, promising to introduce her fiancé as soon as he returned from a trip abroad.

Marcia had spoken to Gower's mother in Gloucestershire when he'd telephoned to break the news, but she called again, saying what she was doing and promising they would both come down for another weekend when John got back.

'I'm very happy for you,' said the elderly woman. 'Very happy that it's you he's going to marry, too. I know you're going to be wonderfully happy.'

'I know it, too,' said Marcia.

Twenty-five

The paramount consideration in everything she did was always to be able to protect and care for Sasha, and with brutal honesty Natalia confronted the fact that she had put that at risk by fantasizing about locating Charlie Muffin. It was the sort of stupidity that had destroyed Alexei Berenkov, and with further brutal honesty she acknowledged that trying to find Charlie through old records had only ever been the remotest of outside possibilities, which she'd always known but chosen to disregard. And now, because of that stupidity, Fyodor Tudin was pursuing her. Pursuing Sasha, too.

For several days her mind remained blocked by conflicting arguments of self-recrimination until she consciously brought the confusion to a halt, forcing herself to separate the different factors, to find a way to safety.

What, then, was there to learn from the débâcle of Alexei Berenkov? On the face of it, nothing more than she knew already. The man had virtually committed suicide by mixing personal feelings with professional activities, welding his pursuit of Charlie Muffin *unofficially* on to the back of a quite separate *official* operation in England. And been discovered doing it. As Tudin could be on the point of discovering her doing, now.

Alone at her desk in the Yasenevo office, Natalia scribbled the two words — unofficially and official — on the pad before her, underlining each several times.

And at last the idea began to harden.

The danger was in using the long-standing resources of the former KGB *unofficially*. But why did she have to do that? Why couldn't she make it perfectly acceptable to any investigation and still hopefully locate Charlie Muffin?

No reason at all, she decided, warming to the idea. She'd actually be doing the job to which she had been appointed!

Under the division of responsibility between herself and Tudin, she controlled intelligence activities in the former satellite countries as well as in the traditional, long-established Western targets. Where it was known, because the London embassy *rezidentura* had reported it, that there was a new Director and deputy Director General of the British external service, just as it was known because it had been publicly announced that British counter-intelligence now had its first woman Director-General. And in the United States the Senate confirmation hearings of the new Director of the Central Intelligence Agency had been publicly televised.

She had every professional reason — a definite requirement, in fact — to order the most exhaustive updating of each organization: so exhaustive that it would be extended to include serving officers. One of whom, she hoped, would be Charlie Muffin.

Unembarrassed, Natalia laughed openly and aloud as the final part of the idea slipped into place, the perfect way to nullify Fyodor Tudin. She immediately summoned secretaries, dictating a shoal of memoranda convening a conference of all the heads of divisions and departments throughout her Directorate. She ensured that the summons to Tudin was the first to be dispatched.

Li arrived at the moment the class was dispersing, causing the same nervous reaction among the students as before: two, both men, whom Snow had regarded as regulars hadn't been back to a lesson after Li's earlier unexpected second visit.

'Nothing's arrived,' said Snow at once. He had planned the encounter: there was something approaching relief that the Chinese had finally come.

'After so long!' frowned Li, stressing the disappointment. 'It's been weeks now!'

'I intended sending a reminder to England but my colleague has been ill.' He wouldn't rush it.

'I'm sorry to hear that.'

'He's better now.' During each of the past three days Father Robertson had gone out of the mission, insisting he needed fresh air. Snow had accompanied him on the first outing. Ironically they had gone as far as the Purple Bamboo Park. Father

Robertson had said he didn't need a nurse after that first day.

'So you can send the reminder now?'

Time to begin his own confrontation, decided Snow. 'The photographs seem very important to you.'

Li shrugged. 'It is pleasant to keep souvenirs.'

'I agree,' said Snow, pleased with the other man's response. 'I would like copies of those *you* took, during the trip.' Snow smiled. 'A mutual exchange, in fact.'

Momentarily Li faltered. 'Is one conditional upon the other?'

Snow decided, even more pleased, that he'd rattled the man. 'Of course not. But there is no reason why I can't have copies, is there?'

'None at all,' said Li, tightly.

Snow was determined that conditional was exactly what the exchange would be: he wouldn't offer anything until he'd seen Li's pictures, and only then match the man, print for print, each tallying with the other, which removed any danger, remote though he'd always regarded it to be. Li couldn't swap the Shanghai pictures because he would actually be *providing* material the Chinese would regard as sensitive. Snow was sorry the escape hadn't occurred to him before. At least it had, at last: so he didn't have anything to worry about any more.

The round-up of students publicly labelled counter-revolutionaries by the Chinese government began in Xingtai and was followed within a day by arrests in Jining and Huaibei. *The People's Daily* carried photographs of two separate groups of head-bowed detainees, all manacled, together with an official statement that more seizures would be carried out to protect the country from civil unrest fomented by foreign imperialists.

Contacted in Paris, where she had been granted temporary political asylum, Liu Yin said it was the purge she had fled from and warned about at her Hong Kong press conference. It would be, she insisted, one of the most extensive and brutal political repressions in the People's Republic for many years.

Statements expressing concern at a threatened suppression of human rights were issued by various foreign ministries in Europe and by the State Department in the United States.

Twenty-six

Ian Nicholson was an anxiously friendly Scot who, in his eagerness to ingratiate, rarely properly finished a sentence or waited for a reply before beginning another sentence. Gower appreciated the attitude if not the one-sided exchanges after the other encounters he'd so far had in Beijing. The housing officer asked twice, phrasing the same query differently both times, if the accommodation was satisfactory. He was bustling on about the purchasing facilities at the embassy commissary ('everything you're likely to need, not just food: difficult to shop locally here') before Gower gave the assurance that his living quarters were more than adequate. On their way to the commissary to stock Gower's refrigerator Nicholson insisted it was necessary to become a temporary member of the embassy social club ('sorry the social life here is so restricted: we do get together with other Western embassy people, of course') and in the same sentence invited Gower to eat with him and his wife ('whenever you like: just say'). The diplomat warned of the risk of money-changers in the street ('happens all the time. Don't deal, whatever you do: the police are damned strict about it and the ambassador doesn't want any trouble') and echoed Samuels' warning about getting lost in the city. Gower was told to register with the embassy doctor ('name's Pickering: bark's worse than his bite') and advised against initially eating out in restaurants and even then not unless they were recommended by other embassy staff ('best to let your stomach become acclimatized in the beginning: wonderful when you get used to it but it isn't your average Golden Palace in the High Street').

By the time of the conducted tour of the embassy ('important to get the layout in your mind as quickly as possible, I always think') Gower had virtually given up trying to make it a two-way conversation.

There were five introductions to other embassy people — four men and a woman — during the tour. Each was as friendly as Nicholson. Gower wondered if they would have been if they had known his true purpose for being in Beijing.

Nicholson tried to press the luncheon invitation in the embassy mess ('everyone will be there: good time to get to know people') but Gower declined, pleading continuing tiredness after the flight, which to an extent was true: he'd awoken while it was still dark, unbalanced by jetlag.

He was eager to get out into the city although not, so soon, to start work. He realized that had it not been for those final training sessions he almost surely would have tried to begin at once. But then, until those final sessions, he hadn't known any better. Now he did. So instead, trying to put into active practice the survival instructions that were supposed to be instinctive, Gower decided that impatient though he was — impatient though the Beijing ambassador and the deputy Director-General in London were — the proper professional action was to orientate himself before even considering anything else.

Although there was to be no encounter beyond the protection of the embassy, he had to venture outside to get the priest to come to him. So he had minimally to know his way around: find the message drops and the signal spot. With his mind on the proper sequence, Gower picked out on the supplied map those designated places, all already memorized in London, recognizing from the plan before him that most were grouped conveniently close around the obvious landmarks, the places where Western visitors would naturally go.

The drops were concentrated around the Forbidden City, with its available labyrinth of alleys and passageways, and the tree-shrouded Coal Hill. He could survey them all by going to Tiananmen Square, the site of Mao's tomb and fronted by the Great Hall of the People: where, in fact, any first-time visitor would go.

He put the map in his pocket and set out forcefully across the embassy courtyard, but recalled at once another warning and slowed to a more sensible pace to prevent the thrusting determination attracting the very attention he always had to avoid.

At the Chinese-guarded gate he actually

stopped, gazing around to establish his directions, settling the immediate places and buildings in his mind, against the memorized map. There was the jumbled swirl of people and bicycles and occasionally vehicles all around, as there had been on his way from the airport the previous day. And among it all was the possible surveillance. Gower brought his concentration closer, even looking from face to face, bicyclist to bicyclist. Impossible, he decided: absolutely impossible. The only obvious, identifiable person was himself, taught to merge into a background into which, here of all places, he could never disappear. *The sort of man that crowds are made of,* he remembered. But not this crowd.

Would he be able properly to reconnoitre everything he wanted, in one day? Perhaps not. If it became impossible, he'd have to spread it over to the following day: set out earlier than this, to give himself more time. Maybe include the Temple of Heaven, to avoid his interest appearing too obvious to anyone watching. Take several days, maybe. Get himself properly established: prepare escape routes, as he'd been instructed to do.

Or should he take so much time? The demand from everyone was that he get out as quickly as possible. Why was he delaying? Fear, of actually committing himself by a clandestine action? Ridiculous! He wasn't frightened. Just the proper edge of apprehension he'd been told was not only natural but necessary. He was obeying instructions; not the briefing instructions but the guidance he'd got, those last few weeks, sensibly identifying his working area, not making any premature moves that might risk everything. Definitely not frightened.

Consciously, obeying the first taught rule, Gower tried to observe, properly to *see*, everything and everyone directly around him. He'd already decided facial characteristics were impossible to work from, in identifying any surveillance. Clothes then. He could utilize obvious physical characteristics — fat or thin, tall or short — but his best additional chance of spotting someone staying close to him had to be by isolating peculiarities or tell-tale points of dress. The anxiety, tinged with despair, deepened. There was colour — garishly bright reds and greens and pinks he couldn't imagine women wearing in the West — but his overall impression was one of uniformity here, too: white shirts, grey trousers, usually grey jackets where jackets were worn at all. When the colour wasn't grey, it was black or blue. The conformity even extended to shoes. All were black and all appeared steel-tipped and maybe even with steel or studs in the heels. Even with the competition of other street sounds, Gower was conscious of a permanent scuffing, tip-tap beat of metal against concrete.

Sure of his direction, Gower changed and altered his route, remembering to make his first deviation to the left, then left again before switching twice to his right down streets to bring himself back on course. Several times, concentrating for the abrupt confusion it might hopefully cause, he halted halfway along a road, feigning the uncertainty of a stranger realizing he had taken the wrong turning and going back the way he had come, intent upon anyone wheeling around to follow. No one did, at any of his staged performances.

Although he had seen pictures and newsreels, the vastness of Tiananmen Square momentarily overawed him. From where he stood the giant memorial photograph of Mao Tsetung was postage-stamp size, the Great Hall of the People and the walled Forbidden City initially of doll's house dimensions. He couldn't guess how many people were there in total — certainly hundreds — but the square still looked comparatively deserted.

Gower set out across it, towards the tomb with its snake of the faithful waiting to make their obeisance. As he walked he was aware for the first time of a fine dust in the air: it was settling on his face and hands and was gritty in his mouth. There was no sun, as there hadn't been the previous day, but heat seemed trapped beneath the blanket of thick clouds, causing him to sweat. Mingling with the dust, it made his skin irritate. He used the act of taking off his jacket, throwing it over one shoulder, to turn fully to look around him. Nowhere, as far as he could see, was there anyone who appeared to be following or watching.

Perhaps he wasn't being watched. Despite the warnings there was no guarantee — and certainly no way of finding one — that surveillance was *absolute*. Perhaps it was a hit-or-miss business: perhaps sometimes it was possible to go out of the legation and move about the streets without any official interest whatsoever. But there was no way of finding that out, either. So the assumption had to be that there was a permanent counter-intelligence attention.

So why was he allowing his mind to drift in a direction it was pointless to follow? A permissible, if naïve, reflection. Now dismissed. Back to reality. The reality which said that somewhere, among the swallowed-up clusters of supposed tourists to the massive, historically bloodstained square, there was a man or men — or women — checking everything he did, everywhere he went.

Gower began to walk the full length of the Great Hall façade, mouth tight against the grit, the aching beginning of protest in his legs. The approach came when he was practically halfway along, the whispering arrival beside him so quick and unexpected he physically jerked sideways away from the man, startled.

'I buy dollars?'

Genuine? Or for the watchers? Working on the just decided assumption of constant attention, Gower stopped, fully to confront the man. As he did so, Gower realized that trying as hard as he had been to pick out people near to him he hadn't spotted this tout, who had to have been close to have made this sudden approach. 'I will not exchange money unofficially. Go away.'

'Best rates.'

Hoping that if there had been an audience the positive refusal would have been witnessed, Gower walked on, refusing to answer the continuing offers ranging through world currencies, almost theatrically ignoring the existence of the man hurrying alongside, steel-protected shoes rattling over the stonework. Despite Nicholson's forewarning, Gower still hadn't expected an approach on his first outing. He was practically at the far extreme of the Great Hall façade before the disappointed money-dealer accepted defeat and broke away. Gower stopped again, watching the man go to stalls at the edge of the square, discreetly to approach a four-strong group of Western tourists, from their clothes most likely American or Canadian. Both men instantly shook their heads, but one of the women felt out to her companion's arm, stopping the rejection. It took about ten minutes to complete the transaction finalized by a conjuror's flick of hand movements as the money was switched from one to the other. The Chinese split urgently away, without looking back. There was no official challenge or intervention. One of the women took a photograph of the disappearing man. There was a lot of laughing and head-nodding approval.

Gower started walking again towards the Forbidden City, guessing he had not allowed sufficient time later to climb Coal Hill as well as explore in one afternoon the world in which former Chinese emperors spent their entire lives.

The Forbidden City *was* labyrinthine. And a blaze of squinting colour, glaring oranges and reds on roofs and walls, the pathways and alleys guarded by statues and carvings of real and mythical creatures: doleful, slumped elephants and head-raised, snarling monsters with tortoise armour and spike-haired lions, squatting with teeth bared in ferocity. Gower walked with apparent aimlessness, in reality following the route set out for him in London. He found the empty brick-space on the bridge over a narrow, carp- and goldfish-filled stream: the crevice into which a single sheet of paper could be slipped, by the haunch of a hunched lion: the overhanging, concealing bush that formed a perfect cache by a refuse bin near a raised and tomb-like rectangle, and another hiding place at the back of a huge storage receptacle in what he took to be a former receiving room of the long-ago emperors.

He neither paused nor showed interest in any of the designated places, deciding as he strolled by that on the subsequent, priest-summoning deliveries a camera would give him the necessary excuse to hesitate and conceal his messages. The ever-changing statues and figures and displays and halls gave him a constant excuse to turn and look around him: not once, from one examination to the next, did he isolate anyone paying special attention to him.

Gower cut the visit short when he judged himself to be about halfway around the sprawling enclave, postponing an attempt upon the hill until the following day. Should he think of secreting a message to Jeremy Snow then? He wasn't sure. Wrong to hurry, came the warning voice in his mind: nothing to be gained by unnecessary haste, everything to lose. His pace, his safety: and the safety, of course, of the priest. Indeed, a positive, professional reason for taking as many additional days as he wanted: watchers would be lulled trailing behind a camera-toting sightseer. He might just carry a message tomorrow. Then again, he might just not.

The eager Nicholson was in ambush when he got back to the embassy and Gower allowed himself to be pressed into their dining together. The wife, whose name was Jane, was a mousy woman who blinked a lot, as if she needed spectacles. She wore a dragon-patterned silk cheong-sam like a banner to prove she had assimilated the local culture. It was too tight, showing the bumps and knobs of her underwear. Gower remembered to ask about laundry and was assured by Nicholson it was excellent: he simply had to hand it to his Chinese houseboy. It reminded Gower to check his room traps.

'Ian tells me it's only a fleeting visit?' said the woman.

'Just checking the local facilities: seeing if anything could be improved,' said Gower.

'Which will throw us together a lot,' said Nicholson. 'That's a big part of my job, knowing what's available here and what's not.'

'I guess it will,' agreed Gower. On the ambassador's direct order he had to go through the pretence with the man.

'So how long *will* you be here?' asked Jane.

Gower shrugged, noncommittal. 'No real time-limit. It's got to be done properly. But I wouldn't expect it to be more than a month.'

None of the room snares had been tripped when he got back to his quarters. He still decided to leave what had been pouched to him from London in the embassy security vault.

After the Prix de l'Arc de Triomphe at Longchamp, which Miller dutifully attended with her, Lady Ann announced her intention to tour the French stables on a bloodstock-buying expedition, which allowed Miller and Patricia Elder almost a month to be permanently together. For only the third time since her affair with Miller began, Patricia moved some of her clothes and personal belongings into the mansion penthouse.

It was obviously the most convenient thing to do, to avoid Patricia having daily to commute to her own house in Chiswick to change her clothes, but Miller was apprehensive at the chance it gave her to press the well rehearsed and too often repeated divorce demands.

Their first night together — the day Gower flew to Beijing — Patricia declared she did not want to go out to eat but to cook for him in the apartment, which she did superbly. Afterwards, huddled together on a couch with brandy bowls in hand, Patricia said this was how it should be all the time and didn't he think so too. He agreed, nervously, waiting for the familiar complaint, but she didn't say anything more. Neither did she the next night, when they ate in again, and just very slightly Miller began to relax.

Perhaps, he thought hopefully, there wasn't going to be a scene: perhaps, having made so many protests, Patricia was reconciled to everything staying as it was. That's what he really wanted: things to go on undisturbed as they were.

'New shoes?' queried Julia.

'And they're killing me,' complained Charlie.

'That's a new shirt, too, isn't it?'

'Needed some new clothes.'

Julia regarded him with her head to one side, which she often did when something particularly caught her curiosity. 'Maybe I should start dressing up.'

'You're fine as you are,' said Charlie.

'I thought you were, too,' she smiled.

'Don't know what you're talking about,' he said.

'Liar.'

Twenty-seven

So large had Natalia Fedova's Directorate become from the increased demands made upon it that a total of thirty deputies and department heads assembled for the meeting, which because of its size was held in the main conference room at Yasenevo.

Natalia supervised everything, even the seating plan around the long rectangular table, topped by a much smaller one to complete the T. There were only two places at the top table. One was obviously hers, as the division chairperson. The other, on her right, was for Fyodor Tudin, a visible display to all of his authority as her immediate deputy.

There were separate seating arrangements to the left of the room for the secretaries and file clerks: it was essential everything be officially recorded. And not just for the archives but witnessed by each senior executive. Natalia was determined against the slightest mistake, believing she couldn't afford to make one.

It was the first complete gathering of chief officials since her appointment, which gave Natalia the excuse to host a brief pre-conference reception, designed to prevent any straggling arrivals in the chamber itself, and to minimize the difference in rank between Tudin and herself. She orchestrated the start so that she and the man entered the conference room side by side. Tudin, a swarthy, belly-bulged man whose permanently red face betrayed the blood-pressure brought on by his drinking, smiled and nodded in private approval at the seating arrangements.

Natalia sat first, however, intent upon the men settling before her. The majority were newcomers to the reorganized intelligence service. She had personally approved nearly all of the appointments, vetting them to ensure they genuinely embraced the changes that had swept both the country and the organization. There were only five, including Tudin, whom she considered old guard, men who mourned the passing of the Communist Party and the absolute power of the former KGB. She wondered if they formed a clique with Tudin in any move against her. It was the way putsches had been organized in the past, and three were nominally under Tudin's direct control, his subordinates in the republic division.

Natalia had prepared her opening remarks as carefully as everything else: throughout she was conscious of Tudin's persistent sighs of condescension, and once she thought she detected a smirk of complicity from a contemporary of Tudin's, a man named Pavel Khrenin. She outlined the increased demands upon their reformed Directorate and described it as one of the most important arms of the now independent Russian Federation, in which it was practically regarded as a separate, autonomous ministry. She was pleased at the way the reorganization was proceeding and hoped it would soon be complete: that was not just her expectation but that of the government they served. She had called this conference, the first of what she intended to be regular sessions, to receive a full assessment from every division and directorate head and to inform that government of what had been already established, what it was hoped to create and what their ambitions were for the future. Here Natalia paused, indicating the scurrying note-takers at the separate table: a full transcript was to be taken and submitted to the President and the appropriate ministers for their comment, which she undertook to distribute to each of her subordinate departments if and when she received replies.

Tudin's final sigh, when it was clear she had finished, was louder and more obvious than those with which he had punctuated her opening address. Determinedly, Natalia refused any reaction. Instead she smiled out into the room, isolating Khrenin to begin the first of the presentations demanded in her convening memorandum. Khrenin was a survivor of the former KGB, although not originally from the First Chief Directorate, and had been appointed to create a new service in Poland. The man appeared startled to be singled out, and started badly: throughout his tone was apologetic for not yet having fully created what was required in the former satellite, constantly stressing the difficulty of establishing a network in a country where anything Russian was derided and anyone identified as having previous connections with the despised KGB faced criminal prosecution.

Not once, while Khrenin spoke, did Tudin sigh. Several times Natalia glanced sideways at her deputy. On each occasion he was staring fixedly down the room, although not directly at Khrenin, his face blank. She wondered if Tudin's attitude was consideration for an ally or the beginning of an unsettled awareness of the coup she planned.

For her own part Natalia decided that Khrenin's miserable apology for his failure in a country for which she was ultimately responsible was personally acceptable. But only just.

Natalia urged the reports on through the former satellites of Hungary and Czechoslovakia and tried to maintain the sequence by going on to the chairman of the German division, now a single unit that included East Germany under the reorganization that she had carried out. All, to varying degrees, argued the difficulties of forming new clandestine structures in countries where they were rejected, but again Natalia decided none of the failings were personally damaging.

As the presentations progressed, Natalia became aware of Tudin shifting uncomfortably beside her, although the admitted failings in the satellite countries reflected upon her as the recognized controller and not at all upon him, as the man answerable for obtaining intelligence from republics within the Commonwealth.

She hoped her deputy's increasing agitation meant he'd seen the abyss towards which he was being irrevocably led. Intent upon heightening his discomfort, Natalia turned sideways and smilingly deferred to him to conduct his subordinates through their accounts.

A considerable effort had clearly been tried to make each report as comprehensibly impressive as possible — which, as one exaggerated recitation followed another, actually focused the awareness of every professional in the room on the fact that in none of the republics was there yet anything approaching even the beginning of an espionage system. Indeed, so obviously embarrassing was it that officers all along the table moved and fidgeted in sympathetic discomfort for those being forced to make the stumbling admissions. A lot stared down at the papers before them, trying to appear occupied in what was written there.

Natalia was one of the few who didn't move. Rather, prepared for this as for everything else, she remained absolutely motionless, letting her face set more and more fixedly as the presentations finally, humiliatingly, petered out. Tudin did not attempt a final summation, remaining stonily quiet, which was an advantage she hadn't anticipated. Seizing it, Natalia stretched the silence: there were audio-recordings being made, as well as verbatim notes, and she knew the echoing stillness would sound far worse than any immediately spoken criticism.

At last she turned to her deputy. 'There appear

to be problems in this division?'

'As there are in the former satellites,' said Tudin, predictably.

'*Acceptable* problems,' qualified Natalia, seeing her opportunity at once. 'And ones that can be overcome. Can you guarantee the republic difficulties can be resolved by your division?' So close and looking directly at him, Natalia could see perspiration bubble out on Tudin's top lip at his recognition of the trap into which he had so easily fallen: already there was a sheen of nervousness upon his forehead and gradually balding head.

'In time,' he said, desperately.

'How much time?' demanded Natalia, relentlessly.

'That is impossible to estimate.'

Natalia looked away from the man, pleased at the chilled atmosphere that had grown in the room, trying to gauge from their expressions the reaction of the other officers to the unexpectedly open challenge. As much the professional survivors of headquarters in-fighting as professional intelligence officers, every one of them was utterly expressionless. Turning back to Tudin, she said: 'I think we have to accept the political realities that exist and what we are expected to provide, in those realities. The admitted, and far less serious, delays in setting up operations in the former satellites are acceptable because those former satellites are much easier to anticipate, politically. This is not the case in the countries that once formed the Soviet Union and now comprise the Commonwealth. Not *one* of them is possible to anticipate. *Each* is unstable and could collapse or be thrown into turmoil by a coup. Virtually each distrusts every other . . .' She paused, anxious not to overplay her hand '. . . If one former republic collapses, the Commonwealth could collapse: certainly it would become more unstable. It is the republics that are the predominant concern of our government and which have therefore to be the predominant concern of this organization. We have to have the facilities and the ability to give the warnings and sound the alarms, in *advance,* so that the President can be prepared. And at the moment we are not in a position to do that, are we Colonel Tudin . . . ?' Natalia hesitated again, not for a reply to a question that was rhetorical anyway but momentarily unsure whether to go on. Deciding to, she said: 'It was because of the importance of getting eyes and ears into these countries that I separated this Directorate as I did: why, believing as I did then in your unquestioned ability, I entrusted you personally to coordinate and create the apparatus essential for our protection.' Natalia staged the final pause. 'I very much hope I have not made a mistake in my choice.'

Tudin was the only man in the chamber whose face was no longer expressionless. The look directed towards Natalia was one of pure and open hatred, and she guessed that behind those hooded, veined eyes he was already planning to initiate whatever scheme he had in mind against her in revenge for such public humiliation.

'I am sure every one of us in this room is grateful for the political insight,' Tudin said. The words strained out from him, as if he had difficulty in speaking, not from breathlessness but from some restriction in his throat.

It was pitiful sarcasm and Natalia contemptuously ignored it. 'I sought an assurance from you, about time.'

'Which I said was impossible to give.' There was the quickest of glances down into the room, and Natalia guessed at brief eye contact with Khrenin: it had certainly been to Khrenin's side of the table.

She didn't try to follow the look. Instead she allowed another moment of silence. When she spoke again, Natalia looked out into the room. 'Then I think I have arbitrarily to impose one. As I said in my opening remarks, these conferences are to be regularly established. I propose they should be at three-monthly intervals . . .' She went back to look directly at Tudin. 'In three months I want to hear from you and your subordinate deputies that networks exist in every former republic which once comprised the Soviet Union.'

Tudin's entrapment was complete and he knew it. He wasn't able to speak, just to nod.

'If, in the interim, you come to believe you cannot fulfil that schedule I expect you to advise me. In any event, I would like weekly progress reports.' Natalia did not think she had left any avenue for escape or evasion: three months was an impossible time-frame and Tudin was going to be racked twenty-four hours a day even to attempt it, before finally having, in the recordable written form she had stipulated, to admit he had failed. And still she wasn't finished with the man.

Once more Natalia turned back to the other men assembled in front of her. While none of them was betraying any readable reaction, Natalia believed she could discern a respectful wariness from some of them: maybe even fear. 'We have considered the immediate past, and to an extent what we hope to create, to make our reorganization complete. To give all of you an indication of how full I want the exchange of information to be at future conferences like this, I want briefly to talk of an active operation I have already initiated, among certain overseas *rezidentura*.'

She watched several of the division chiefs prepare to take notes.

'Some years ago, I was involved in a specific operation to identify a member of the British external service,' continued the woman. 'For reasons that do not concern this conference, the operation was not a complete success. But recently I consulted the file to remind myself of it, because of official appointments that have been made in the British SIS, MI5 and the American Central Intelligence Agency. Learning from the mistakes of that earlier failed attempt, I have ordered London and Washington to create the most definitive and exhaustive records in all the past and recent history of this Directorate, not just upon the Director-Generals and Director of the British and American organizations, but upon as many division heads and active serving officers as it is possible to identify . . .'

Natalia looked briefly sideways, to Tudin. He was sitting with his mouth slightly open and staring not at the table before him but at some spot on the floor beyond. Natalia's impression was of someone absolutely stunned. To account for the brief attention upon her deputy, she said: 'I have initiated the programme in those two countries because of the recently announced appointments to which I have referred and because *rezidentura* are fully in place and operational in embassies there. When we are properly organized in the former satellites and republics, I want similar tracing programmes conducted there. As I said at the very beginning, this new Directorate is being invested practically with the status of a ministry. I intend it always to qualify as such, if not actually in name.'

Natalia stared around the room, beginning to feel the strain of her performance. 'Any questions?'

No one spoke.

She'd done it! Natalia decided, exultantly. She'd devastatingly reversed any threat from Fyodor Tudin, virtually making his future in the Directorate impossible. And she had evolved a foolproof way to locate Charlie Muffin by openly using the entire resources of the Russian Federation's intelligence service. Indulging herself, Natalia decided she had managed the sort of Machiavellian manipulation of which Charlie himself would have been proud. Abruptly, quite unprompted, the sort of recollection she had been seeking for so long came with that idle reflection. It was incomplete and hazy but she was sure it could be important: a long-ago conversation, when he had been here in Moscow. Something about his having a bedridden mother, who at that time would be missing the regular visits he made. He'd talked about the home she was in: described something particular about the part of England where it was situated. But what, she asked herself, desperately: a half-memory wasn't any good. No good at all.

Within an hour of returning to her office, the satisfaction at defeating Tudin and the hope that the long-sought recollection was coming at last were washed away by a new and far more immediate crisis.

Natalia realized that the tempo at which the demand was channelled to her was clearly speeded by the official enquiry she had earlier made at Mytninskaya, coupled obviously with her rank: the delay, from the initial approach, was less than two days, which for Russia was amazingly fast.

What she expected was to be told by an aide that Eduard had finally tried to find her at the old apartment. She was even beginning to consider how to react to an approach she had already de-

Twenty-eight

Gower awoke within thirty minutes of his usual time, pleased at the apparent recovery from jetlag. As he made instant coffee, he planned his day: he'd climb Coal Hill to explore the drops there, revisit the Forbidden City to get the necessary places marked indelibly in his mind, and in the afternoon pick a route to take him past the Taoist temple where the routine to bring Jeremy Snow to the embassy had to begin.

Begin today? Gower sat with his elbows on the narrow kitchen table, both hands around his cup, considering his own question. It was still too soon. He hadn't yet visited two of the three places with which he had to familiarize himself. And there was that much-repeated insistence from his last, unnamed teacher always to set up an escape route before ever thinking of beginning anything. At that moment he hadn't started to consider how he and the priest were going to get out. But what was there to consider? There was only one conceivable way: by air. So there were air guides to be consulted, reservations to be made, routes to be chosen.

Ridiculous, then, to think of leaving a signal and filling a drop today. It would have to be spread over several days, at least. Certainly a week. Not a delay of nervous reluctance, Gower assured himself: anything but. It was a professionally required period in which to work properly to guarantee the demands imposed from London and from here. He *needed* that amount of time — might need more — to get an awkward priest to safety and remove any risk of exposure and political embarrassment. And to remove also, of course, the risk of harm to the priest.

Gower wished the self-doubt was not so readily there, always waiting on the sidelines of his mind, too swift to intrude itself into any uncertain thought.

He tried mundane activity to slough off the introspection, tidying the kitchen and making his own bed in advance of the room-boy's attendance. He had just finished setting his snares when there was a peremptory rap on the door, startling him.

'You were away from the embassy all day yesterday, apart from the time you spent with Nicholson,' declared Samuels, scarcely bothering with any greeting. 'Have you forgotten what the ambassador said he wanted?'

Gower had. 'Sorry?' he queried, hopefully.

Samuels sighed, with predictable condescension. 'You are supposed to be surveying the facilities of the embassy.'

'And also concluding what I've been sent here to do as quickly as possible,' countered Gower, ignoring his earlier reflections.

'We have Chinese staff: gardeners and cleaners. And security officers we know about on the gates as well as those we don't know about, elsewhere,' said Samuels. 'It is important you visibly appear to be fulfilling a proper function.'

After the specific London instructions about protocol and the avoidance of offence, Gower accepted he had to defer to what amounted to an order, although he didn't enjoy taking orders from a man like Peter Samuels. 'Nicholson said he expected to spend some time with me.'

'He's your man,' agreed the political officer. At once there was the reversal of attitude that had occurred the previous day. Samuels smiled and said: 'Everything OK?'

'The map was useful: thanks for the suggestion,' said Gower. 'I . . .' he stopped, realizing what he was going to say, then decided he wasn't disclosing anything. 'I had a look around the Forbidden City. Might go again, later.'

'Fascinating,' agreed Samuels, seeming positively friendly. 'You could spend a month there and still not see all of it.'

Taking advantage of an encounter he hadn't expected, Gower said: 'I might want to look at what was pouched to me from London.' Conscious of the wariness that instantly came to the other man, Gower hurried on: 'Not to keep here, in these quarters. I just want to check it through.'

Samuels nodded, slowly. 'I'm going to be in my office all day. Come there when you're ready. Let's go and find Nicholson, shall we?'

The gabbling Scotsman, whose appointed position emerged as the junior lawyer in the embassy's legal department, was as effusively affable as the previous day. Totally unprepared for what he was being called upon to do, which he acknowledged to be an oversight, Gower asked Nicholson, with the experience of a resident, to decide the inspection by taking him to those facilities in the embassy the man believed most in need of improvement. That brought them back at once to the accommodation wing, for which Gower was grateful, reckoning he could prolong the charade in that one section for enough of that day to comply with Samuels' insistence, without needing to spend any longer in the embassy itself. He trailed behind Nicholson, genuinely agreeing that the majority of the fittings and furnishings were out of date and inadequate, apologizing to the wives upon whom they intruded in some of the occupied flats. He listened patiently to their more forceful complaints after he was introduced as a Foreign Office inspector: in two flats he dutifully sat and drank the offered coffee, sympathetically nodded and tut-tutting, all the while feeling the fraud that he was.

It was close to noon when they recrossed the forecourt to the main building, and with the morning wasted Gower agreed to lunch with Nicholson in the embassy mess. On their way there the persistent lawyer-diplomat detoured to enrol Gower as a temporary member of the social club. Inside the dining-room there was virtually a moving line of introductions: when Nicholson announced Gower's proclaimed purpose for being there nearly everyone grumbled that the survey was long overdue. As he had that morning with the aggrieved wives, Gower felt vaguely disconcerted at deceiving so many people so obviously, but supposed he shouldn't: it had to be all part of the job to which he was still adjusting. Halfway through the meal, he saw Samuels enter and take a seat at the far side of the room. The political officer ignored him. Gower guessed the mood pendulum had swung back in the opposite direction.

Gower pleaded the need to get the problems he'd discovered that morning into a preliminary report to avoid continuing the pointless exercise in the afternoon. They made arrangements to resume the following morning. Gower declined the offer to eat again with the Nicholsons that night.

Remembering his protective idea of the previous day, believing it showed he was thinking and acting as he should, Gower went back to his quarters to collect his camera before setting out for the second time. Sure of the direction from his earlier excursion and knowing, too, that he would not be able to pick up any follower directly outside the legation, Gower moved off without pause towards the Forbidden City. He measured his pace today and once away from the embassy repeated the attempt to discover company, deviating from the shortest route and then suddenly backtracking on himself. Yet again no one reversed direction in obvious pursuit. Close to the square he tried again, halting abruptly at a street-stall he had already isolated, using sign language to buy a covered carton of yoghurt and staying there to drink it, able while he was doing so to turn this way and that like the interested first-time visitor he was, surveying everyone around him. He could recognize no one drinking or loitering around the stall whom he had seen before, closer to the embassy. No one moved off when he finished his drink to continue towards the square. All around him, the steel-tipped shoes tapped and chattered, like pavement cicadas.

Today Gower ignored the Great Hall, immediately re-entering the Forbidden City. He checked himself just in time from taking the same route as before, instead following different paths and alleys and carefully not stopping at two of the designated message spots. At the others he used the convenient camera as an excuse to stop and study them in detail: remembering the incriminating problem of the pictures the priest had taken, Gower was careful with the exposures it was protectively necessary to take, each time shooting so that the concealment he was detailing in his mind was on the peripheral edge of every frame. He spent longer in the City than he had on the first occasion, lingering and photographing a lot of other locations with apparently more concentrated interest than he'd shown in the places for which he was really visiting the site.

Coal Hill, built from the earth dug out to make the moat for the Forbidden City, was a rolling hump conveniently covered with trees and shrubs and close-knit bushes, surmounted at its very top by a traditional pagoda with three tip-cornered roofs, one on top of the other, like a nipple on a breast. It was laced by paved walkways and in places guarded, like the Forbidden City, by armoured lion figures and hard-shelled monsters from myths he did not know.

Gower climbed steadily towards the top, but not directly, meandering from path to path to find his drops, turning frequently not just to search behind him but using the always pointless check to gaze out from the elevation afforded by the hill out over the ancient city spread out below.

There were two places established on the hill. One was by a tulip-lamped light standard, where a message could be slipped beneath the rotund bottom of a permanently fixed rubbish bin. The other was just two paths to the left, on one of the statues, where the right front paw of one of the snarling lions had lifted slightly with the aged distortion of the metal, creating a barely visible but very usable crack into which a single stiff card could be inserted.

He would use a drop on Coal Hill, Gower determined, positively: perhaps the lion cache or then again maybe the tulip light. He didn't have to decide until the very moment he left the signal by the temple. Whichever it was, Coal Hill had the better concealment, both hiding places surrounded by shrubbery.

Gower was oddly encouraged by the choice of

Coal Hill, seeing it as a further step towards completing his assignment. He had only the temple site to reconnoitre and there couldn't be any problems there, any more than there had been at the Forbidden City or where he was now. Once he'd positioned the flower alert he could remain within the security of the embassy until he went with the priest to the airport: in his growing confidence, Gower had no doubt Father Snow would at last do what he was told. Incriminated by the photographs he had to produce, the priest had no choice.

His mind upon the pictures, Gower started back down the hill, remembering to keep his pace that of a sightseer leisurely ending a visit, not someone in any, sudden hurry. He did not make any attempt to discover if he was under surveillance: he was doing nothing covert, so there was no reason to bother with a pointless exercise. It was a relief to feel as self-assured as he did. He knew everything was going to work out exactly as it should: he'd be back in London very soon, with Marcia. She'd expect a souvenir, he realized abruptly: it would be a mistake if he did not take her back a present. Easily achieved, though, without it becoming an unnecessary interference with what he was in Beijing to achieve. He'd ask Jane Nicholson to shop for him: the sort of cheongsam she'd worn the first night at dinner. He wasn't sure it was what Marcia would choose for herself, but it was something she could use to lounge around the flat. By now she would have given up her own apartment: knowing her he guessed she would already be making plans for the wedding. One of the first things he'd have to do when he got back was buy her an engagement ring. He wanted it to be something special: whatever she wanted, without giving a damn about the cost.

Samuels was in his office as promised when Gower got back to the embassy. The political officer went with him to the basement security vault, authorizing his access to the officer on duty there. Gower remained inside the vault to examine the package, wanting only to look at the photographs with which he had to force Snow's departure. The alterations had been expertly done: to Gower's untrained eye it was impossible to detect any tampering. He replaced them inside the envelope and resealed it, returning everything to the security official and rejoining Samuels in the tiny outer room.

As they walked back up the stairs together, Samuels said: 'You've become a very popular person here. Everyone thinks you're going to get a lot of improvements made around the place.'

'I'm embarrassed about it,' admitted Gower.

'That's the only embarrassment we want,' said the diplomat.

Charlie finally got his confirmation of an affair between Peter Miller and Patricia Elder at precisely eight-thirty on a surprisingly sunny Wednesday morning in early March.

And in addition got far more than he expected.

He was perfectly hidden from the spectacular bordering mansions on the inside of the hedge that surrounds the park, and at that precise moment was finally deciding he'd wasted far too much effort over the past weeks chasing a personal impression that he should at last admit was wrong.

And then they emerged from the private exit of the penthouse.

They were not initially together. Miller came out first, alone, but hesitated after two or three paces, looking back into the still open door and eventually stopping, to wait. Patricia Elder followed. There was a brief conversation, with both consulting their watches, before they began walking together down the outer circle.

Charlie began to smile, knowing that familiar flush of satisfaction at a hunch turning out to be a hundred per cent right, which was always a feeling he savoured, wishing there'd been more of them in a troublesome life.

Almost at once the expression — and the satisfied feeling — faltered and died, never properly forming.

It was the movement of a camera that caught his eye, in an inconspicuous black Ford parked beyond his concealing hedge, less than five yards from where he stood: a camera aimed by one of the two men to take the last photograph of the disappearing Director-General of Britain's external intelligence service and his deputy as they turned into Chester Gate, to reach Albany Street.

The Ford started up immediately, trying to move in the direction opposite to that taken by the oblivious couple: it had to pause, because of a passing van, conveniently enabling Charlie to take the number.

Charlie remained where he was for several moments before slowly moving off deeper into the park, towards the boating lake. An enquiry agent, hired by a suspicious Lady Ann? Or was it something professionally far more serious? A private detective agency could probably be easily confirmed from the registration number. It was just possible to check the other alternative, too, if a person remained an awkwardly suspicious and genuine bastard who didn't believe in virgin births, that there was something good in everybody, or in New Realities for the future.

The taxi got Charlie to Notting Hill in fifteen minutes. He ambled into the tree-lined avenue linking the Bayswater Road with Kensington High Street and dominated on either side, with a few exceptions for millionaire residents, by the London embassies of foreign countries. He showed no reaction whatsoever at identifying from the registration he had so recently recorded the black Ford parked neatly among three other vehicles in the forecourt of what had become the Russian, not the Soviet, embassy.

Reaching Kensington, Charlie hesitated on the pavement, thoughts momentarily refusing even to present themselves for consideration. What the

307

fuck was he going to do about that, he asked himself, wishing he knew.

His feet hurt, too, from walking the entire length of the embassy row.

Twenty-nine

The traditional animosity between the respective policing agencies had only minimally lessened since the transfer of the renamed KGB to the control of the Interior Ministry, which also governed the Militia, but Natalia guessed from the tone of his voice that the man to whom she spoke would have travelled out to the Yasenevo suburb if she had asked. She didn't. The policeman formally introduced himself as Mikhail Stepanovich Kapitsa, a senior investigator in the organized crime division, in the thick, frequently coughing voice of a heavy smoker: twice their telephone conversation was interrupted by the sound of a match scraping into life. The man agreed they could meet at once: it was better to get everything sorted out as soon as possible, didn't she think?

Natalia hesitated at the moment of departure, aware before knowing the circumstances she could be entering a situation of enormous personal danger, danger far greater than she had so far faced from Fyodor Tudin.

Decisively, still in her own office, she ordered her official, chauffeur-driven Zil. In addition, as she went through the outer secretariat she made a point of recording a visit to Petrovka. The chauffeur was a pool driver with a Georgian accent and a painful-looking boil on a thick neck. Natalia remembered Tudin was Georgian. The man, hand constantly on his horn, insisted on bulldozing down the central road lanes which in the past had been reserved for government vehicles. Anxious to get to Petrovka, she didn't object.

A uniformed officer escorted her to the second floor. Kapitsa's office was fugged with the anticipated smoke, an ashtray on a cluttered desk overflowing, a half-burned cigarette smouldering in it. Kapitsa picked it up as he sat. His dark blue suit shone with wear and there was a snow-line of ash over the front. The left lapel had a burn hole that looked ancient, the cloth frayed around its edges.

'I appreciate your contacting me,' embarked Natalia cautiously.

The man smiled. His teeth were yellowed by nicotine. 'We're closer together now as colleagues than we ever were. But it's not going to be easy. To be honest, at the moment I can't think of a way.'

A man of the past, accustomed to deals and arrangements, guessed Natalia. 'What's happened?'

Kapitsa nodded, lighting another cigarette from the butt of its predecessor: as an afterthought, he offered the packet to Natalia. She shook her head. Kapitsa said: 'Organized crime has become a serious problem in Moscow. And greatly increased since the changes that were supposed to provide things that haven't been available.

And still aren't now, unless you go to a Mafia outlet . . .' He shrugged, apologizing in advance. 'The order has been given, for a major crackdown . . .' Another shrug. 'Market forces can't fill the shops and we can't fill the work rosters with enough men to do the job we're told to do. So the Mafia go on winning: we haven't — and won't — get it under control.'

Natalia was curious at the generality. It would be a mistake to hurry him.

'We do the best we can, of course: we've got to. We're publicly accountable now, not like before.'

Natalia detected the nostalgia: definitely someone immersed in the past and mourning it.

'Occasionally we get lucky. Like this time. It's one of the known Mafia families, the Lubertsy. They're young. Violent. Trade in a lot of drugs brought up from the southern republics: across the Polish border from Italy, too. There were two kilos of heroin and ten kilos of marijuana, all from the south. There was a lot of medicines, as well: to be sold to people who know what they want but can't get it through hospitals or from their doctors who prescribe it. We're still carrying out tests but we think the medicines have been adulterated, to stretch the size and value of the shipment . . .' The man paused, to light another cigarette. '. . . Adulterated medical drugs kill sometimes, instead of saving lives. Or maim. Certainly aren't effective, in doing what they're supposed to do . . .'

Natalia couldn't contain herself any longer. 'What's Eduard's part in all of this?'

'Organizer,' said the man, bluntly. 'He hasn't admitted it, but there's no doubt he was in charge. It was a big load, in total. Four lorries. We don't know where they originated: no one will say. It was on the Serpukhov road.'

'Only narcotics and medicines?'

Kapitsa shook his head. 'Quite a lot of domestic electrical stuff, mostly German. That will have definitely come through Poland. Clothing, too. Jeans, naturally.'

'How did the interception happen?' This wasn't just potentially dangerous; it could be catastrophic.

'Luck, like I said. We chose the Serpukhov direction because we heard drug shipments had come by that route before. Put up a road-block five nights ago and they drove straight into it.' There was a quick, satisfied smile. 'There were only eight of us: should have been double that at least if we'd known what we were going into. There were twelve of them.'

'They fought? Resisted?' Natalia tried to push back the sensation of numbness threatening to engulf her, clouding her reason.

Kapitsa's smile remained. He shook his head. 'They weren't even worried. I was there, in charge. They laughed at me: asked what arrangements were necessary to solve what they called "a little problem".'

'*They* asked?' pressed Natalia.

The man gave an apologetic shrug. 'Eduard asked.'

'*Were* there weapons?'

'Enough for a short war. Handguns. Small-arms. A nine-millimetre machine-gun, in the rear vehicle.' The smile now was sad. 'There's enough spare military weaponry to put a gun in every home in Russia. They're probably there already. But you know what the irony was: they weren't carrying the guns to oppose the police! They think they can bribe their way out of that sort of difficulty. The guns were to fight any interception by rival gangs.'

Natalia shook her head, disbelievingly. But she *couldn't* be overwhelmed: sit there numbed. She had to think: think beyond what she was being told about her own son in this stinking office in this stinking police station. She had to think of Sasha.

'So you can see my problem?' invited Kapitsa, hopefully.

Natalia regarded the man with renewed caution, alert for a pitfall. 'I'm not sure that I do.'

The investigator frowned, disappointed. 'This is an incredible opportunity for us to show we're doing our job. One we never thought we'd get . . .' The man hesitated, both for another cigarette and for Natalia to respond. When she didn't he said: 'But one of the people we have in custody — the organizer, it seems — is your son.'

'Yes,' Natalia agreed, slowly. She had to assume Fyodor Tudin would find out: protect herself against how the man might try to use the information.

Kapitsa spread his hands towards her. 'There must be a way, somehow, to avoid the difficulty.'

Natalia's first thought was that Kapitsa was seeking a bribe, although not one offered as openly as it had been on the Serpukhov road. Cautiously she asked: 'What did Eduard say, when you wouldn't take money?'

Kapitsa didn't reply at once, recalling in detail. 'He seemed to think it was the beginning of negotiation at first. Kept smiling, very friendly. That gave us the time to collect the guns. Then he got angry. Not frightened. Angry. Asked me if I had any idea what I was doing, and when I said I did he told me who you were. Said it was a waste of time to make a seizure so why didn't I save myself a lot of unnecessary trouble, take the road-block down and that would be the end of it. That if I wanted the bribe, I could still have it.' Kapitsa shook his head. 'He was carrying $5,000, in notes. Called it his passage money, in case they got stopped. He told me to help myself.'

Definitely not asking her for money, Natalia decided. 'Which you refused again? Arrested him?'

'The only reaction to that — from them all, not just Eduard — was shock. Two tried to hit out, but it wasn't anything like a fight. The others were actually angry at him: they thought he had made a mess of the bribe negotiations. We've had to put him in a separate cell.'

'Here?'

'Yes.'

'Can I see him?' To see him would give her time to try to think what she had to do. She desperately needed time.

Kapitsa hesitated, uncertainly. 'I thought we might decide how to handle things first.'

'I'd like to see him,' she insisted.

The investigator spoke briefly into a telephone almost drowned under a wash of put-aside papers, and as they walked side by side down the corridor said to her: 'I'm having him put into an interview cell, away from the detention block. It's not very pleasant. No reason for you to be embarrassed. Or upset.'

'You really are being most considerate.' Sasha. That's who she had to think about, above and beyond everything else. Only Sasha: keeping Sasha safe.

'I've got children,' said Kapitsa. 'Two boys. I'm terrified they might go wrong some day.' There was the familiar shrug. 'It's the job, I suppose. Seeing it happen everyday.'

The interview room was still in the basement, but sectioned off from the main detention area behind a thick wall into which just one barred communicating door was set. Smell and noise permeated out: to Natalia it sounded like the rumbled shuffling of animals herded together, which she supposed was a fairly accurate description.

There were two solid metal doors on either

side of a central corridor, each with a round Judas-hole at head height. The holes were covered from the outside by a swivelling metal plate. Kapitsa led her to the first door directly to their right, nodding as they approached an officer sitting at a bare desk just inside the communicating entrance to the main cell block. At once the man rose, sorting through keys on a large ring attached to a body chain around his waist. As the officer found the right key Kapitsa said: 'I'll leave you here. Just call for the officer when you want to come out.'

'No!' said Natalia, quickly. 'I think you should be with me.'

'What?' The investigator stood looking at her, face creased in bewilderment.

'It's a Militia responsibility: we're virtually colleagues, as you said.'

'But . . .'

'I think it's best. It's what I want.'

The door swung open and Natalia hesitated before pushing forward into the cell. Had she not known it was Eduard, Natalia would not have recognized the man as her son. When she had last seen him his hair had been shorn tight to his skull, making him almost bald. Now it was very long, practically shoulder length, and waved, which she couldn't remember it being even before the army, when he'd been at university. His face was stubbled, not with an attempt at a beard but where he had been denied shaving material. There was a gold band in his left ear. If he wore an earring there would be more jewellery. She guessed everything else would have been taken away, along with all the other personal possessions, when he was received into the jail. All his clothes, which she supposed he'd been allowed to retain because he had not yet been formally charged, appeared to be from the West: Levi jeans, leather loafers, an expensive-looking leather jacket and a wool shirt, open at the neck.

Eduard was at a table chained to the floor, in the very middle of the room. There were chairs either side of the table, also chained down, but still with some movement, which he was using as much as possible, going back on the rear legs and rocking slightly back and forth, easily confident. He didn't attempt to get up when his mother entered.

Instead he smiled up from the tilted chair and said: 'At last! I thought you'd forgotten me!'

Kapitsa gestured politely towards the facing seat, but Natalia didn't take it. Even from where she stood she could detect the sour smell that she'd earlier got from the main detention block minutes before.

'It wouldn't have been difficult to forget you.'

Eduard's expression faltered, but only slightly. Looking pointedly at the investigator near the door but still addressing Natalia he said: 'We need to talk. Just the two of us.'

'I've asked him to stay.'

'Why?'

'It isn't going to be a problem.'

Eduard came forward at last, settling his chair. 'You sure about that?'

'I think so.'

'Good!' he said. The smile came into place.

My flesh and my blood, she remembered. She wished she could feel more: feel anything. Still her flesh and blood. 'How long have you been back in Moscow?'

'It must be over a year.'

'You did not contact me?'

There was a passing attempt to look serious. 'Meant to. Decided to get established first. Got busy, you know how it is.'

'You're in a hell of a mess.'

The seriousness now was genuine, Eduard's eyes going between Natalia and Kapitsa. 'I'd really like to talk to you alone.'

'I don't think so.'

'I need your help!'

For the first time the complacent arrogance slipped, and Natalia was unsure whether Eduard's anguish was at having openly to plead or at having allowed the fear to show. From the look he directed at her, she guessed it was a combination of both. 'There are things to think about.'

'What things?'

'It's not that easy.' She heard Kapitsa shift behind her.

'You're still in the KGB or whatever it's called these days?'

Natalia hesitated. 'Yes.'

The smile returned. 'You'd be surprised at the

effect it had when I told him' — Eduard nodded towards Kapitsa — 'your name. You know what I think? I think you've climbed even higher up the ladder than when you and I were last together.'

'Much higher,' Natalia conceded.

'That's good.'

'Is it?'

'Things *must* be easy for you.'

Now Natalia gestured behind her, to the investigator. 'It's not just a matter for me. There's the Militia position to consider.'

'What about my position to consider?'

'That's what I'm doing,' said Natalia. *Adulterated medical drugs kill sometimes. Or maim.* The investigator's words echoed in her mind, loudly, like an announcement with the volume turned up. My flesh and blood, she thought: Eduard is my flesh and blood.

The expression was sly now. 'We don't want any embarrassment, do we?'

'I'm not sure I understand that.'

The back and forth chair came down squarely again. 'You're obviously *very* important now: much more than before. Everything's public in Moscow these days: openness is the official policy . . .' There was a hesitation, staged and theatrical. '. . . Very easy for people in important positions to be embarrassed: damaged by the embarrassment even . . .'

The noise of Kapitsa shifting behind her was louder. 'All of that is very true.'

319

Eduard sighed. 'So we'd better get this problem cleared up, before it goes any further. I've been in this shit-hole for five days.' There was a nod in Kapitsa's direction. 'Why don't you have a talk?'

She had to estimate how exposed she was. 'You're with a Mafia gang? The Lubertsy?'

Eduard sniggered. 'Don't be melodramatic! I work with businessmen.'

'What sort of business?'

Eduard's shoulders went up and down. 'All sorts. Providing what people always want.'

Natalia used his ambiguity. 'When you formed your consortium with these Lubertsy business-men, did you tell them I had a rank and influence in what was then the KGB?'

Eduard's smirk was conspiratorial. 'It's normal business practice, to provide references. Assure colleagues of one's good standing.'

Natalia guessed he would have seen every West-ern gangster film to be shown in Moscow: the attitude and the words were virtually a parody. 'Is that why you were appointed an organizer: put in charge?'

'Recognition of natural ability.' There was an-other disparaging head movement, towards Kapitsa. 'The offer I made still stands, if the money hasn't already vanished from wherever it's supposed to be safeguarded here. No reason for anyone to lose out. Everyone stays happy. OK?'

Natalia gestured again to the man behind her. 'We have to talk. See what can be done to make everything work out right.'

'Of course you do,' agreed Eduard. 'Just be quick, OK?'

For a moment Natalia stood looking down at Eduard. Then she turned, quickly, and followed Kapitsa out. Once inside his office, the man lit yet another cigarette and said: 'It's difficult to know what to do: what to suggest. I can't see how we can take him out of the case and still proceed against the others. That's my problem.'

Natalia decided that Kapitsa was honest according to the convoluted standards of bygone Russian bureaucracy, disdaining blatant bribery but prepared to compromise and make deals with people he considered to be in the same business, linked by a professional freemasonry. She halted at the thought. Was it really a bygone time? Or still the way Russia operated, despite the supposed second revolution? 'I need time. There is a lot to consider: to be worked out.'

'I can leave it to you, to come up with something?' The man sounded relieved.

Natalia nodded. 'Have you filed an official Militia report?'

Now Kapitsa smiled, believing he understood the significance of the question. 'Only provisionally. No identities. Technically the investigation is continuing.' He examined the end of his lighted cigarette, as if it were important.

'So there are no names, on any official document?' persisted Natalia.

'No.'

'Could I have a copy?'

'Of course.' He burrowed into the paper mountain, producing a case report surprisingly quickly.

'I'll be in touch very soon,' promised Natalia. 'It must be handled properly: to everyone's satisfaction.'

'That's exactly what I want,' assured Kapitsa.

Natalia slumped in the back of the Zil returning her to Yasenevo, head forward on her chest, totally absorbed in the new crisis, but thinking beyond it. How good was Tudin's personal spy network? A question she couldn't answer. But she'd taken an official car to the Militia headquarters. And very openly announced it to her secretariat, as she left. So she had to assume he would learn about it from those sources, if he had no others. Which he probably did. She would have liked to have somebody else with whom to talk it through: somebody whose mind would have been less cluttered by conflicting loyalties and doubts.

The reflection inevitably brought her thoughts to Charlie, who'd had the quickest and most analytical brain she'd ever known. Charlie, who'd always been able to consider things from every angle: see the dangers that no one else could . . . The reminiscence was never finished, blocked by something else.

The memory was abrupt and totally illogical — a bizarre trick of her mind — and physically startled her into coming bolt-upright from the way she had been sitting. But it was there: all she wanted. The unformed recollection that had refused to come after her conference confrontation with Fyodor Tudin filled her mind with utter and complete clarity. She could remember the words: even what she'd been wearing and what they had been doing. It had been here, in Moscow, long before he'd had to leave, disappointing her for the first time. It had been a caviare celebration, at Mytninskaya, for no better reason or excuse than their happiness together. Perhaps it was the association of Eduard and Mytninskaya that had finally prompted the memory. Or the fact that they'd eaten caviare, because it was that which caused Charlie's seemingly innocuous conversation. About his mother being in a home for the elderly near the most famous salmon-fishing river in England: in England, not Scotland. And he'd recounted an anecdote of English privilege, about a fishing club so exclusive it had first call upon the town's best hotel, ahead of the general public.

Natalia became aware of the driver's attention, in the rear-view mirror, and settled back upon the cushions again.

She had it, she told herself. The way to find him, providing his mother was still alive. And she'd already put in place the operation to make it happen.

Which still left the crisis of Eduard.

John Gower did not, after all, venture out into Beijing on the fourth day, remembering the edict about escape routes.

Airline reservations need not be in the names recorded on the passport, so under false identities Gower made confirmed bookings on direct London flights for the sixth day, leaving the intervening twenty-four hours to contact the priest. As protective insurance against any additional delay that he could not, at that moment, anticipate he repeated the reservations, under other different names, on the two succeedings days.

It had been the uneventful visits to the Forbidden City and Coal Hill that convinced him it would be pointless going to the Taoist temple without activating the system: not to do so *would* be putting the positive commitment off, which practically amounted to cowardice. The next day he'd trigger the signal and then fill the already chosen lion figure on the hill, to complete the routine.

And wait for Snow to come to him at the embassy.

According to the London briefing, Snow had been told to check at three-day intervals, but Gower didn't have a starting-point for his count, so he had to allow that full period for the priest to respond. He remained momentarily unsure whether he could chance the reservations so soon or whether to extend over several more days. No need for an immediate decision, he decided: if Snow didn't appear, bookings could still be made. For the moment he could leave things as they were.

That night he accepted the dinner invitation

from the Nicholsons. Jane agreed at once and enthusiastically to shop for the cheong-sam. After an animated discussion, he chose blue for the colour and said he thought her sizing would fit Marcia. He hoped Marcia's underwear wouldn't be quite so obvious if she ever did wear it.

Jeremy Snow grew increasingly frustrated as he monitored the constantly empty signal spot by the temple, until finally he began to think London had taken him at his word and withdrawn, ending their relationship.

Most frustrating of all was the acceptance that there was nothing he could do, to restore things as they had been before; as he wanted them to be again. Walter Foster had gone and London had clearly not appointed a successor. Which left him in a vacuum, with no one at the embassy he could approach to try to put things right. His very dilemma showed the stupidity of the system that London had insisted upon, and Foster adhered to, so rigidly.

Snow followed the too familiar route by the temple, seeking the signal that wasn't there, and afterwards walked almost for a further hour before going back to the mission to rid himself of the anger. He still got there before noon.

'Have you seen the *People's Daily*?' greeted Father Robertson. 'The dissident arrests have started in Beijing.'

Snow took the offered newspaper, at first not properly concentrating. And then he did. There was a photograph of three manacled men being led from a police van. One of them was Zhang Su Lin, his underground information source and English-language student until a year ago.

For the first time Snow felt a bubble of genuine uncertainty. It became difficult for him to breathe properly, although not bad enough for any medication.

Thirty

'You could have done something with yourself, you could. Been a doctor. Went to grammar school, didn't you!'

'Yes, mum.' Charlie was surprised how well she was holding on to reality today. And had been, for weeks now.

'What *do* you do? I forget.'

'Clerk, in a government office.'

'Girl's job,' dismissed the woman, scornfully. The rear of the bed had been cranked up, to put her in a sitting position. She wore the knitted bedcoat Charlie had bought the previous Christmas over her nightdress, and one of the nurses had carefully crimped and prepared her hair the way she liked it done. She smelled of lavender, her favourite. He'd have to remember that, next Christmas.

'Get a lot of holidays,' said Charlie, letting the conversation run, most of his mind elsewhere, conducting the private debate about his Regent's Park discovery.

'No money, though, is there?'

'Not a lot.'

'That's why you're a bloody tramp!' she said, triumphantly.

'Yes, mum.' It was an accusation made on average at least once during every visit. His mother had always been extremely clothes-conscious. Ironically, considering his constant concern for his painful feet, her particular delight had been shoes: he could vaguely remember the floor of a bedroom closet completely covered with pairs that overflowed from a shoe-rack. He hadn't expected Julia to notice the effort he'd made, with new shoes. They were settling in now but they really had hurt like hell at first.

'No wonder you never got married.'

'No, mum.' She'd forgotten Edith and there seemed no purpose in reminding her. Charlie wondered what Julia was preparing for that evening: she'd invited him to eat in her house for the first time.

'Your dad was a smart man.'

'I'm sure he was.'

'Give me my handbag! There! Under the cabinet.'

Charlie did as he was told, watching her fumble with veined hands through a bag crammed with long-ago letters, most still in their tattered envelopes.

'There!' she said, in further triumph. 'There's your dad. Officer in the navy: lieutenant or something. Always smart, he was.'

Charlie took the picture. It had to be the sixth she had produced of a man she claimed to be his father. He had not seen this one before. It was of a stiffly upright, unsmiling officer in an army uniform. He wondered where she got them all from: he supposed they had all been men whom he'd been told to call uncle when he was young. He definitely couldn't remember this one. 'Good-looking man,' he agreed.

'Name was George. He could have got you into the navy, if you'd wanted. Had a lot of influence. Knew admirals.'

It was almost time to go. 'Everything all right? Nothing you want?'

'They've stopped my Guinness,' complained the old woman. 'Won't let me have any now. Used to, but not any longer.'

'Why not?'

'Don't like me.'

'I'll fix it,' promised Charlie.

'It's the matron: she's the one.'

'I'll talk to her. I have to go now.'

She hardly seemed to notice when Charlie kissed her goodbye. He stopped at the matron's office on the way out, gently asking if there was a problem over Guinness, and was told by Mrs Hewlett that the nightly allowance for those who wanted it was two bottles but his mother was demanding more, which they didn't think was good for her. Charlie said he was sure they knew best.

He was glad to get back into the hire car, with the prospect of a two-hour, solitary journey ahead of him in which to think. But think about what, any differently or any better than he'd already examined the question from each and every side? There was not the slightest doubt that his only course was to report the hostile Regent's Park surveillance upon the Director-General and Patricia Elder. It was his duty, in fact, enshrined in all the regulations and conditions under which he was supposed to work.

Which would destroy them both. There'd be an internal investigation, admissions demanded, discreet and accepted resignations hurried through, damage limitation at its very British best.

But what damage limitation was there for Charles Edward Muffin? None, he acknowledged, miserably. As there never seemed to be. If he did what he should do and alerted internal security and counter-intelligence and Christ knows who else that Peter Miller and Patricia Elder were being targeted, the first and most obvious demand would be how the hell he knew. And to answer that honestly — to say that for weeks he had been unofficially and privately targeting them himself — would bring in roughly three seconds the most inglorious end it was possible to imagine to an inglorious career. In fact his ever-painful feet — or his ass — wouldn't even touch the ground on his way out.

So what was more important, the security of a service to which he remained genuinely dedicated? Or the security of his ass, to which he was equally if not more devoted? An impossible dilemma, decided Charlie. Which was what he'd decided every time he'd thought about it since watching the silly buggers parade for the benefit of a Russian camera with a long-focus lens.

They *were* silly buggers, Charlie determined,

contemptuous at them and himself and at everything. Deserved whatever happened to them. Which was not really the consideration. What happened to them was immaterial. It was the blackmail danger that existed to the organization they jointly controlled.

The fast dual carriageway from Stockbridge joins the motorway at Basingstoke, and Charlie picked up the dark grey Ford behind him about a mile from the junction, automatically connecting the vehicle with that in which the two Russians had sat that day, taking their photographs. Black then though, not grey. He slowed, concentrating. The following car dropped back, keeping the same distance behind him, about fifty yards, with two other vehicles, a red van and an open sports car, in between. Had the Ford been behind him since he'd left the nursing home? He didn't think so, but he wasn't sure. No cause for an over-reaction, simply because his mind was locked on surveillance conducted from the same make of car. He kept to the inside lane to join the motorway. So did the other vehicle and the intervening van; the sports car burst by in a blast of exhaust noise. Charlie ignored the first turn-off but took the second, without any indication, stopping unnecessarily at the roundabout below. Nothing followed him. He still made the full circle, very slowly, before going back up the link to rejoin the motorway. Far better to have been safe than sorry, he reassured himself.

Would Miller and the woman be destroyed if

he reported what he'd seen? Not necessarily: there was an escape. He knew, because he'd seen it. But what *proof* did he have, of anything; of hanky-panky in a millionaire penthouse or that it was known about by a foreign country whose operatives still appeared to wear the black hats supposedly no longer in fashion? None, he recognized: not a fucking thing. So if they didn't admit an affair — and Charlie was prepared to bet a pound to a pitch of shit they wouldn't admit *anything* — where was he? Figuratively twisting in the wind with piano wire around a very tender part of his anatomy, displayed for the crows to feast, a disgruntled, cast-aside officer making entirely unfounded and libellous accusations about superiors against whom he had a grudge for prematurely ending his career. Justifiably ending his career, if he was prepared to make unsupportable accusations like that.

Not an immediate decision to agonize over any longer, although he knew he would. There was nothing he *could* do, in any practical sense.

There was another Ford behind him. Grey, like the last one. Or was it the *same* one? He'd been passing the Fleet service station, concentration on two levels, and become instantly aware of it emerging from the filter road to come in behind him. Had it been waiting? It looked the same as the first car. But then any grey Ford would look the same as the first car, sitting as it was still fifty yards behind him. He should have pulled into a layby before the earlier avoidance, to get the registration number as it went by. Still time. He saw the emergency telephone that would provide the excuse well over two hundred yards in front. He slowed, getting closer, but without using the brakes that would have flared the stop-lights. He only did that at the very last moment, uncaring of the blast of protest from the immediately following car, remembering how it had happened to Gower. There was only one man in the Ford that passed: he was balding and wore a sports shirt and went by apparently quite unaware of Charlie, who had the pencil and paper below the window level to note the number.

He stopped after counting ten grey, black or brown Ford cars on the rest of the journey, although he allowed every one to go by him. Charlie snake-looped into London, turning off at Acton, going sideways to Hammersmith and on into Fulham before switching northwards again, but going right through the centre of London, where the traffic was heaviest and most concealing and where he was able to judge his crossing of two intersections on amber, so all the following traffic had to stop at red. The hire car return was in Wandsworth: Charlie changed subway trains three times to reach his station. He had the Duty Room at Westminster Bridge Road run a trace on the Ford number: it was registered against the car pool of a fish processing plant in Hull. They confirmed the Hull outlet genuinely existed, although an examination of the British Company Register revealed it to be a subsidiary of a Belgian conglomerate headquartered in Bruges. Charlie thanked the Duty Officer and said he didn't want them to go to the trouble of taking it any further, in Belgium.

Julia cooked pheasant. Charlie was glad he'd taken Margaux. Quite soon into the meal, she said: 'Whatever it was, I'm glad it's over.'

'What?' frowned Charlie.

'You're like your old self tonight. The last couple of times you haven't been altogether with me, have you?'

'Something on my mind,' admitted Charlie.

'Anything you can talk about?'

It would have been interesting to discuss it with Julia. Except that it would have disclosed how he had used her, in the very beginning. And might do again in the future: forever trapped by his own double standards. 'Over, like you said.'

'How was your mother?'

'Bright enough.' He smiled. 'Told me I'd never get a girl-friend.'

'Won't you?' she asked, not smiling.

Charlie was uncomfortable at the seriousness with which she was looking directly across the table at him. Quickly he said: 'I'm thinking of asking for an interview with the deputy Director.'

She looked away, breaking the awkwardness. 'Why?'

'About time I was assigned someone else, don't you think?'

She turned down the corners of her mouth.

'I never got the impression they were going to come through on a conveyor belt.'

Charlie was suddenly struck by a thought quite apart but at the same time closely connected with his uncertainty over the past few days. 'If there was any change at the office . . . if Miller and Elder left or were transferred . . . would you expect your rather special situation to stay as it is there?'

Julia frowned. 'I wouldn't think so. Why do you ask?'

A further reason for doing nothing, Charlie accepted. 'Nothing,' he said.

Her frown deepened. 'What *is* going on?'

'Nothing,' he repeated. 'Honestly.'

Patricia Elder had moved her clothes out gradually as their time together came to an end, so there were only her washing things and make-up left by the last day. At breakfast Miller suggested he go on ahead, leaving her to check everything as she normally did at the end of any period they spent together at the penthouse.

Patricia went through the sprawling apartment room by room, although knowing it wasn't necessary because she'd removed the traces of her having been there as carefully as she'd removed her clothes, over the preceding days.

She went through the master bedroom last. All Lady Ann's cosmetics were arranged on the expansive dressing-table, laid out with the precision of instruments upon a surgeon's operating tray:

Miller's wife was an extraordinarily neat and tidy person, as he was.

The Jean Patou *Joy*, the perfume Lady Ann always wore, was in the middle of the line, its accustomed place. Patricia preferred Chanel, which was not so heavy. She slotted her bottle in alongside the other perfume: it seemed perfectly to fit the symmetry of the orderly arrangement in which Lady Ann delighted.

'Everything OK?' asked Miller, when she got to the office.

'All fixed,' said Patricia.

The Russian *rezidentura* at the London embassy justifiably considered it had achieved a remarkable success with its discovery and proof of a relationship between the head of British external intelligence and his deputy, although accepting with some regret that it would not now be considered so usefully important as it once might have been, in the old days of the KGB.

The *rezidentura* hoped that success would balance the partial failure with the man named as Charles Edward Muffin, the lead to whom had come *from* Moscow, which might have indicated particular interest.

The apologetic account to Moscow acknowledged that the guidance of a famous salmon river and a unique fishing club had successfully led to a nursing home in the small Hampshire town of Stockbridge in which an elderly woman with the same name as the man they had to trace was a permanent resident. They had been fortunate locating and so quickly identifying him from the Moscow-supplied photograph. They could offer no reasonable explanation for his having turned so unexpectedly off a motorway on the return journey to London, although later, when the observation was resumed, he had stopped by an emergency telephone, so there might have been problems with the car, which had been hired and not in the name they knew to be his. Against the possibility of the observation having been suspected, the pursuit had been abandoned at that point.

The *rezidentura* sought further instructions about maintaining surveillance upon the nursing home, for a subsequent visit, although pointing out that the demands of the operation were stretching the London resources to the absolute maximum.

From Moscow Natalia ordered no further time or effort to be expended on this one man: the tracing operation had to concentrate on others.

For the moment — perhaps for a very long time — telling Charlie about his daughter had to wait. She still had to evolve a foolproof way to deal with the problem of Eduard.

Thirty-one

John Gower was sure there was no significance in his waking virtually in the middle of the night, long before dawn: certainly it wasn't nerves. Very little to be nervous about. Probably still hadn't recovered from jetlag as well as he'd hoped. Definitely not unsettled by it. The opposite. Gave him a lot of time to think things through, go over what he had to do that day. Scarcely needed a lot of time. All very simple; very straightforward. Everything already sorted out in his mind. Didn't need what was in the security vault, not yet. Maybe tomorrow. Or the day after. Which would mean what London regarded as sensitive being here, in his rooms. No problem. He was positive his rooms hadn't been searched. Every trap he'd set had remained in place, unsprung. Damned good room-boy. Everything clean as a new pin, laundry perfect and nothing touched. No need to study special maps, for reminders of the drops: he'd already decided where to leave his summons. Only the temple still to find that morning. Just needed the photographs, for when the priest responded. They'd be meaningless, if the room-boy *did* see them. After today he wouldn't be going outside the compound, not until the moment he finally left for the airport. And he would have handed them over to Snow long before then.

Everything fitting properly into place, all in the right sequence. Easy. Pity he couldn't make any recommendations towards the improvements necessary here, when he got back to London. People had trusted him. Didn't like deceiving them, after they'd been so kind. Hoped they wouldn't criticize him personally: hoped they'd decide it wasn't his fault but budgetary restraints and penny-pinching back in London. Might be an idea to prepare the ground. Say something about trying his best but financial approval having to come from higher up. Nicholson was the gossip of the embassy, the man to spread it around. Hope Marcia liked the cheong-sam Jane would be buying today. What would Marcia be doing right now, this very minute, thousands of miles away? Planning the wedding, most likely. Wasn't sure he'd like her going away so much when they were married. Important she had a career of her own, of course. Extra salary would be useful in the beginning, too. Just try to rationalize the travelling. Have to talk to her about it. Be seeing her soon now. Just over a week at the most. Sooner maybe. Christ, he wanted to be with her so much: to get out of this place and back where he understood at least something of what was happening around him. Not nervous, though. Knew what he was doing: what he had to do. Everything in place. Easy. Today was the day. He felt good. Relaxed.

Gower got up when the light was just beginning to break, orange and yellow fingers feeling cautiously across the sky. This early there were no clouds, the blueness uninterrupted but very pale, practically white. He stood at the window for several moments, gazing out over the deserted, utterly quiet courtyard as the dawn hardened the outlines and shapes of buildings and trees and shrubs. He'd think back to this moment when his career began, so it was right he mark it all in his mind, always to remember. But only a recollection for himself, he realized, quickly: there would be no one else with whom he could fully share its importance or meaning. Enough that he should do it for himself.

It was when he was bathing, luxuriating with time to spare, that Gower realized an oversight, a gap in his preparation so big that his initial reaction was to laugh in disbelief rather than become annoyed at himself. The temple signal was fixed for him. But what about the actual summons to bring the priest to him? Gower lay with the water growing cold around him, running words and phrases through his mind to convey the appropriate urgency. And in the end dismissed them all. There was no need to convey any sort of urgency. According to the London briefing, it was Snow who was demanding instant personal contact, threatening any future cooperation. All the man needed to know was that someone had come from London to meet him and understand where that meeting was to be. All so easily fitting together, thought Gower, again: the perfect jigsaw puzzle.

Its coldness drove Gower from the bath. He towelled warmth back into himself but still in his robe went into the sitting-room for his brief-case, the way it was secured and the arrangement of its entirely innocuous contents one of the traps he'd daily left since his arrival. The interior was ornately sectioned and partitioned and pocketed: Gower had worked out himself the pouch for stiff-backed, blank memoranda cards. Slowly, determined on the legibility of every letter, he printed in the centre of the white rectangle 11, Guang Hua Lu, Jian Guo Men Wai. Very gently Snow bent the card back and forth between his fingers, testing its tensility, satisfying himself it was rigid enough to slide into the gap beneath the lion statue without buckling and jamming. In the bedroom, his suit still on its hanger, Gower eased the card into the top pocket of his jacket, careful not to bend it.

The sky had remained clear from the early dawn and the unexpected sun bore down, heavy on his back and shoulders as Gower left the embassy. On a convenient island in the middle of the traffic system outside the embassy he took off his jacket, but slung it over his shoulder rather than doubling it across his arm, to avoid losing the prepared card from his top pocket. The route memorized from the printed map seemed different when he tried to follow it in practice, road connections and turnings either too close or further away than

341

he expected them to be, so finally he stopped again, needing to consult the city plan in conjunction with the landmarks around him. According to the map the temple should have been quite close, but he was beginning to think it was widely out of scale or proportion. Gower saw the money-dealer preparing to intercept him as he crossed a wide, multi-laned thoroughfare, the man quick-stepping this way and that like a rugby full back anticipating a long dropping ball as Gower dodged between the bicycles. Gower was shaking his head before he reached the man, repeating the refusal as the dealer scurried along beside him, babbling the different rates for what seemed to be the majority of world currencies. Towards the end Gower's rejection became a matching, dull-voiced chant. The tout finally gave up, stopping abruptly and hurling, soft-voiced but vehemently, a one-word accusation at him. Gower wished he could have remembered it, later to ask Nicholson to translate.

He saw the tip of the temple roof ahead, but none of the building, and decided the Taoist shrine had to be in the next street, if not the one beyond. Minutes away: minutes until everything was put into motion. Leave the signal, plant the summons at Coal Hill and get back to the embassy. Safe. Should he tell Samuels when he got back that it was all drawing to a close? He was tempted but the warning about telling nobody anything immediate overrode the impulse. Could it have been only two months since he'd gone through those final, demanding sessions with the man with bad feet, sickeningly aware how gauche and un-prepared he'd really been? Did the prohibition about disclosing things extend backwards, *after* an operation? He'd like to talk to the man about the Beijing mission when he got back to London: let him know how successful it had all gone. *Was* going; not over yet. Almost.

Gower pushed forward, easing his way through the shoppers. The street connected with a slightly wider road cutting diagonally across about two hundred yards beyond a tiny, two- or three-stall market. Gower paused at the junction, looking expectantly to his left. He could see much more of the tip-pointed roof but not the temple itself, hidden by other buildings in another side-street three hundred yards further down, but on the other side.

Gower waited for a break in the traffic to cross, so that he could turn without any hesitation when he reached the street he wanted. Bicycles plied in either direction and Gower had the impression of a river again: of walking along the bank of a fast-flowing waterway in which occasionally an out-of-place car floated by. People jostled, behind and against him, so that he had constantly to twist to his left and right to avoid colliding.

He turned abruptly, without pause, when he reached the street. His imagery still on a river, Gower thought this was like a backwater: there were far fewer people, far fewer bicycles and no cars at all. The only stall was that selling threadbare blooms, for the temple. Four he remembered: orange, to be placed on the left of the offering shelf on the shrine. The theatricality of it all suddenly struck him as absurd: no one would believe it if he ever did tell them. The seller was a woman, shapelessly layered despite the heat in brown and black, a shawl over a smock over a dress. There was a black cowl covering her head and her face appeared to be caving inwards on a toothless mouth. Gower smiled and pointed to the flowers he wanted, holding up six fingers. As she gathered them, he assembled the foreign exchange currency in readiness, holding the money out for her to help herself. She took the money before offering the meagre flowers. Gower moved towards the pots and troughs, variously filled with scraggy contributions.

He never reached them.

It started with a shout: an alert, not a challenge. At once there was a matching yell, like a reply, and then a whistle sounded and people were running at him, not just from the main road but behind from further up the side-street. There were uniforms — blue, he thought, and then khaki — and a very thin man who reached him first lashed out, hitting him in the chest. It would not have been hard enough to knock him over if the troughs hadn't caught him behind his knees, tripping him backwards. The first jar into his back was where he fell into someone's knee but the second blow, into the side of his face, was a deliberate kick. Everyone seemed to be shouting at once, too many people trying to grab at him: there were several more kicks and two obvious punches before Gower was able to turn on to his hands and knees to get upright. Before he fully succeeded, hands did get to him, finally pulling him from the ground.

One voice persisted louder than the rest, gradually forcing the uproar to subside. The squad pulled back, creating a tiny space, but stayed in a tight, enclosing circle.

The loud voice belonged to a thickset, neckless man in one of the khaki uniforms. Gower couldn't detect any insignia of rank.

'Spy!' Although it was now comparatively quiet, the man still shouted, in English.

'I am attached to the British . . .' Gower tried, but there was a sudden thrust in his back, winding him so that he couldn't finish.

'Spy!' yelled the man once more.

Hands grabbed at Gower again, thrusting him forward. He staggered, wishing his attempt to recover his breath didn't sound like a whine. His head was bent forward in the strained, gasping effort: he saw the signal flowers trampled underfoot. There was a windowless van blocking the street where it joined the larger road. A lot of people were anxious to push him inside. Gower fell at the last moment, pitching full-length on the metal floor, but scrabbling up before he could be kicked any more. He just managed to get on to one of the metal benches that ran along either side before the van lurched away with a jerk that would have thrown him off his feet again.

Gower remained doubled up, arms across his body, face hidden so they couldn't see his eyes and mouth squeezed tightly closed with the determination with which he was fighting against his bladder collapsing. No, he prayed: please God, no!

It happened but it wasn't much: not enough for the wet stain to show for them to know how frightened he was.

Panicked desperation drove Fyodor Tudin personally to go to Petrovka, although he didn't at the moment of arrival properly know why the Militia enquiry had been made at Mytninskaya, only that it had something to do with the boy: knew even less how to explain his coming there at all. So initially he didn't attempt an explanation, clawing for guidance from the reaction of the policeman. He judged himself lucky with Kapitsa: one of the old school, only knowing the old ways.

'I expected her to come back: not somebody else.' The room was thick with cigarette smoke.

'Is that what she said?' He had to feel out with every word, like someone walking across a frozen lake unsure of the thickness of the ice.

'Something about needing time to work out what we were going to do.'

Good but not good enough: not quite. 'That was all?'

Kapitsa frowned. 'You haven't discussed it with her?'

Tudin thought he knew the way, although the personal risk was appalling: but then all the risks he faced were appalling. 'I'm here on behalf of the Agency as much as for General Fedova: we've got to work out the proper balance, to avoid embarrassment to the Agency as well as General Fedova. You see that, don't you?'

The investigator remained doubtful. 'I would have thought the two were virtually the same.'

Tudin nodded. 'For the moment, until everything is sorted out, this meeting — this discussion — must remain strictly between ourselves.' Still hardly good enough, he conceded.

The policeman's uncertainty was still obvious. 'But we're talking of some arrangement, aren't we: something acceptable to everyone? Everything settled to everyone's satisfaction?'

It was like a signpost, lighted before him. 'Is that what she said?' he chanced, tailoring his reply from the investigator's attitude.

'Not precisely: it was definitely to that effect.'

Gold-dust, thought Tudin, ecstatically: sparkling, glittering, life-saving gold-dust. 'That an arrangement could be found?' he pressed.

'Yes.' There was another hopeful smile. 'We want to cooperate as much as possible, of course. Within reason. We need a prosecution.'

We both do, thought Tudin. 'Everything will be worked out.' He smiled, leaning forward, man to man. 'It's important wires don't get crossed: what arrangement was General Fedova considering?'

'She didn't say. It was actually the boy who first used the word arrangement. She agreed that one had to be found.'

Tudin guessed his already flushed face was an even deeper red, in his excitement. He couldn't have expected it to be this good: not in a million years. Striving to keep his voice level, he said: 'What did Eduard say?'

Kapitsa shrugged, as if disassociating himself from the remark. 'Seems he's boasted about his mother's position, in the KGB and in the new security agency: let the Lubertsy Family know he'd be protected if ever there was any trouble.'

'And she agreed that he would be?' Oh God! Oh dear, wonderful, rewarding God! Careful. Calm down. Shouldn't get too euphoric; too carried away. This was the chance, the incredible, unimaginable chance to destroy the bitch absolutely, and he had to drain every last drop that was available.

The shrug came again from the policeman. 'She wanted time to think: to fix it. Eduard was very upset, later. Still is. He expected to be released at once.'

Dare he see the boy? Try to get him to repeat the claim, even in some sort of legal, devastating affidavit? Yes! he decided, positively. Already, at this stage, there was probably enough for an internal agency investigation into the propriety of what she was doing, but Tudin wanted more than that. Regulations existed for an officer to lay a formal accusation of abuse of power against another before the ultimate chairman, and at that moment this was the course upon which Tudin determined. He'd get his evidence and confront her face to face, be her prosecutor at their own mini-trial. Eduard could be forced to testify, lured by the promise of immunity. And this disgusting, smoke-stained man would quickly realize whose side he had to take. It would all have to be handled with infinite care but he knew he could do it. He could bury her, Tudin concluded, triumphantly: bury her alive. 'You've helped a lot.'

'What would you have us do?' asked Kapitsa.

'Just give us a little more time. And remember, no mention of this visit. It's not important for her to know how concerned we are. How much we want to protect her.'

That night Fyodor Tudin got very drunk.

Thirty-two

Only two men travelled with him in the van. One was the thickset officer who had appeared to be in charge of the arrest. The other was a civilian, a thin, bony man in a black, Western-style suit who made frequent gestures as he talked. There was a lot of conversation between the two of them. Although he could not understand what was being said, Gower got the impression the civilian was in some way superior to the officer, whose attitude was deferential.

Gower guessed from the length of the journey that he was being taken outside the city. He was glad of the time, using it to recover. He remained hollowed out with fear but it was lessening: certainly he'd pulled back from the collapse that was still making it uncomfortable to sit on the cold metal bench. He hoped there wouldn't be a visibly damp patch when he stood up.

Had to think! Had to work out what had happened — what *was* happening — and decide how to confront it. Remember all the interrogation resistance! Think! *Always take, never give,* he remembered. Say the minimum at this stage then. Make the protests necessary for an innocent diplomat but no more: wait to see what the accusations were. What could they be? Difficult to

350

anticipate yet. He had to assume Jeremy Snow had been arrested: confessed about the Taoist temple and what they used it for. But Snow couldn't have identified him, either by name or description, because the priest didn't have either! So there was nothing personally incriminating against him. Couldn't be. Deny anything and everything. Certainly any knowledge of a priest named Jeremy Snow. Which wasn't cowardice. Or abandoning the man. It was common, practical sense. Snow had been told again and again to run. And arrogantly refused. He was the architect of his own destruction. Now it all came down to damage limitation. Interrogation resistance. Vital they weren't able to link him with anything, to form a provable connection with the embassy. *A good liar tells the fewest lies.* Important to remember that. Important to remember everything. He was in a difficult situation but that's all it was, difficult. Not disastrous. Possible, even, to extricate himself. Thank God for this journey, giving him the chance to think. Not frightened any more: properly apprehensive, properly alert, but not frightened. Ridiculous to have pissed himself. No one would ever know. Make the necessary protests of an innocent diplomat, he thought again. Now was the time: to wait might indicate an acceptance of guilt.

Addressing the officer who spoke at least some English, Gower said: 'I demand an explanation for this illegal detention. I am an accredited British diplomat, guaranteed protection in your country

351

according to the Vienna Convention.'

It was the civilian who answered. 'Be quiet. You are a spy.' The tone was extremely soft, almost difficult to hear: the sibilants hissed.

'That is a ridiculous accusation!'

'Quiet.' The hands made a damping-down movement.

'I demand the embassy is told of my arrest.'

The plainclothes man ignored him, saying something instead to the uniformed officer. The thickset man shrugged, looked directly at Gower, then back to the other, shrugging a second time.

Enough, judged Gower: no more. He wondered how much further they had to go. They seemed to have been driving for almost an hour. He wished he'd thought to time it, when they'd set off. Too frightened then: not thinking properly. Recovered now. He could get himself out of this: sure he could.

Because he had belatedly fixed the time, Gower knew it was a further fifteen minutes before they stopped. Gower emerged into what appeared to be a huge area of single- and two-storey barracks: where he stood there was a group of taller buildings which he guessed marked the centre of the camp. Soldiers piled out of a van which had obviously followed them from the city: there were other men in a variety of uniforms moving around the buildings. Between a gap separating two of the barracks Gower could see a group of men drilling.

The black-suited civilian herded Gower into the

block outside which they had halted. They went the full length of the block, along a corridor of closed doors on either side, encountering no one on their way. It was absolutely quiet. The walls were yellow and dirty: their feet squeaked on the rubber composite floor. The plainclothes man opened a door at the far end of the corridor without knocking or giving any warning. Another Chinese sat at a table, waiting. The man was bespectacled and wore a buttoned-to-the-neck tunic. He appeared very young: younger, decided Gower, than he was. As he got further into the room, Gower saw two more Chinese at a side-table, behind the door: there was recording apparatus on the table and both men had notebooks opened before them.

The man who had travelled with him in the van indicated a chair directly opposite the already seated man. Gower hesitated, unsure if he should obey or if he should make another protest, finally sitting down. He was pleased at how calm he felt. There was no discomfiting wetness, either: he had forgotten to look behind him in the van, to see if he'd marked the metal bench.

'You will tell us your name,' declared the open-faced man at the table. 'Mine is Chen Hong Qi. You will come to know me.' The English was better than that of the escort in the van.

'I am an accredited British diplomat, attached to Her Majesty's embassy in Beijing. I demand immediate access to my embassy. And an explanation of this outrage!'

'Name.' The tone was practically conversational.

'I am required by no protocol applicable here to supply my name to you.'

'Name,' persisted the young man.

They couldn't deny him access to the British embassy, Gower thought. They would need a name to give to the legation, when they made contact. 'John Gower,' he supplied at last. The ambassador and the political officer would finally go apoplectic when they heard: both would regard it as *precisely* the type of problem they had so fervently wanted to avoid.

'What is the reason for your being in Beijing?'

'I demand immediate communication with my embassy!'

'Turn out all your pockets.'

'No!'

There was a sigh. 'We will allow you to turn out your pockets yourself. Or you will be forcibly searched.'

'It is improper for you to threaten any physical assault or restraint.'

'Empty your pockets.' The tone now was not so much conversational as dismissive, a weariness at having to deal with an irritant.

The man who had travelled in the van was standing beside the notetakers. Now he pushed himself away from the wall, as if expecting to receive an order. Gower realized for the first time that the squat man in the khaki uniform had not come into the room. *Take, don't give.* But why not? He was carrying nothing incriminating: nothing that could even be twisted to be made so. Taking his time — consciously moving more slowly than was necessary — he started stacking the contents of his pockets on the table between them. There was a flare of anger, instantly subdued, when the man flicked open his wallet and looked curiously for several moments at the photograph of Marcia. The printed card he had intended leaving beneath the lion statue for Jeremy Snow was the last thing he put upon the table.

The original escort came further from the wall, standing beside the other Chinese as they went through everything. As they did so, initially unspeaking, Gower suddenly wondered if the thin man in the black suit was the suspicious Mr Li who was demanding the photographs from the priest. Both took a long time over the street map of Beijing: Chen held it before him, twisting it to the light, seeking any markings. It was impossible to infer anything from their facial reactions, which were minimal anyway, but towards the end of the examination Chen grunted and Gower decided they were two very disappointed men. There was a staccato exchange of Chinese between them. Picking up the card, the man said: 'What is this?'

'The address here in Beijing of the British embassy.' And utterly meaningless to you, thought Gower.

'Why?'

'I do not know the city: I needed the address

with me if I got lost.' An explanation against which it was impossible to argue.

'You bought flowers, by the temple?'

Careful, thought Gower: very, very careful. The one action that might cause him difficulties. 'Yes.'

'Why?'

The lie had to be one from which he would not deviate. 'For my room, at the embassy.'

'You were going towards the shrine, where flowers are displayed.'

'I was curious. I wanted to look at the shrine.'

'You were going to put flowers there.'

'Nonsense! I have told you why I wanted them.' They'd seized him too soon, Gower realized, abruptly: just minutes or seconds too soon! If they'd waited just a moment longer he *would* have arranged the flowers and not now been able to explain them.

'You were going to leave a signal,' insisted Chen. 'You are engaged in counter-revolutionary activities in my country.'

'Preposterous!' rejected Gower. When were specific charges going to be put against him, maybe even with Jeremy Snow being identified by name?

'Our courts deal leniently with counter-revolutionaries who confess.'

'There is nothing whatsoever for me to confess,' rejected Gower. 'I demand to be released. The strongest possible protests will be made by my embassy to your Foreign Ministry.'

'Why did you come to Beijing?'

No danger here if he maintained the established lie. 'To examine the facilities that exist at the embassy, for British diplomats and employees.'

'That is not true.'

'The embassy will confirm it.'

'Tell us the true reason for your being here.'

'I have already done so.' If they had something better, something provable against him, they would surely have produced it by now!

'Admit what you're here for!'

Gower remained as he was, refusing to speak.

'Answer me!' Chen's voice was becoming louder.

Desperation, determined Gower. Dare he risk the open confrontation? It might give him some indication if they really had anything against him. 'I have answered your questions, which according to my legal status I am not required to do. I did so to show my cooperation, over what is clearly a mistake. But not any more. I demand to be able to speak with my embassy.'

'We know what you have done, since you have been in Beijing,' said the Chinese. 'And we know *why* you did it. What you hoped to achieve.'

Bluff, dismissed Gower. They had made a mistake, seizing him too quickly. Now their only hope of making a case would be if he stupidly gave them a confession. Gower slumped as best he could in the straight-backed chair, trying to convey an impression of relaxed confidence.

The man who had been in the van said something from his place near the wall. Chen's reply was sharp and irritable. To Gower he said: 'Take off your clothes.'

'What?'

'Take off your clothes.'

'I absolutely refuse!'

Chen sighed. 'Do it yourself. Or be stripped.'

It was an established questioning technique, to demean a man with his nakedness, recalled Gower. But he'd gone through it, in training: knew how to refuse the embarrassment. He stood, actually having to feign the reluctance, worried only there might be a yellow stain on his underpants. It wasn't much. He stood with his hands cupped in front of him, expecting the examination to continue. Instead one of the men by the recording apparatus picked a bundle Gower hadn't noticed before from a side chair, carrying it to him. Gower stared at the trousers and slipover top. They were striped, white and blue: at first he thought the stiffness was because they were made of canvas, but then he detected the human smell and realized it was from months, even years, of unwashed wear by others. 'I will not wear these!'

Chen shrugged, as if he were uninterested, going himself to open the door to a military escort outside.

'I want my embassy informed about this!' Gower tried, once more.

The man gave a hand-flicking, discarding gesture. The escort formed up around Gower. With no alternative — still naked — he allowed himself to be led away. Close to the door through which he had originally entered, he was jostled down echoing stone steps into what was obviously a basement detention centre. There were solid metal doors along either side. Again, as in the corridor above, there was no sound from behind any of them.

Gower was prodded towards the middle cell, entering but instantly stopping on the threshold, gagging at the stench. There was a concrete bunk to his left, forming part of the wall out from which it was built. There was no pillow and only one thin blanket. Against the far wall, facing him, there was a small table, fronted by a stool. The gagging smell was coming from an uncurtained, open hole in the corner furthest from the bed, a stink of never-emptied sewage so bad that Gower retched and thought he was going to have to go to it to be sick. He only just managed to avoid it, swallowing the bile, recognizing that what he had thought to be the black stains of excreta all around the edge of the hole was, in fact, a cluster of gorging flies. There was a shove from behind and someone threw the sweat-starched tunic after him.

Gower edged on to the concrete ledge, arms tight across himself again, willing the revulsion to go. It still took a long time for him to be sure he wouldn't be sick. If the embassy reacted with the outrage that it should, he could be out of this obscenely vile place by the evening. He hoped to God he was: he couldn't imagine spending a whole night there. Certainly not being able to sleep. Hurry, he thought: dear God, please hurry.

It was to be some hours, slumped in growing despair on the rock-hard ledge, before Gower accepted he wasn't going to be freed, because the embassy hadn't been told of his detention.

It was bitterly, damply, cold. At first Gower tried just to use the blanket, twitching at the movement of whatever lived in it against his skin, but he began to shiver violently, so at last he was forced to put on the tunic. It was much too small for him: the top was like a straitjacket.

Would the embassy hurry to find him, when he was missed? That would be the ordinary reaction to the disappearance of someone accredited to the legation. But he wasn't regarded as ordinary by an ambassador who considered him a nuisance and would regard him as a positive liability after this.

There was no guarantee they'd do anything quickly. Gower was still shaking, but it wasn't solely from the cold any more.

Thirty-three

It was the attentive Ian Nicholson who raised the alert, although with no immediate urgency: at first Nicholson regarded the problem as no greater than that of a visiting Foreign Office colleague getting lost in a strange and unaccustomed city, without the ability to speak or read the language to seek help. Initially Nicholson even hesitated about mentioning it at all, and having decided he should he was uncertain whom to tell, because it was not a situation he had encountered before. He finally determined upon the senior security officer, Alan Rossiter, who was as uncertain as Nicholson and for the same reasons. It was late afternoon, minutes before the embassy was officially closing for the day, before Rossiter finally spoke to Peter Samuels and the sensitive bells began to jangle.

Samuels ordered the security man and Nicholson to remain on the premises for a possible discussion with the ambassador. Samuels held the senior legal attaché, Patrick Plowright, for the same reason, without offering an explanation.

'This could be everything we feared,' judged Railton, when the political officer disclosed Gower's absence. The ambassador was away from his desk, fidgeting in front of the fireplace and the largest of the carpet wall hangings, striding back and forth but only briefly, not more than four or five steps in either direction.

'We don't know that it's bad at all, at this point,' cautioned the political officer. 'He apparently indicated to Nicholson that he would be back around mid-day. He hasn't arrived.'

Railton looked unnecessarily at his watch. 'He's been adrift for six hours then?'

'If he *is* missing,' said Samuels, trying to calm the other man. 'There could be a dozen reasons why he hasn't returned yet. We just don't know: can't know.'

'Damn them!' said Railton, vehemently. 'Damn these stupid services with their cloak-and-dagger rubbish! You're right: we *don't* know what the hell the man was up to. So we can't formulate any sort of response!'

'We haven't been asked to make one yet,' pointed out Samuels.

'What have you done, so far?'

'Told Rossiter and Nicholson to stand by. Plowright, too.'

Railton nodded approval, 'Quite right. Best to confine it to as small a group as possible. We should tell London, of course.'

'Should we?' queried Samuels. 'Tell them what? Gower didn't log an official return time. Just mentioned casually that he would be back.'

Railton stopped his up-and-down promenade. 'Damn the man and all he represents! This could be awful: disastrous.'

'I don't think we should tell the others what Gower's real function was,' warned Samuels. 'Not unless there is something official, from the government here. In which case they'll learn anyway. For the moment I recommend we do nothing too prematurely, either within the embassy or with the authorities, outside.'

Railton nodded again. 'Quite right: nothing premature. Just prepare ourselves. Call the others.'

By the time they assembled, Nicholson noticeably nervous, Railton was re-established behind his impressive desk, showing no signs of the agitation of a few minutes before. He waved them to gather chairs for themselves, conveying the impression of a casual discussion, not a matter of any urgency. He smiled towards Nicholson, furthering the young man's uncertainty, and said: 'Now what do we think we've got here?'

'I am not sure, sir,' said the Scot, immediately apologetic. 'Maybe I've been too hasty. I'm sorry . . .'

'Rather have a reaction than no reaction at all,' encouraged Railton. 'I just want to get everything clear in my mind. Tell me exactly what this man Gower told you, about getting back.'

'He's eaten with us a couple of times: Jane's buying a dress for him to take home to his fiancée. At dinner last night he said he was going out into the town, but would certainly be back for lunch. We arranged to eat together in the mess.'

'A *definite* arrangement, then?' pressed Railton.

'I thought so.'

'Did he say anything else?' came in Samuels.

Nicholson thought about the question, before answering it. 'Not about today,' the man shrugged. 'He mentioned that he expected to be going home very shortly.'

There was a silence.

Samuels said: '*Certainly* be back by midday?'

'That's what he said,' agreed Nicholson, frowning at the need for such constant repetition.

'And that he was going home very shortly?' echoed the ambassador.

'Yes.'

The ambassador's hands began moving around the desk, as if he were anxious to employ them. 'Did he say *where* he was going?'

Nicholson shook his head. 'Just out.'

Rossiter noisily cleared his throat, a reminder of his presence. 'Beijing is confusing to a newcomer: very easy to get lost. He could very easily turn up in a while.' Rossiter looked the military policeman he had once been. He sat oddly to attention, all three buttons of his jacket done up, hair shorn almost to the point of baldness up to the very top of his head.

'I am not, at this stage, regarding this as sinister,' insisted Railton. 'I have no reason or cause to regard anything as sinister.'

'Can we explore that?' came in Plowright, quickly. Plowright was an unsettlingly diminutive man, just inches from being dwarflike. It was the embarrassing absence of stature that had taken him into the diplomatic legal profession, rather than any practising career before a Bar behind which he would have looked ridiculous. Plowright always dressed, as he was now, in the black jacket and striped trousers of his profession: customarily, in introducing himself, he identified the Inn of Court in London through which he had been called to the Bar, as if proof were necessary that he really was a qualified barrister.

'What do you mean by exploring it?' demanded Samuels.

'This man Gower was here to carry out a survey of embassy facilities?'

'Yes,' agreed Samuels.

There was another silence.

'*Was* he?' demanded the senior lawyer, at last.

'I'm not sure I understand that question,' evaded the ambassador.

Plowright had found that because of his smallness people tended to diminish him in everything. It annoyed him. He sighed. 'The most obvious explanation at the moment for what's happened is that Gower has got lost: that he'll reappear, hopefully very shortly. For which we will all be relieved and grateful. But if he doesn't . . .' The man paused, seeking a legal nicety. '. . . if for some unfortunate reason there is a difficulty in which I have to become officially involved, I need to be fully acquainted with the *true* facts. And *all* of the facts.' He looked rapidly between the ambassador and the political officer, waiting to see which would reply.

'I am not sure . . .' started Samuels.

'. . . I think we all are, in this room,' cut off the senior lawyer. 'I am not familiar in this or any other embassy to which I have been attached with facility officers travelling thousands of miles to perform a function that could be more than adequately fulfilled in half a day by any second secretary.'

Samuels gave no reaction, but the ambassador shifted uncomfortably. A diplomat happy nesting in the thicket of diplomatic ambiguity, Railton said: 'My advice from London was that John Gower was a facilities officer. It is as such that he is accredited.'

'So you know of no other reason, apart from his becoming lost, why he has not yet returned to this embassy?'

'No,' said Railton, thinly.

'There are other possibilities, beyond his having simply lost his way,' suggested the security officer. 'He could have fallen ill, been taken to hospital somewhere. Or been involved in an accident, which could also have put him into hospital.'

'They are possibilities,' agreed Samuels. Now he was thin-voiced. 'But in either event I would have expected official contact. He would have been carrying documentation identifying him as English even if he was unconscious or incapable of communicating.'

'Couldn't we contact the obvious places — hospitals or police stations — just in case?' asked Nicholson, ingenuously. 'We surely can't just sit around and wait, expecting him to surface?'

'No!' said Samuels, too sharply. 'I don't think we need to go outside of this embassy for the moment.'

'He could be *hurt!*' persisted Nicholson.

'No!' endorsed Railton. 'We wait.'

'How long for?' asked Rossiter.

Railton looked at his political officer for guidance. When Samuels said nothing, the ambassador said: 'Tomorrow. We'll give it twenty-four hours. If he hasn't come back by then, we'll start making enquiries.' He looked to each of them. 'In the meantime, I don't want this spread about the embassy: it's very easy here for rumours to become ridiculously outlandish. For the moment this remains a matter between ourselves. And that is an official instruction. Understood?'

There were various head movements and sounds of agreement from the men assembled in the room.

'I want everyone standing by, obviously . . .' Railton nodded towards the political officer. 'Peter and I might decide upon another conference, whatever happens, tomorrow . . .' The ambassador looked between Nicholson and Rossiter. 'I want you obviously to monitor his quarters, in case he comes back. If he does, I want to be informed immediately, irrespective of the time.'

Samuels remained behind, after the others left. In pointed reminder, Samuels said: '*Certainly* back for lunch. And that he was going home very shortly.'

'I felt like an idiot,' complained Railton. 'And

what the hell did that gnome of a lawyer think he was up to?'

'Being professional, as he saw it,' suggested Samuels.

'I think we should tell London,' said Railton, reaching a reluctant decision. 'If everything turns out all right, then so be it. But I don't want the Foreign Office and the Foreign Secretary caught unawares if it's *not* all right. They've got to be prepared, as best they can be. Get whatever guidance there is from Gower's people. *I'd* like whatever there is, too.'

Samuels nodded, accepting the instruction. 'Shall I express our concern at this stage? Or merely make a report?'

Railton remained head bent at his desk for several moments. 'Express our concern,' he said, looking up. 'A simple report might lie around undistributed for days. If we indicate concern, it'll get some reaction: get it sent to the right departments.' The diplomat paused before adding: 'I just know it's going to be bad. Disastrous.'

'I think you are right,' said Samuels, at the door. 'I think Gower has been arrested. So God knows what the end is going to be.'

The wording of the cable did result in it being instantly directed across the river from Whitehall to Westminster Bridge Road: Peter Miller was alerted by telephone in advance of its actual arrival, so Patricia Elder was already with him when it was delivered.

368

'No official denunciation or protest,' Patricia pointed out. 'There would have been, if he'd broken.'

'We can't anticipate the severity of the questioning,' said Miller. 'But we've got to try to minimize that as best we can. The only way is the strongest possible protest: make them apprehensive of treating him badly. I'll give the Foreign Office briefing personally. Gower's cover is one hundred per cent: the line has to be that he's an innocent diplomat, wrongly detained.'

'There's too much we don't know,' protested Patricia. She nodded towards the message. 'What's their guidance?'

'To make every possible enquiry!' said Miller, contemptuously.

'We're hamstrung, not knowing *any* of the circumstances!'

'If it were unarguably incriminating there *would* have been a public announcement by now,' insisted Miller.

'It'll be the most unholy mess if Gower breaks.'

'He was the most resistant to interrogation, in his entry course. He won't break easily.'

Natalia felt herself in the middle of a tightrope with both ends fraying, not knowing which way to dash to safety. It all had to be perfectly coordinated, and at the moment it wasn't. The Federal Prosecutor, who was responsible for any prosecution of Eduard, had acknowledged her approach and then written in greater length, and the previous day there had been a telephone call which she had avoided, with an innocent message left with a secretary for her to return the call, to arrange a meeting. Natalia did not think she could put it off much longer. Two days, she decided. Three at the most. That was the maximum she could allow herself. Just three days.

In his office further along the same corridor and on the same level at Yasenevo, Fyodor Tudin was finalizing the plans he was sure were going to get rid of Natalia Fedova for ever. He was very excited.

Thirty-four

Fyodor Tudin took every possible precaution, fully aware just how dangerously he was initially exposing himself, with no chance of correcting any mistake once he started. He had to get it all right the first time.

For the second and all-important visit to Petrovka he chose the most senior assistant from his own secretariat to take the notes and formulate the affidavit, but called a lawyer from the general Directorate pool with whom he had no provable association, to lessen any accusation of a clique or cabal, conspiring against the woman.

The lawyer's name was Anatoli Alipov, and as soon as the man entered his office Tudin concluded he was ideal for the official inquiry he was going to demand. Alipov was a slow-moving, slow-talking man of about forty-five, grey-haired and dark-suited, the personification of a solid and dependable legal figure.

'It is punishable, under legal statute?' questioned Tudin, after explaining the reason for the summons.

'Most definitely.'

'And under the regulations of our service?'

'Even more definitely.'

Tudin smiled, satisfied. 'We'll press for both.'

'There will need to be corroboration,' warned the lawyer.

'It will be provided,' guaranteed Tudin, confidently. The Militia investigator would have no choice, to save his own neck. And he'd know it, the moment the situation was spelled out to him.

'I dislike this sort of business,' protested the lawyer. 'Bad for the service if it becomes public: continues all the overhanging prejudices against the old KGB as a self-protecting organization above all laws or criticism.'

'No!' challenged Tudin, at once. 'It'll prove the very reverse: that when corruption and abuse is discovered, it's legally and publicly prosecuted under the new democratic system by which this country is now being run.' Which was the ultimate beauty of the whole thing. Natalia Nikandrova Fedova wasn't going to be destroyed by any connived or manipulated coup.

Alipov said: 'If that's how it's to be done, then I agree with you.'

Tudin telephoned Petrovka to warn of his return, but without saying there would be others with him, and Kapitsa's unsettled surprise was obvious when they got to Militia headquarters.

'There is a problem?' questioned the investigator. A comforting cigarette clouded into life.

Tudin shook his head. 'We'll obviously need a statement, won't we?' he said, intentionally ambiguous, hurrying to prevent Kapitsa thinking too fully about what he was being told: once he had the boy's deposition it wouldn't matter, but at this critical moment Tudin wanted the investigator's unquestioning cooperation, not any suspicious objections. 'We've got to get something written down: recorded. You see that, don't you . . . ?'

'I suppose . . .' Kapitsa started to agree, but Tudin bustled over him, close to bullying.

'. . . While we're doing that, I'd like a copy of the written record of the investigation so far.'

'Yes, but . . .'

'Doesn't matter what sort of order or shape it's in. Just the bare facts are all we need. We'd like to see the boy now: get it all over with.'

Kapitsa hesitated before stumbling: 'Yes, of course. No problem. I'll do . . . take you down . . . of course.'

Tudin reassessed his earlier opinion. The investigator was not just one of the old school, which was invaluable enough in itself: in addition Kapitsa was — rare for anyone in the Militia — intimidated by what he clearly still considered to be the KGB, with all its power and influence. Which in these very particular circumstances was valuable in the extreme. 'Good! . . . Good . . . !' he urged, backing gratefully from the smoke-fogged room to bring Kapitsa out with him: once he'd attained access to the boy, Tudin considered himself inviolable. Dutifully Kapitsa allowed himself to be drawn out, leading them downstairs: they had to wait in the interview cell for Eduard to be brought to them.

He arrived complaining loudly, practically bursting into the room in the expectation of confronting his mother, jerking to a halt at encountering strangers. 'What's this?' he demanded.

Tudin, who throughout a long career in the former KGB believed himself to have developed into an excellent if amateur psychologist, instantly categorized the stale-smelling, newly bearded man in front of him. Characteristics: bombast and pretension. Approach: initially soft, quickly aggressive. Affect: eggshell thin, defensive arrogance easy to crack. Outcome: whatever he wanted it to be.

'Sit down.' Tudin was soft-voiced, inviting.

'I want . . .'

'Sit down!' Immediately loud, intimidating.

Eduard sat abruptly on the chair he had occupied during the meeting with his mother. He made no attempt to push it back upon its rear legs this time.

To the Militia officer Tudin said: 'We'll handle this now. I'd like you to assemble the arrest reports. Have everything ready for when we leave.'

Kapitsa backed out into the corridor, nodding agreement. Tudin felt the satisfaction ballooning inside him. Done it, he thought: got here without argument or suspicion from the one person who might have obstructed him! So he was there: he'd virtually won.

'Who are you?' Eduard tried to make the question demanding, but his voice wavered and Tudin detected it.

'Eduard Igorevich Fedova?' The soft approach was back.

'You're from my mother's department?' said Eduard, smiling expectantly.

The idiot was making it even easier. 'Yes,' Tudin agreed, honestly.

'Thank God for that! Why has she left me this long?'

'That's what we've come to talk about.' Tudin gestured the note-taker to the chair directly opposite Eduard, the only one available.

Eduard looked up at Tudin. 'What's this? What's happening?'

'What's got to happen,' said Tudin. He had to avoid leading as much as possible. It was too late now to wonder if he should have established in advance some questioning routine with the lawyer: he wished he had thought about it earlier.

'I don't understand what's going on here!' protested Eduard.

'Do you understand why you've been arrested?'

The frown creased the younger man's face again. 'Of course I do! What sort of a question is that?'

The arrogance had to be extinguished. Suddenly loud-voiced, Tudin said: 'A question you've got to answer! Properly! Like you've got properly to answer every other question that's put to you by us today. You've got to understand something, Eduard Igorevich. Your mother can't help you. I can.'

'What is this?' Eduard repeated. The indignation was very weak.

'Why do you think we're from your mother's department?'

'Obvious, isn't it?'

Tudin decided he had to lead this fool, just a little. 'You were in charge of an illegal convoy of narcotic and medical drugs, as well as black-market material.'

Eduard's eyes went between the note-taker and Tudin. He said nothing.

'Answer me.'

Eduard's shoulders moved up and down. 'I haven't been charged with anything yet.'

'If you don't start behaving properly — sensibly — you *will* be charged. The combined offences carry a maximum penalty of forty-five years' imprisonment. Think about that: forty-five years. You'd be sixty-eight years old when you were released . . .' Tudin sniggered. 'Not really possible to imagine something like that, is it?' Tudin knew at once the barb had deeply embedded itself.

Eduard's tongue came out snakelike over his lower lip and he was frowning again, trying to grasp the import of what he was being told. Striving to find a way out from the pressure, he said: 'Tell me what you want me to do. To say.'

'In your own words — as fast or as slowly as you like — I want you to tell us everything leading up to your arrest on the Serpukhov road.'

The flickering smile came at last. 'I don't think I can talk about what happened on the Serpukhov road — if indeed anything *did* happen on the

Serpukhov road — until I have had a chance to talk with a lawyer.'

Tudin suppressed his fury at this juvenile posturing. 'What about after you were brought here? And your mother came to see you?'

'What do you want?' wailed Eduard. 'What does she want me to say or do? Help me!'

He had to take the risk. Tudin said: 'That's what it comes down to, Eduard Igorevich. Helping you. That's what your mother was going to do, wasn't it?'

'*Going* to?' snatched the younger man, catching the ball that Tudin threw him.

Getting there, thought Tudin: it was slow but he was getting there. 'We know about your meeting here. What was said: all of what was said.' Beside him Alipov shifted, and Tudin wondered if it was at what he was saying or merely weariness, at having to stand for so long. They really *should* have discussed the approach, before this confrontation.

'So?'

'Tell us what she promised you: what you always understood your protection would be, if you got arrested . . .' Tudin nodded towards the waiting secretary. 'He'll take it all down.'

'You're not *from* my mother, are you?'

'I've already told you, she can't help you,' stated Tudin, flatly. 'I can. But you've got to cooperate.'

'How can you help me?' demanded Eduard, quickly again. The tongue reappeared, more nervously than before. And he was beginning to

377

perspire, worsening the already long-unwashed smell.

'Immunity,' declared Tudin, shortly. Alipov shifted again. Tudin hoped the lawyer didn't interrupt or try to introduce caveats. Tudin knew himself so close to success he felt he could reach out to touch it.

Eduard's nervousness remained, but there was a slyness now. 'What's happened to my mother?'

'She's exceeded her authority. By undertaking to protect you.' It was an exaggeration but only he knew it: and it wouldn't be an exaggeration when he'd made his complaint, based upon what this snivelling, self-serving little bastard was shortly going to tell him.

Eduard's smile was hopeful. 'You said immunity.'

'If you make a full statement, about everything she said to you . . . tell us about why you were so sure you would always be protected by her . . . I'll intercede on your behalf.'

'I couldn't do that without talking about why I'm here,' bargained Eduard, smiling longer this time. 'That's more serious for me than anything involving my mother. The two are too inextricably mixed up, anyway.'

'I'll get you immunity from any criminal prosecution, too,' conceded Tudin.

'No accusations about anything?' pressed the young man, determined to clarify the deal he was being offered.

'None.'

It took two hours. Alipov quickly broke in, at the beginning, to stop Eduard performing for an imagined audience, insisting instead upon a cohesive account, stopping and questioning the lank-haired man every time he veered off on a self-important tangent. It took another hour for the deposition to be typed, over Eduard's signature. Tudin witnessed it, as the interrogator. Alipov signed, as the independent legal arbiter.

Eduard said: 'I've done all that you wanted?'

'Yes,' agreed Tudin.

'I want to get out of this shit-hole.'

Tudin had not expected such an immediate demand but he was prepared for it. 'I'll arrange it as quickly as I can.'

Kapitsa was waiting in his second-floor office. 'I didn't expect you to be so long.'

'Read this,' demanded Tudin, curtly, offering the deposition.

It took Kapitsa three cigarettes to get through the document. He came up hesitantly and said: 'Where is this going to be used?'

'Before an inquiry into the activities of General Natalia Nikandrova Fedova,' declared Tudin. 'You will be required to testify as well.'

There was a further moment of uncertainty. Then Kapitsa said: 'Yes. I understand.'

Late that evening, when they were quite alone back at Yasenevo, the lawyer said: 'What authority do you have, offering that lout immunity from prosecution?'

'None,' admitted Tudin, casually. 'I'll recommend it, like I said. If the Federal Prosecutor doesn't agree, that's fine by me. Eduard Igorevich can be prosecuted. But *after* he's testified against his mother.' It was a wonderful feeling to have won: like the best drinking experience he had ever had.

It was the smallest class for a very long time, only three students, and they were all evasive and uncomfortable when Snow questioned them about the others, variously insisting they did not know the reason for the absences. Li arrived in the middle of the lesson, sending the familiar frisson through the room, and the priest accepted the pointlessness, quickly ending the session.

'I have my photographs,' announced the man, offering the packet. 'I am very pleased with them.'

Snow accepted the folder, without opening it, not knowing what else to do or say.

'Aren't you going to look?'

Snow shuffled with forced slowness through the pictures, sure he was remaining impassive, mentally matching print for print, realizing that nothing Li had taken during their journey had been omitted.

The Shanghai prints were last. There were five, the same number that he had taken of the warships and proudly sent to London. But there were no warships in any of these shots. The positioning was the same and the lighting was the same and the time of day was the same but Snow knew *they* were not the same. The innocuous and quite meaningless photographs had to have been taken subsequently, after the flotilla had sailed.

'Now I can have mine, in exchange, can't I?' smiled Li.

They'd anticipated him, Snow accepted: beaten him. 'I would hope so, very shortly,' he said. How? he wondered.

Thirty-five

It took several hours for Gower to get hold of himself and fully comprehend the psychological pressure being imposed upon him. Finally, thankfully, he began to draw on the interrogation resistance in which he had done so well in training — and which had been further refined during those last, unorthodox sessions — and to concentrate upon behaving professionally. He'd faltered, admittedly: initially forgotten everything he'd ever been taught, all the training he'd undergone. But now he'd recovered: now he could fight back. Win.

So far it was almost classically textbook: there were even elements of it dating back as far as 1953 and recorded by men taken prisoner by the Chinese during the Korean war. He knew all those techniques. And others that followed later. So he could anticipate them: not completely perhaps, but enough. Fear — of the unknown, of what might happen next — was the first, eroding, intention of every interrogation. Once fear was instilled, every other collapse was inevitable, simply a matter of time. But it wasn't going to happen to him. Not now he'd collected himself. There was apprehension, naturally. But no longer the panicked emptiness that had made him piss himself, in those first few moments. He could think ahead: guess what was coming. And what he could guess, even incompletely, wouldn't be erodingly unknown.

The filthy, shit-smelling cell and the lice-ridden, stinking uniform were very much part of the ritual, calculated to degrade him into the deepest despair as quickly as possible. There was no toilet paper, if he was forced to use the fly- and excrement-encrusted hole. Water would be fouled, to give him dysentery. He'd have to expect any food to be rotten, to achieve the same illness: possibly even maggot-infested, openly to revolt him. And for as long as he was detained, he'd be denied any washing facilities. Not allowed to shave.

From the concrete shelf, Gower at last surveyed the rest of the cell in the necessary detail, seeking how they would watch him, surprised when he couldn't detect any electronic device in any part of the ceiling or upper walls. All that was obvious was the round Judas-hole, in the solid metal door. He stood at last and went entirely around the cell to look more closely and still found nothing. There would be the minimal warning, from the covering scraping back, when they looked. He would have to be prepared to move quickly to conceal from them any indication that he'd regained control. My advantage, decided Gower.

Moving about the cell brought him close enough to the lavatory hole to hear the permanent buzz of the flies. Revulsion could be eroding, although not as much as fear. Equally essential that it be controlled: overcome. Alert for any sound from the door, he forced himself towards the hole, tensed against the stench and the sudden cloud swarm disturbed by his approach. More insects rose up about him in protest when he began to urinate. As he did so, he was aware of a positive scratching, from inside the hole. How many rats would there be, he wondered.

Gower was back on the concrete ledge when the observation point scraped open. He was sure he hunched forward, arms around himself in the near broken pose they wanted, before anyone looked in. Gower remained unmoving. It was several moments before it scraped loudly closed again.

Gower started his mental count from that observation, remaining bent, intent on gauging their routine. Roughly every fifteen minutes, he estimated, after the third inspection. Part of a careful pattern constantly to disconcert him by the noise and by his becoming unsettled at how frequently he was being watched. But counter-productive because he could match his pattern to theirs and move around the cell, even relax as much as possible, in between their checks.

Think ahead, he reminded himself, as he exercised. There would be the tainted food some time. They might even make him beg for the infected water, to demean him. He'd have to do that, if it became obvious they expected it: had to take the greatest care against their realizing he was resisting them. What else? Noise, he remembered. It would get worse as the night progressed, to keep him awake. Sleep deprivation was inextricably linked with fear, in the very beginning: the mentally strongest man, indoctrinated with every resistance skill ever devised, could be reduced to a puttylike automaton if he were continuously deprived of sleep longer than seventy-two hours. It was important that he get as much as possible, before the noise disturbance became louder and more sustained, which he knew it would.

Gower did not attempt to stretch out full-length. He was crouched forward at the next Judas-hole check but didn't bother to move after the visor screeched shut. Instead he remained as he was, although as far back on the shelf as possible to support his back, trying to doze. He was never wholly successful, never lapsing into a proper sleep, but he didn't want to do that because it would have been a dangerous mistake: he drifted in a half consciousness, resting but aware every time of the rasping scrape of the peep-hole, alert enough when it came to the louder sound of the door opening to be awake and looking at who entered. The bow-shouldered, bowed-headed man carrying the food wore a stained and shapeless tunic like him, obviously another prisoner. There was a guarding soldier either side. The food slopped over the edge of the bowl when it was dumped on to the table. The soldiers looked at him, expressionlessly. The food-carrier didn't try. Nothing was said by anyone. The sound of the door slamming shut was still echoing in the corridor when the covering metal was slid back from the observation point.

For a moment Gower remained undecided: he did not feel genuinely hungry and did not want to arouse suspicion by appearing so, after such a comparatively short time without food. The hole remained uncovered longer than at any other time and so Gower moved eventually, going across to the table.

He had grown used to the lavatory in the corner. The smell from what was being offered as food was quite different but equally revolting. The bowl contained a predominantly grey liquid, but it was glutinous, slimed on top. There were things floating or suspended in it but Gower could not tell what they were supposed to be: they appeared transparent, as jellyfish are transparent, and when he looked closer he saw that like jellyfish there were black blobs or spots on some parts of whatever it was. There was a cup beside the food, half filled. Gower was prepared for the water to be discoloured, maybe even with detritus floating in it, but it was unexpectedly clear.

Aware of the eyes upon him, Gower stood with his back to the door but in front of the table, so the food tray was hidden from his onlooker. He visibly went through the motions that from behind would have seemed to be his bringing the cup to his mouth but, sure his face was hidden from outside, kept his lips tight, barely letting the water wet them. It didn't taste sour or bad, but he still didn't drink. There was no spoon to eat with, so Gower lifted the food bowl, but still hidden from outside did not let it even touch his mouth. He tried to avoid inhaling, fighting against the bile building up in his throat. He made four or five lifting and head-back swallowing movements, then replaced the bowl. The visor swivelled shut as he sat down on the ledge. Gower rose at once, pouring half the water into the lavatory to make it appear to have been drunk, then emptied most of the viscous slops after it. The flies rose and settled: there was excited scratching from inside the clotted rim.

Gower drowsed through four more doorway checks before the louder noise began. There was a lot of activity in the outside corridor, sounding like squads of men moving up and down to bursts of shouted orders, and then two separate loudspeakers started up with contrasting, discordant wails, one clashing against the other. It was so raucous that Gower almost missed the rasp of the peep-hole opening. He didn't have to prepare himself. He was sitting up, awake, his hands actually to his ears against the cacophony. He remained like that but with his head bent, no longer able to doze but with his eyes closed, still resting after a fashion, despite the row.

He hadn't expected the middle-of-the-night resumption of the questioning, but it was one of the standard procedures so Gower was not disorientated by the abrupt entry of an escort squad, although he tried to appear confused. He kept up the pretence when he reentered the room where Chen was waiting.

The table was clear now, all his belongings gone. The recording operators looked to be the same men. The black-suited man who had been present at the arrest wasn't there any more, and on this occasion the three-man escort remained inside the room.

'We have proof that you are a spy,' announced Chen, at once.

'I am not a spy,' rejected Gower. Although the Chinese was wearing the same tunic it appeared freshly pressed. The man's open face gleamed with cleanliness and there was the obvious fragrance of a heavy cologne. Gower recognized it all as another attempted psychological twist of the screw, for him mentally to compare his predicament with that of his questioner. He edged forward on the table separating them, for Chen to catch the odour seeping from him, hoping to offend the man.

'The flowers were a signal.'

He was supposed to be muddled, remembered Gower. He blinked and made several attempts to form his words before saying: 'Told you earlier what they were for.'

'Tell me again!'

'My room at the embassy.'

'Liar!'

More word-searching. 'Demand the embassy be told. I have the right of access.'

'Tell me who you were signalling and I will inform your embassy where you are. And why.'

Gower dropped his head, not sure if he could conceal his full reaction to what the other man had disclosed. If they wanted him to provide a name, they *hadn't* arrested Snow! 'Not signalling anyone,' he mumbled. 'Here inspecting embassy facilities.'

'What is the importance of the Taoist shrine?'

'Not important. It seemed unusual. I was interested.'

'We've set a trap,' announced Chen.

Gower decided he couldn't respond: show any reaction at all. He moved his shoulders, barely shrugging, but said nothing.

'We're putting flowers at the shrine.'

'I don't understand.'

'Yes, you do.'

Gower shrugged again.

'We're going to make the signal you were supposed to give. Trap the others.'

Could it work? Possibly. The colour of the flowers had to be right. And the precise position, in the troughs. The significance of the colour would probably be obvious but they wouldn't know where to put them. But would it matter if the signal was wrong and the priest ignored it? Snow — a Westerner — would arouse suspicion merely by being there if they expected a Westerner: risk almost automatic arrest. Still no personal danger, Gower reassured himself, recalling his reflection at the earlier confrontation. Snow didn't know *him:* couldn't name him. But was there any safety there, either? If Snow were seized, merely for being in the same area, and under interrogation disclosed that the flowers were a signal, then the connection was established. And Snow hadn't been trained to resist interrogation. There was nothing he could do. If it happened — and Snow broke — he was lost. 'I don't understand,' he repeated.

'It would be better for you if you confessed now.'

'I am a diplomat. I want to talk to my embassy.'

'You're guilty.'

Gower stayed silent.

'You're a fool.'

Still silence.

'We just have to wait,' said Chen.

Charlie knew immediately from the expression on Julia's face that there was a crisis. She stood unspeaking at the door of her house for several moments before backing away, for him to enter.

'What?' he demanded.

'Gower,' she said. 'They've swept up your apprentice.'

Thirty-six

The gesture of pouring Charlie the Islay malt she was buying specifically for him now was practically automatic: that night Julia poured for herself, which was not: normally she didn't drink whisky. Charlie accepted the glass but put it at once on the side-table before leaning forward from his facing chair to bring them very close. He reached out for her hands to direct her entire concentration upon him.

'Every detail,' he urged. 'Everything you know.'

'Very little,' apologized the girl. 'Nobody knows anything. He went out of the embassy in Beijing, telling people he would be back around midday. He never arrived.'

'Beijing?' queried Charlie.

'That was the assignment. China, to bring out someone we think is under suspicion: liable to arrest.'

'What about an announcement? An accusation?'

'Nothing yet. We're making official representations, enquiring about his whereabouts. As a missing diplomat, of course. That's why I'm telling you now: you'd have learned anyway, in a few hours. The idea's to create a fuss: the Director thinks it might make them cautious about the pressure they'll put on him.'

'Bollocks,' said Charlie. 'They'll do what they like. It's China, for Christ's sake! They don't care about Western opinion.'

'I'm sorry, Charlie,' said Julia, sadly. 'Really very sorry.'

Charlie was grateful but indifferent to sympathy for himself. 'Gower will be a bloody sight sorrier. Hardly anything of what we did . . . what he did before, at the proper training schools . . . prepared him. Why the fuck did it have to be China?'

'There's a hell of a flap at the Foreign Office. The DG — and Patricia — have made a lot in their memoranda about Gower's resistance to interrogation.'

Charlie shook his head. 'It's not the same: never can be. You can go through all the motions . . . authentic physical stress . . . beating . . . drugs . . . sleep deprivation. . . all of that. But it's not the same. You can always hold on to the fact that it's a war game: that it'll stop sometime. That insurance isn't there, for the real thing. And the Chinese are good at it. They've been doing it longer and better than anybody else.'

'You think he'll break?'

'I *know* he'll break. Everyone does . . .' Charlie was looking away from her now, deep in reflection. 'It shouldn't have been Beijing, not the first time. He wasn't ready. That was wrong.' His voice was distant: he wasn't really addressing the girl whose hands he still held.

'It was pretty shitty luck,' agreed Julia.

'Luck never enters into it.' Charlie looked up, abruptly. 'What about the person who's exposed?'

Julia shook her head. 'Not a lot. He's a priest: told to get out but wouldn't.'

Charlie frowned across at her, concentrating again. 'Why send *in?* Why didn't his Control in Beijing simply tell him to get out?'

'The relationship collapsed. We brought the Control out a long time ago. A damage-limitation move, if the priest was arrested.'

'What damage limitation, with Gower in the bag?'

She nodded in further agreement, at Charlie's outrage. 'No one anticipated this.'

Charlie stayed frowning. 'Is that the way it's being put forward?'

Julia nodded.

More damage limitation at Westminster Bridge Road than ten thousand miles away in China, thought Charlie, bitterly. '*If* the priest was arrested?' he echoed.

'There's been nothing about that, either,' conceded Julia. 'But there is something.'

'What?'

'He had a dissident source, about a year ago. A man named Zhang Su Lin. He's one of a number of dissidents who've been arrested in the past few weeks. There's a purge going on.'

Charlie was silent for several moments. At last he took his drink, sipping it. Then he said, distantly again: 'This could be a full-scale, eighteen

carat, one hundred per cent disaster. With political and every other sort of fallout all over the
place. And with Gower buried under it, right
at the very bottom.'

'I wish I could think of something practical
to say.'

So did Charlie. But he didn't know enough:
supposed he'd never know enough. Only sufficient
to make the judgement he'd just reached, which
hardly required the political acumen of the age.
'The official reaction, if there is an accusation,
will be absolute denial?'

'It's standard,' reminded Julia. 'I guess that'll
be it.'

Charlie wondered how a girl named Marcia
whom he'd never met would feel seeing newspaper and television pictures of a cowed and
brainwashed lover humbled in a court on the other
side of the world. He smiled across at Julia.
'Thanks, for bending the personal rules. Can you
go on doing that? Just about Gower. I want to
know much more than what's going to be made
officially public.'

Julia didn't reply at once. Then she said: 'Just
about Gower.'

'Poor bastard,' said Charlie, reflective again.
'Poor, frightened bastard.'

'I'm glad it's not you,' said Julia, unexpectedly.
'That's selfish, I know. Doesn't help anyone. But
I'm so glad it's not you.'

Refusing to pick up on her remark, Charlie
instead practically echoed the threat of John

Gower's interrogator. 'All we can do now is wait.'

It wasn't to be long, for any of them.

The British demands brought about the uproar.

The Chinese ambassador to London was summoned to the Foreign Office personally to receive the request for information about John Gower, described as an accredited diplomat on temporary secondment to Beijing. The interview was timed to the minute to coincide with the visit to the Chinese Foreign Ministry in Beijing of Sir Timothy Railton. The request the British ambassador formally deposited was worded identically to that collected by his Chinese counterpart, in London. The press release was confined, for reasons of practicality, to London. It began by expressing the concern of the British authorities in the Chinese capital and of the British government in London at the apparent disappearance of Gower. The British government were unable to offer any explanation for his not returning to the embassy and could only infer the man had become ill or been involved in an accident which had so far prevented his being properly identified.

The press statement was issued quickly after the simultaneously delivered information-seeking notes, so there was a gap of several hours before the Beijing answer. The delay was sufficient for media interest to begin, although initially with no suggestion of espionage overtones: the disappearance of a young and new diplomat in this still enclosed country, the one remaining communist superpower in the world, was enough to justify newspaper curiosity.

That curiosity erupted into near hysteria with the Beijing announcement that John Gower had been arrested as a spy engaged in counter-revolutionary activities against the State, activities which had already led to widespread arrests of dissidents throughout the country. Within twenty-four hours the newspapers discovered the existence of Marcia Leyton: the innocent vicar who had christened her confirmed the wedding preparations and the media cup was filled to overflowing, a spy sensation they never imagined possible after the end of their self-entitled Cold War, complete with a perfect human-interest angle.

All the pictures of Marcia were of a bewildered and confused girl. She broke down at the only press conference she attempted to give, so the denial that her fiancé had any connection whatsoever with any intelligence service was issued by the family solicitor. Traced to Gloucestershire, Gower's mother confronted the press on the lawn of the decaying mansion and insisted it was nonsense to describe her son as a spy. The Chinese had made a terrible mistake which they should rectify immediately.

It was on the day of the televised press conference during which Marcia broke down that Charlie was called to the ninth floor of Westminster Bridge Road.

There was another summons made that day, in Moscow. It demanded the appearance of Natalia

Nikandrova Fedova before Vadim Lestov, the chairman of the Federal Agency for Internal Security. No reason was given.

Natalia finally made the telephone call she had delayed. It was the third day of the deadline she had imposed upon herself.

Thirty-seven

Natalia was ordered not to the traditional head-quarters of the former Soviet intelligence apparatus at Lubyanka, but to the nearby White House, the seat of the new Russian government. There Vadim Lestov maintained an office suite in which he spent most of his time, in preference to the ochre-painted mausoleum so closely associated with KGB oppression.

Only when she approached the inner sanctum of the intelligence division, close to Lestov's suite, was there any reminder of the old KGB security mania, but even here the officers who carried out the mandatory screening were young, open-faced and comparatively friendly, not the stone-featured automatons she could remember from when she first joined the service, which now seemed so very long ago.

Natalia felt completely alone and frighteningly vulnerable, without any indication of what or who she was going to confront. At this moment — this very last moment — the precautions she'd attempted, working blind, always having to guess where and how Tudin's attack might come, seemed woefully inadequate.

A man was waiting to receive her in an ante-room, gesturing her at once towards high, divided double doors. Natalia was disorientated the moment she entered. She had expected an office, with maybe just Lestov or Tudin waiting inside. Instead she walked into a small conference room already arranged as an examining tribunal. There was a table across the end of the room. Lestov sat in the centre, flanked by his two immediate deputies, Vladimir Melnik and Nikolai Abialiev. A bank of tables to the left already harboured a recording secretariat of three men and two women. There were two rows of chairs facing the three blank-faced members of the committee. Fyodor Tudin was already occupying a seat in the first row, on the left. Eduard was directly behind. Mikhail Kapitsa was in the same row, but separated from Eduard by two empty chairs. Also in that row sat a third man whom Natalia did not know.

Her escort indicated the chairs to the right, separated from the others by a central aisle. Mustn't become disorientated, confused by the unexpected! she told herself. She'd make mistakes if she let this tribunal hearing unsettle her. No reason why she should be unsettled. Her original KGB training had been as an interrogator, accustomed daily to being faced during debriefings with situations for which there had been no primer or rehearsal. It was at one such session that she'd met Charlie Muffin for the first time!

As she reached her designated place, Lestov said: 'This is a preliminary disciplinary examination, of complaints from Fyodor Ivanovich

Tudin, under regulations governing the security service of the Russian Federation. If those complaints are found to be justified they will be laid before a full tribunal hearing. Any such findings will in no way interfere with quite separate criminal charges that might be considered appropriate by the Federal Prosecutor.'

Tudin, the outdated traditionalist who only knew well trodden routes, had moved as she'd anticipated, pursuing her through the organization's regulations first! Natalia felt a surge of relief. There was still a lot more she had to understand and perhaps prepare herself against.

When she did not respond Lestov said: 'Do you fully understand what I have said? Why you have been brought before us?'

'Absolutely.' She didn't welcome the irritation in his voice. Natalia came slightly forward, concentrating entirely upon the chairman, needing his attention, which at that moment was upon the documents laid out before him. Natalia supposed she had either met him formally or been in his presence among others on about four or five occasions since their respective appointments. It had been Lestov who officially confirmed her as chairman of the external directorate. He was an inconspicuous, undistinguished man who nevertheless conveyed an impression of the authority he clearly possessed. Head-bent as he was, the thinning hair was more obvious than she could remember from their previous encounters. He was not a career intelligence officer. At one time in the turmoil of fledgling Russian democracy, which still didn't properly exist, Lestov had served as Interior Minister, but had been dismissed because he was considered too liberal. Natalia hoped the charge had been true. Not having expected an investigating panel she certainly hadn't prepared herself for the sort of prosecution that was clearly intended.

At that moment, fortunately, Lestov came up from his papers, looking enquiringly at her.

'Will I have the opportunity to question the accusations I am going to face?'

Lestov went briefly to the men on either side of him. 'Within limits. There is no reason for this to be a protracted examination.'

Already judged guilty, decided Natalia, worriedly.

At Lestov's nod, Tudin hurried to his feet. The man was more florid-faced than usual, and Natalia guessed at a combination of nervous excitement at appearing before his ultimate superiors at last to destroy her, and an excess of alcohol in premature celebration. He'd dressed for the occasion. His suit was immaculate and there was the pose of a man in command in the way he was standing. Twisted sideways, Natalia could easily see Eduard as well. He wore the same clothes as in the detention cell and they were creased, but he was clean-shaven and the near shoulder-length hair was no longer lank and greasy, so he'd been allowed to shower. His belongings had been returned to him. As well as the earring she had seen there was a heavy gold watch on his left wrist and a gold identity chain on the other. There were two rings on his left hand, one dominated by a large purplish-red stone, and one on his right: from where she sat it seemed to be in the shape of a face or a mask. The dishevelled Mikhail Kapitsa, deprived by the formality of the proceedings of the habitual cigarette, was blinking rapidly and frequently brought his hands to his face, as if troubled by an irritation. His frowning look towards her was one of confused bewilderment.

Tudin avoided any flamboyant speech or mannerisms: his attitude was practically the opposite, an address delivered in a flat, sometimes almost boring monotone, with few hand or body movements. He listed precisely by their subheadings and numbers the regulations governing the Agency under which he was bringing the accusations, which he summarized as abuse of power and condoning corruption. In addition he itemized the criminal statutes he contended Natalia had broken.

The man quickly sketched Eduard's youth at Moscow University before gaining a junior officer's commission in the Russian army which had ended with the scaledown of the military.

'Returning to Moscow he became a criminal, joining a recognized Mafia syndicate known as the Lubertsy,' declared Tudin. 'He told his criminal associates — as he will tell you here today — that he was in a particularly privileged position. His mother was a high-ranking official in the

State's security service. Her rank and influence put him beyond the law. If he were ever unlucky enough to get arrested, he could call upon his mother to intercede to prevent any prosecution or conviction . . .'

Tudin paused, and despite his control the man was unable to avoid darting a satisfied look between mother and son.

'An arrest did happen, through brilliant detective work by Militia Investigator Mikhail Stepanovich Kapitsa, who will also testify before you today . . .' Tudin turned quickly, identifying the detective with a hand gesture. '. . . Eduard Igorevich Fedova was seized, with eight other members of a gang of which he was the leader, in possession of narcotic and medical drugs and a considerable amount of black market material. Fedova's first action was to offer Investigator Kapitsa a substantial bribe. Which Kapitsa of course refused. At that point, Fedova identified his mother. He told Investigator Kapitsa it was quite pointless the man attempting any sort of criminal prosecution: that his mother would prevent it. And he demanded to see her . . .'

Tudin coughed, his voice becoming strained, but also wanting the minimal pause, for effect. Looking directly up at the assembled committee, he said: 'Natalia Nikandrova Fedova was contacted on the eighteenth of this month. Within an hour of a telephone conversation between her and Investigator Kapitsa, she arrived at Militia headquarters at Petrovka, to do exactly what her son had always insisted she would do, intercede upon his behalf to block any prosecution against him.'

It was impressive and convincing and Natalia felt a dip of uncertainty. There was no protest she could make, but the whole balance of the inquiry was unfair, weighted against her. Realizing he had finished, Natalia said quickly: 'I would like to ask Colonel Tudin some questions.'

There was a peremptory, practically dismissive nod and Natalia tried to remain unruffled by Lestov's clearly preconceived acceptance of the accusations against her.

She turned fully to confront her accuser, who came around in his turn to face her. He was impassive but still red, his attitude one of assured confidence. She was a long way from matching it, because she hadn't expected the quasi-legality of an inquiry with witnesses arraigned against her and she still hadn't properly adjusted. She tried to clear her throat but failed, so when she started to speak her voice was ragged and she had to stop and start again. A smirk flickered momentarily around Tudin's mouth.

'You are my immediate deputy, in the external directorate of the Russian security agency?'

Tudin hesitated, cautiously. 'Yes.'

'As such I have delegated to you particular authority concerning the new independent republics of the former Soviet Union?'

The caution was longer this time. 'Yes.'

'At a recent conference of all department and

division heads did I have cause strongly to criticize your performance? And to insist upon substantial improvement within a stated time period?' The smirk flickered again, and Natalia decided the man imagined she was attempting a defence in an indefensible situation by introducing internecine and irrelevant squabbles.

In immediate confirmation, Tudin turned invitingly towards the committee, visibly shrugging. Lestov responded with worrying speed and obvious impatience. 'Is there any purpose to these questions? They have no bearing on what we are considering here today.'

'They — and the attitude of Colonel Tudin — have *everything* to do with what is happening here today,' argued Natalia, as forcefully as she felt she could. She was directly arguing against her chairman, she realized.

Lestov's mouth tightened, but he nodded curtly for her to continue.

'Was there disagreement between us?' resumed Natalia.

'I regarded it then and I regard it now as a department matter. I do not consider it has anything to do with these proceedings.'

Natalia's voice caught again when she began to speak, but this time she did not regret the apparent uncertainty. 'The conversation between myself and Investigator Kapitsa was a private matter: quite unofficial?'

Tudin smiled openly at what amounted to an admission of what he was accusing her of. 'Exactly!' he said, triumphantly. 'In an official Militia inquiry you intruded unofficially to save your son!'

There was a stir from among the men comprising the examining panel. Natalia tried to remain unruffled. 'How did you discover that contact between myself and Investigator Kapitsa?'

Tudin's caution returned. 'Rumours,' he said shortly.

'The directorate has an internal security division. It is not your function or responsibility to respond to rumours or gossip or suspicion of internal wrong-doing within the directorate.'

For the only time since the inquiry began, Tudin looked uncomfortable. 'I regarded the matter as one of the utmost seriousness: one that had to be handled by someone with the authority I possess, to avoid any intimidation.'

'Isn't the truth of the matter that you were spying upon me, as your superior, because of your resentment of my holding that position and because of my criticism of your inadequacy to fulfil the job to which I had appointed you?'

'No!' denied Tudin, loudly. 'I admit — and if the committee should require an apology then of course I offer it — that I did not strictly follow the procedures laid down for investigating matters of this sort. My only reason for doing so was quickly and effectively to prevent an abuse of power and authority. Which I have done.'

Natalia slumped down, stranding Tudin neither talking to her nor to the committee, but to the empty space in between. She hadn't obtained an admission — as he had from her — but she hoped to have established doubt in the minds of the three men sitting in judgement upon her.

The unidentified man whom Tudin called first gave his name as Anatoli Alipov and his position as a lawyer with the security agency who had witnessed and formally taken the affidavit from Eduard. Alipov's account was formal, nothing more than assuring the committee that the incriminating statement had been properly obtained.

'What reason did Colonel Tudin give for your going with him to Petrovka?' she demanded, when her turn came to question.

'Legally to conduct the taking of an affidavit.'

'An affidavit to serve what purpose?'

Alipov considered his reply, a careful lawyer. 'To establish there had been an abuse of power according to our internal regulations.'

'Which you considered to *be* established?'

There was another gap, for consideration. 'Yes.'

'Was that all?'

'No.'

'What else?'

'To give an opinion on possible criminal action, too.'

'What was your opinion?'

'That there was a case to be made.'

As she sat, Natalia glanced unexpectedly sideways and caught the look of smiling satisfaction upon Eduard's face, and when Tudin called him by name there was a swagger about the way he stood. He rested his hands upon the chair-back in front and at the beginning looked about him, and Natalia got the impression he regretted not having a larger audience before which to perform.

Tudin led.

The facts, from the moment of the interception on the Serpukhov road, were essentially the same as she had heard from Kapitsa, and there was a basis of accuracy in the account of the conversation she'd had with Eduard and which Kapitsa had witnessed, at her insistence. But it had all been subtly exaggerated, inference hardened into substance, innuendo presented as positive fact.

It sounded convincing and devastating.

Eduard adamantly repeated that he had never doubted her protection: at Petrovka his mother had assured him he would be freed and no action taken against him. His deepest regret was that his mother now faced this and possibly further, more serious inquiries. He had never openly asked her to be his protectress. He wanted to cooperate in every way he could, which was why he had made the affidavit. He hoped his mother would be leniently dealt with, at this and any other investigation.

She was quickly on her feet, but having risen she did not immediately speak, regarding her son steadily. How could she have ever had any emotion or love for this creature standing before her, thinking about him in the same terms — my flesh and blood — as she thought about Sasha?

Her only feeling now was one of loathing hatred.

'Where do I live?' Natalia demanded, harshly.

Eduard blinked. There was shuffling in the room. Eduard said: 'What?'

'Where do I live?'

'I don't . . . I thought Mytninskaya but it wasn't.'

'When was the last time you came to Mytninskaya?'

'I don't . . .' started Eduard, then stopped. He shrugged. 'Some time ago.'

'How long have you been out of the army?'

Another shrug. 'Quite a while.'

'Have you come to Mytninskaya to see me during that time?'

There was no longer any swagger or superciliousness. Eduard was suddenly aware it was not as easy as he imagined it to be, and was leaning slightly towards her. Tudin was half turned, but unable to provide any guidance, from his awkward position. Guessing the direction of her questioning, Eduard said: 'I tried, but you weren't there.'

He was improvising! Natalia realized at once, from long-ago experience. He was lost without guidance from Tudin and he was improvising as he went along! 'When did we last meet, *before* you left the army?'

'Can't remember.'

'The dates of your leaves and furloughs would be a matter of existing record, on army files,' she warned heavily. 'It was six months before you left the army, wasn't it?'

'Maybe.'

Natalia was too far away to be sure, but she suspected there was a sheen of perspiration on her son's face. Sweat you bastard, sweat, she thought. 'What rank do I hold?'

'Colonel. That's what it was.'

'Not what it *was*. What *is* it, now?'

'Not sure.'

'Where do you live?'

'Tverskaya.'

'In what? An apartment?'

'You should know! You've been there often enough!'

Natalia realized that her son was really remarkably stupid. 'Is that what you're telling this inquiry? That I've visited you there?'

'You know you have.'

'That's not true, is it?'

'You know it's true! That's where we reached our understanding!'

Tudin was turned away from Eduard now, head lowered towards the floor, and Natalia wondered how the man could have possibly imagined he would succeed with an attack like this. At once she answered her own question. The ways of the past, she remembered: once an accusation as blatantly false as this could have succeeded. 'Tell the inquiry about that understanding.'

'Already have,' said Eduard. He'd been tensed but now he relaxed, believing he had beaten her.

It was important to inflate the confidence, in

the hope that it would burst. 'Let's do it again. You were sure I'd get you out of Militia custody?'

'That's what you'd always said you'd do.'

'When I came to Tverskaya?'

Eduard smiled. 'Yes.'

The balloon was becoming stretched, decided Natalia. 'What did I say, when I saw you in the cell?'

'That it wasn't just a matter for you: that you had to consider the Militia position.'

That was a fairly accurate recollection, she conceded. 'How long had you been in detention when I saw you?'

'Five days.'

'When were you released?'

'This morning.'

'That is the agreement, is it? Your release in return for talking to this inquiry today?'

Natalia had hoped to get the over-confident, unthinking admission, but before Eduard could reply Tudin hurriedly stood. 'I should tell the committee that I have today sent a full report to the Federal Prosecutor, recommending immunity in return for this man's cooperation. At the moment, technically, he remains in Militia custody.'

It was the perfect rebuttal of what Natalia was striving to establish, that a freedom deal had been reached between Eduard and Tudin in return for Eduard's testimony, and briefly Natalia was numbed by the despair of being so easily thwarted. For several moments her mind blocked and she couldn't think how to continue — but more importantly how to win — this exchange with her son. And then her mind did start working again and the despair lessened, although she suspected everyone — the committee headed by the security chairman, and Tudin and Eduard and Kapitsa — would believe she had failed miserably to establish any sort of defence. Briskly she said: 'We weren't alone in the detention cell, were we? Investigator Kapitsa was there all the time?'

'Yes.' Eduard's caution had returned.

'He witnessed everything?' A great deal depended on the honesty of the detective, Natalia realized: more than she'd anticipated until this moment.

'Yes.'

'Did you want him to be there?'

Eduard shrugged. 'It was a matter for you. I didn't mind.'

'You didn't suggest he should leave?' Natalia concentrated not upon her son but upon Kapitsa when she asked the question. The detective was frowning.

'No.'

Kapitsa's frown deepened. Dear God, thought Natalia, don't let him have reached any agreement or understanding with Tudin, as Eduard obviously has. 'You identified me as your mother to Investigator Kapitsa the moment you were stopped on the Serpukhov road?'

'That was what you'd always told me to do: announce it at once to prevent any investigation becoming established.'

Natalia intruded the pause, wanting the silence. Then she said: 'So it had to be done quickly? You were to be got out quickly?' Natalia saw Tudin stiffen.

Eduard said: 'Yes.'

'But it was five days before I came to Petrovka.'

Eduard appeared to realize the danger. He nodded, nibbling his lower lip, not replying.

'Was it not five days before I came to Petrovka?'

'Yes.'

'If we'd always agreed to move quickly, why do you think it took five days for me to come to you?'

'You tell me!' said Eduard, defiantly.

'I will! You didn't have an address to contact me, because there had been no meeting between us for almost two years, had there? Just as there was no understanding or agreement between us, to look after you if you got into trouble.'

'Always said you'd help!' insisted Eduard, desperately. In front of him, Tudin was rigid, head predictably down over his papers.

Destruction time, decided Natalia: she was savouring the moment, even delaying for the pleasure of it. 'Why do you think it was that when I promised you protection, which you say I did at Tverskaya, I didn't tell you I'd been promoted to General, which would have been a much better guarantee than if I had remained a Colonel? Or why, during those visits, did I never give you my new address? And how did I *know* you lived

413

at Tverskaya, when we hadn't had any contact for six months *before* you left the army? Eighteen months before you even *had* somewhere to live at Tverskaya!'

There wasn't any impatient shifting from the panel now. In fact there was no movement or sound at all in the room.

Natalia pressed on, relentlessly. 'Colonel Tudin promised there would be no prosecution if you came here today, didn't he? That's the deal, isn't it? Give evidence against me — incriminate me — and you'll go free!'

'He said he would recommend it,' said Eduard, trying to stick to what they had rehearsed.

'It's with Colonel Tudin that you have an arrangement, isn't it? Not with me? There's never been an understanding or arrangement with me.'

Again Tudin came to his feet before Eduard could reply. Tudin said: 'This evidence is becoming distorted: twisted. The facts are that General Fedova went to Petrovka and in front of Investigator Kapitsa, who has still to address this committee, undertook to prevent a prosecution.'

Tudin was floundering. Natalia didn't think she'd won yet, not as absolutely as she intended, but the hostility from the panel wasn't so easy to discern any more. She said: 'The distortion of this matter is not mine. It's that of Colonel Tudin, for the reasons I have already brought before you. I ask you to insist my question is answered.'

'Well?' demanded Lestov, of Eduard.

'Colonel Tudin promised to recommend leniency,' said Eduard, doggedly. 'There was always an understanding between my mother and me prior to any undertaking from Colonel Tudin.'

Natalia risked the silence that lasted until there was a positive shift from the men at the table before saying: 'So what happened to our understanding? Why did you have to wait another six days in custody after I had been to Petrovka before you were released, to come here? Released upon the instructions of Colonel Tudin?'

Before Eduard could respond to a question she didn't want answered anyway — believing her intended effect was best achieved *without* an answer — Natalia sat down. The gesture left her son standing as ineffectually as she wanted him to appear and Tudin having to grope to his feet, to indicate that Eduard's testimony was finished. But Natalia remained ready, believing that the inquiry was swinging in her favour, and when Tudin moved to call the Militia investigator she rose up, stopping him in mid-sentence, asking if she could recall the lawyer. The agreement from Lestov was immediate, which she took to be a good omen.

Alipov rose, as demanded, and Natalia said: 'You were present at Petrovka when the affidavit was taken?'

'Of course. That's why I was there.'

'At that meeting what promise or undertaking was given to Eduard Igorevich Fedova?'

The lawyer hesitated, looking momentarily at Tudin's unresponsive slumped back. Then, visibly, he straightened as someone straightens having made a decision. 'That there would be no prosecution.'

'By whom was that assurance given?'

'Colonel Tudin.'

'Had there at that time — or at any time up until this moment — been any consultation or approval of that amnesty from the Federal Prosecutor?'

'Not as far as I am aware.'

'It was given entirely upon the authority of Colonel Tudin?'

'Yes.'

'Before or after the taking of the affidavit?'

'Before.'

'So the amnesty was an inducement for the testimony?'

Tudin moved to rise, but before he could do so Lestov waved the man down, refusing the interruption.

'I do not believe there would have been a deposition without such a promise,' capitulated the lawyer.

As she sat to end the re-examination, Natalia was sure that at least one person had abandoned Tudin. Surely the investigator would have realized by now which was going to be the winning side and be anxious to join it. All he had to do was tell the truth.

Very soon after Kapitsa began to talk Natalia

decided there *had* been an attempt at a slanted rehearsal but that it was failing because of the Militia investigator's effort to distance himself from this unofficial prosecution which was so obviously going wrong.

Kapitsa's nerves were clearly stretched by his enforced deprivation of nicotine. His hands fluttered in constant movement over the chair-backs and he kept squeezing his eyes shut, in an exaggerated blinking expression. He exposed himself as someone prepared to compromise and bend any legality in a stumbling effort to explain why he had contacted Natalia, openly saying that Eduard — and the men arrested with him — clearly expected Natalia's intercession to block any prosecution. The admission opened the way for Kapitsa to insist that throughout his discussions with Natalia he had always asserted the need for a prosecution.

'Did you expect General Fedova to remove her son from any proceedings?' demanded Tudin.

'I felt I should discuss the matter with her before formulating any charges,' allowed Kapitsa, miserably.

'To what purpose?' pressed Tudin.

'I left General Fedova to decide that.'

'Have you ever brought prosecutions against a high-ranking official — or any member of the family of a high-ranking official — in the State security service?'

'No.'

'Do you expect to?'

Kapitsa looked forlornly towards Natalia. 'No.'

'Did you expect Eduard Igorevich Fedova to be removed from the situation in which he found himself?'

'Yes,' said Kapitsa. His voice was barely above a whisper.

'What, exactly, did General Fedova say to you after she left the detention cell at Petrovka?'

Kapitsa did not reply at once, and Natalia hoped he was searching for the most innocuous remark she might have made.

'That she would be in touch very soon,' he recorded accurately.

It was the ideal moment for Natalia to come into the examination, and she seized it when Tudin sat down, apparently satisfied. 'Did I get in touch with you very quickly?'

'No.'

'Have we met at all from that moment, until today.'

'No.'

It was not Kapitsa's fault he was appearing so ineffectual. It was the fault of a far too recent favour-for-favour system and the blind jealousy of a man like Fyodor Tudin, and of no one being really sure whether Russia was going to go forward into new ways, in all things, or fall backwards into the familiar mire of the past. Natalia felt a surge of sympathy for the man who'd acted in the only manner he knew. She said: 'There was more discussion between us, after I had been to the cells, wasn't there?'

Kapitsa's face furrowed, in the effort for recall. 'Yes.'

'Did I not say that my son's arrest — and the interception of the convoy — had to be handled properly, to everyone's satisfaction?'

Kapitsa nodded, eagerly. 'Yes. And I said that was what I wanted.'

Natalia was glad the man had picked up on her offer, recognizing at the same time how he had sanitized his original reply. 'So we were discussing a prosecution?'

She wondered if Kapitsa's search for a reply she wanted was as obvious to the panel as it was to her. 'Yes. That's what I understood.'

'Did I *ever*, at any time, say or indicate to you that I was going to prevent or stop a prosecution of my son?'

Kapitsa's hesitation was greater than before. 'No.'

'I will not lead you on this question,' warned Natalia. 'I want you to recall, as precisely as possible, the remark my son made about embarrassment.' You're a detective, trained to remember things, thought Natalia: for God's sake remember this!

There was a long silence. The man's hands fluttered for things to do and touch. 'He was talking about telling me your name and position . . .' groped Kapitsa. 'You agreed, when he guessed, that you had a higher rank than the one he knew . . .' The investigator straggled to a halt.

Go on, go on, thought Natalia: she wanted it all. 'Yes?' she encouraged.

'. . . He said something about there being much more openness in Moscow . . .' Kapitsa's face cleared. 'And then he went on that it was very easy for people in important positions to be embarrassed: damaged by embarrassment even . . . and that we didn't want any embarrassment . . .'

Natalia gave no outward signal of her relief. She had to risk leading now, to ensure the man answered correctly. 'Did you interpret that remark as a threat?'

Seizing her guidance, he said: 'Yes. It was clearly that.'

Enough, decided Natalia. She believed she had weakened Tudin's attack sufficiently. Now there had to be the *coup de grâce*. She thanked Kapitsa, dismissing him, but remained standing to avoid losing the momentum. Addressing Lestov, she said: 'If this is the end of what amounts to a prosecution against me, I ask the committee's permission to call evidence of my own.'

'A witness?' queried Lestov.

'The Federal Prosecutor, Petr Borisovich Korolov,' confirmed Natalia, formally. The stir went through everybody in the room.

The publicity over John Gower's arrest was greater in the *People's Daily* than in the Western media — most of the front page was devoted to it, with a government statement about foreign

420

conspiracies and counter-revolutionary crimes published verbatim — so Jeremy Snow learned of the seizure within forty-eight hours of it happening.

The Taoist temple was not named, but the district of Beijing was, which was sufficient for Snow to realize that he had not been abandoned and that an effort was being made to reach him through the prearranged system.

The priest's satisfaction was momentary. Not *was* being, he told himself: *had* been. By someone now in custody. Which left him as stranded as ever. It was obviously pointless — dangerous, in fact — to go anywhere near the shrine again, for any other signal, which he had intended to do that day, maintaining the imposed three-day timetable. Or to any of the message drops, which might have been filled and be waiting for him. And anyone going to the British embassy now would risk automatic association in the minds of the permanently watching Public Security Bureau.

With a stab of helplessness, Snow accepted that he didn't know what to do.

And then, quickly enough for him to have considered it some kind of superior guidance, which he refused to countenance because it would have been an ultimate blasphemy, he did see a way. Partially, perhaps: but still a way. The final inevitable, irrevocable blurring of everything, he recognized at once. So he wouldn't do it: couldn't do it. Not inevitable and therefore not irrevocable.

He couldn't prostitute his faith and its tenets. *Wouldn't* do it.

It would still be a way out, though, partial or not. Once he pacified — perhaps deflected was a better word — Li Dong Ming. He'd try to think of something else: anything else first. Didn't want to sacrifice all integrity.

Appropriately Snow's prayer came from the Book of Lamentations. *Oh Lord,* he thought, *thou hast seen my wrong: judge thou my cause.* Blasphemy, he thought again: therefore utterly *in*appropriate.

Thirty-eight

'You've seen the newspapers? And television?' greeted Patricia Elder. She was not sitting at her desk but standing before the window with its distant view of the Houses of Parliament. She was wearing the high-necked, dark green coat dress she had been wearing the morning Charlie had seen her leaving the Regent's Park penthouse with Miller. It was difficult to imagine her without it, with her legs in the air. But perhaps they didn't do it with her legs in the air. Miller looked a prosaic, missionary-position player.

'Of course,' said Charlie. A time to listen and a time to question, he thought. For the moment, it was the mouth shut, ears open routine, but the question was burning to be asked. What was he doing here on the ninth floor, practically as soon as a crisis had erupted on the other side of the world? Julia didn't know either, not even when he'd arrived minutes earlier. To his enquiring look she'd simply shaken her head. She'd gestured towards the intercom, too, to warn him it was on.

'It's a disaster,' declared Patricia.

How much of a disaster was it being for John Gower? 'I only know what I *have* read in the newspapers,' he prompted.

'We don't know much else. As far as we can gather he was picked up three days ago. The Chinese announcement gave no details apart from the accusation. We aren't being allowed access.'

Was it reassurance she wanted? 'His interrogation resistance was supposed to be good: we touched upon it but not in any situation of duress. Which is the only real test.'

'How long?' she demanded, brutally objective.

Charlie turned down the corners of his mouth. 'Impossible to estimate, without knowing what they're doing to him: without knowing *how* they caught him and if he was doing anything to make his guilt obvious and undermine any denial. The more innocent the circumstances of the seizure the easier, obviously, it'll be for him to hold out.'

'Maximum?' she persisted.

'It's a pointless exercise,' refused Charlie. 'If he feels he can resist because they don't have enough, maybe two weeks. Three at the very outside. If he was compromised at the moment of detention, far less: he might be breaking already . . .' Charlie hesitated. 'I still don't know what he was doing there?' It was a testing invitation, to tell him far more than the simple answer, which he already knew anyway.

Patricia moved away from the window, sitting at last at her desk and looking down at it for several moments, as if reaching a decision. And then she told him, disclosing Jeremy Snow as a priest and talking of the man's refusal to accept he was compromised and of the incriminating

424

photographs. She even identified Li, not simply by his family name but in full, as Li Dong Ming.

Charlie listened intently to every word, analysing every word, unasked queries flooding into his mind, but he was always ahead of what she was saying, the one query above all the others echoing in his head. Why? Why was she giving him details of an active operation he had no right to know about under the compartmenting system by which every intelligence agency operated? It wasn't enough that the person swept up had been someone he'd supposedly trained: not enough by half. So why?

'That's the catastrophe,' the deputy Director concluded.

'Do we know enough to consider it that?'

She frowned at him. 'In the last few months the Chinese have rounded up at least twenty dissidents: it's probably more. One was once Snow's source: perhaps the best one he ever had. How's it going to look with an English Jesuit who's acted for us as a freelance for three years and John Gower, someone officially attached to the British embassy, in the dock there with them?'

'Are you sure it's going to get as bad as that?'

'It can't,' insisted Patricia, autocratically. 'A way has got to be found.'

Now it was Charlie who frowned, wanting the remark straightened out. 'A way has got to be found to do what?'

The deputy Director stood suddenly from her desk, resuming her position in front of the window. 'Gower went to Beijing with instructions to make one last attempt to get the priest out. If Snow went on refusing, he was to be abandoned: he was freelance and deniable. Gower isn't. Any more than William Foster was deniable, which was why we withdrew him, to break the link in the chain to the embassy.'

'Which hasn't, as far as we know, been established yet?' anticipated Charlie. Surely not! he thought: surely he hadn't answered the question about his own future! Hope surged through him.

'Not as far as we know,' she agreed. She looked directly at him.

Charlie looked directly back: this was very definitely not talk time.

She said: 'We hoped for better, from Gower. Your apprentice.'

Bollocks, rejected Charlie: she wasn't going to stick any of this on him. 'You don't know what happened to him yet. *How* it happened.'

'He got arrested. After being trained by you, someone supposed to be so good. Someone who'd never been picked up.'

Bollocks again. 'China is the most difficult country in the world to work in. Always was. Always has been. It shouldn't have been a first assignment: certainly not an assignment where things could go so easily wrong.'

'I've told you how he was specifically ordered to operate. No personal risk. At any time. He screwed up.'

'Inquest thinking,' rejected Charlie. 'I thought

the problem was the immediate future: like the next three weeks, if Gower holds out that long.'

'It is,' Patricia agreed. Her eyes hadn't left him.

'So what are you going to do?'

'Send you in, to prevent a disaster. You're the Never-Been-Caught man whose very first pupil did just that: got caught. Whether he gets twenty years in a Chinese jail depends entirely on preventing any link being established, between Gower and Snow. We were prepared to abandon the damned priest. Now we can't. Your job is to get him out, so the Chinese can't establish any connection. What happens to Gower depends on you.'

He was back! Back and working properly! Reality dampened the euphoria. 'None of this is my responsibility.'

'It's a mess, for you to clear up. Or to keep from becoming a bigger mess than it is.'

Get it official, Charlie told himself. 'Does this mean I'm restored to the active roster?'

Patricia Elder hesitated. 'For the moment.'

Charlie supposed she showed some integrity in being honest. 'On trial?'

'You're being given the opportunity.'

Jesus, he wanted it! All Charlie's regret and nostalgia of the past months concentrated into one consuming awareness that he wanted, under any circumstances or conditions, to become actively operational again. He'd accept the terms, whatever and however they were offered: anything to get back. 'What have you done, already?'

The deputy Director shook her head. 'You're supposed to be the expert. Tell me what *you'd* do. Give me something to put to the embassy.'

Flattering, thought Charlie. 'According to the embassy, Gower left everything in the security vault?'

'It's one of the straws we're clutching, that there was nothing incriminating on him when he was picked up.'

'Authorize my access to it: I'll probably still need the photographs. Advise them of my arrival, with a request for every possible facility, as and when I call upon it.'

'They won't agree to that sort of *carte blanche:* not the embassy nor the Foreign Office here. They just won't like it.'

'They'll like a bloody sight less a full-scale trial of Britons in the dock of a Chinese court: they haven't got any choice but to help.'

'I'll try,' promised the woman, doubtfully.

'And announce through the Foreign Office the intention to send out an official, to enforce the protests of Gower's innocence. There'll have to be a visa application, too: to provide them with a name.'

'What?' From her window-ledge vantage point the deputy Director was looking at him in head-tilted surprise. 'But that . . .'

'. . . will give them someone to look out for,' completed Charlie. 'It won't be me.'

The woman came back to her desk but did not immediately sit at it. Instead, shaking her head, she leaned across to face him. 'I'm not sure I'm following you here.'

Charlie smiled. 'I don't want anybody to.'

'I want more than that.' Patricia sat, slowly.

'If the Foreign Office will agree, make it one of their own men. A lawyer would be the obvious choice. Let him work with the legal representative in Beijing, then pull him out.'

The head-shaking refusal grew. 'You *must* have embassy cover: diplomatic protection.'

'Like Gower did!'

'That's a cheap shot, which doesn't get us anywhere,' rejected Patricia. 'From what we're getting from Beijing, there was nothing the embassy *could* have done. But at least, for Gower, we can mount every diplomatic protest *because* he was accredited. There's no question of your going there as a loose cannon: it's absolutely out of the question.'

'The embassy is what they'll be watching!' argued Charlie. 'If you link me to it in a visa application you'll alert the Chinese I'm coming. And so soon after Gower's seizure, the connection is inevitable.'

'It's a point,' she conceded, with seeming reluctance.

'Just allow me a few days, without provable links to the embassy: as a tourist. Tell the embassy I'll present myself, when it's necessary. But nothing radioed or wired. Everything by pouch.'

'You think our cipher's insecure!'

Charlie sighed. 'Everyone's cipher is insecure. Use the diplomatic bag. Please!'

'There's no reason why it shouldn't be done that way,' she agreed, in further concession.

'I'll want to look at the duplicate prints of all that Snow photographed, along with the rest of the file. And see Foster.'

'What for?'

'I don't know, not until I've talked to him,' said Charlie, matching her awkwardness. 'There's no reason why I shouldn't see him, is there?'

'If he'd done the job properly, we wouldn't have this crisis,' said Patricia, bitterly.

'I don't want to learn his mistakes,' said Charlie. 'I want to know how to avoid them.'

She hesitated, momentarily. 'You should know that Foster's finished, because of this. He'll be retained but never given any responsibility again.'

'Better not appoint him a special, end-of-course instructor of how to survive,' said Charlie.

The cynicism went badly wrong. 'We didn't choose very well last time, did we?' she said, sourly.

Charlie decided, impatiently, that this was childish, yah-boo stuff. He regretted starting it in the first place. 'Gower had a fiancée. Marcia. I don't have a surname. She's been on television and in the papers.'

'So?' frowned the woman.

'She'll be as frightened as hell. Not know what's going on.'

The frown remained. 'You think she should be told?'

Now she was initiating the childlike remarks.

'I think when she tries to find out she shouldn't be fobbed off by some metal-voiced Foreign Office robot with the usual load of bollocks. But convinced as much as possible that everything is being done to help the man she thought she was going to marry!' said Charlie, irritated.

The smile was brief but with neither humour nor sympathy. 'Didn't you tell me once that you'd never let any personal feelings intrude?'

Bugger her, thought Charlie. 'Gower might appreciate it. He's probably doing his best for you at the moment.'

'Let's hope it's better than he's done so far.'

'How did it go?' demanded Peter Miller.

'He practically bit my hand off,' said Patricia. She'd gone immediately next door after Charlie Muffin's departure, nervously surprised there'd been nothing from Miller *before* the encounter. The previous night Ann had been due at the Regent's Park penthouse, her first visit since they'd spent the week there together.

'Nothing you didn't expect?' The voice, as usual, was blandly neutral.

Patricia didn't respond at once, although the hesitation was not to consider the question. She shouldn't show any expectation: certainly not apprehension. 'Not really, although he wasn't quite as overwhelmed as I thought he would have been. Very quickly began making demands.'

'Difficult ones?'

She forced a smile. He should have said something by now! Miller didn't smile back. 'He wants to avoid the embassy at the beginning. And he asked for a decoy to be sent.'

'What did you say?'

Maybe his wife hadn't come after all. Or maybe — although hard to believe — the perfume hadn't been discovered yet. Against which was the fact that he hadn't made any move to kiss her, which he normally did, when they met for the first time in the day. She desperately wished now that she hadn't left the bottle: taken the risk. 'Agreed to his being solo, at first. Left the decoy idea for us to think about.'

'It's not a bad idea.'

When was he going to talk about something other than about this damned assignment interview, which he should know without asking would have gone quite satisfactorily? 'He wants to talk to Foster.'

The Director-General came forward over his desk, hands steepled before him. 'What did you say to that?'

'Agreed. What else?' Was she imagining the brittleness in his voice? Why had she done it?

Miller nodded. 'No reason why he shouldn't, I suppose.'

'Every reason why he *should:* it's an obvious thing to do.'

'You tell him we're sidelining Foster?'

The perfume couldn't have been found yet: that was the only explanation. She nodded to the question. 'There were some wisecracks: except they weren't very wise. He made himself look stupid. And realized it, too.'

'That's a word that's been in my mind overnight,' said Miller.

Patricia looked at him, in apparent incomprehension. At last! 'What word?'

'Stupid.'

'I don't understand.' She wished he hadn't called it that, although she supposed that was how it would have seemed.

Without taking his eyes from her, Miller reached sideways into a drawer. He lifted out the half-used bottle of Chanel and placed it on the desk between them. 'Yours.' It was an announcement, not a question.

Patricia, who believed she'd prepared herself for whatever he might say but now wasn't sure, about anything, half lifted and then dropped her hands, in a gesture of helplessness, and said: 'Yes, but . . . I don't . . . where . . . ?'

'On Ann's dressing-table.'

'That's not possible! I tidied everywhere!'

'Right in the very middle of Ann's things. As if it had been placed there.'

'That's not right . . . I mean I'm not saying it wasn't there . . . what I'm saying is I *couldn't* have left it . . . I'm sure I couldn't . . .'

'Didn't you miss it?'

Her hands rose and fell again. 'No. It's not the only bottle I have . . . another at Chiswick . . . it just never arose . . .'

Miller looked steadily, blankly, over the desk.

Say something! she thought. Say something, please, something I want so much to hear: shout even, if you're angry, although you never shout, no matter how enraged you get, do you? When he still didn't speak, she said: 'Was it bad when she found it?'

'She didn't find it,' announced the man, calmly. 'I did.'

No! The failure wailed so despairingly through Patricia's mind it was as if she could hear her own voice moaning it. The smile was practically impossible, like what she had to say. 'Thank God!'

'I always check, after we've been there. Before Ann comes.'

'Always?' It was right that she should show some affront.

'Always,' he echoed.

'What does that mean?' she demanded, disappointment fuelling the annoyance. 'That you don't trust me?'

'It means I'm extremely careful. Fortunately.'

'Would it have been so bad if Ann had found it?' Wrong! The word, a warning this time, reverberated through her mind like the earlier despair. She knew it could harden any suspicion he might have, but at the same time she wasn't sorry she'd said it, either.

'Did you intentionally leave it, Patricia?' There was no anger in his voice: no emotion in the way he was speaking at all, which she found more unsettling than if he'd raged at her.

'NO!' She knew she was reddening but that

didn't matter because it could have been in anger at the accusation. 'How can you ask me a question like that?'

'It seems perfectly valid, to me.'

'I don't think so! I thought there was trust between us. Love, too. Maybe I was wrong.' Patricia realized she was coming dangerously close to the edge, confronting him more forcefully than ever before. And he'd avoided her question, as he always avoided her question.

'This isn't the way Ann is going to be told.'

'How is it going to be?' she demanded, not able to hold her anger. Why? Why did he have to be so bloody careful! Why couldn't the precious, cosseted, protected Lady Ann have been the one to find it?

'Properly. Calmly. With my telling her.' The voice droned, the man utterly in control of himself and his feelings.

'After the boys finish at university! Or has some other schedule arisen I don't know about yet?'

'You're putting a strain on things, Patricia.'

'Is that a threat?' Of course it was! Back off: she had to back off! She couldn't risk losing him!

He shook his head. 'A statement of the obvious.'

Oh no! He wasn't ending it: surely he wasn't doing that! The fear surged through her, far worse than the despair and disappointment and anger, so that she felt physically sick. Don't let him end it! She didn't have anyone else: any chance or hope of anyone else. She'd trusted him, relied upon him: given up other friendships that might have led to something. What little she had of Peter Miller was *all* she had, of anyone. 'It was a mistake, the perfume. I honestly didn't realize I'd left it. I'm sorry. And glad it hasn't caused the upset it could have done.'

Miller pushed the bottle further towards her, across the table. At last he smiled. 'You'd better take it, hadn't you?'

Patricia did so, slipping it into her pocket to conceal it as she went between their two offices. It bulged, too noticeably, so she took it out again, covering it in her hand.

'Let's do it my way,' he said.

'All right.' Which was how they'd always done everything. His way. To his convenience. And always would, she supposed, miserably.

Thirty-nine

They reconvened within twenty-four hours. Natalia guessed the delay would have been much longer but for Vadim Lestov's previous role as Interior Minister, to whom the Federal Prosecutor had been responsible and with whom a known friendship had gone beyond officialdom, so that favours could be demanded and met.

Natalia entered the inquiry room on the second day feeling none of the uncertainty of the first occasion. She got there early but Tudin, the lawyer and her son were already ahead of her.

Petr Korolov came in with the three-man committee, a permitted gesture to make clear his equal stature. Korolov, whom she had met on only two other occasions, lowered himself on the front row but not immediately beside her. He looked at her, though, briefly smiling. He was a plump, shiny-faced, balding man corseted in an ill-fitting, waistcoated suit, the sleeves and trousers too long, so that they bagged at wrist and ankle.

'This examination will be concluded today,' declared Lestov.

So there had been some ante-room discussion, Natalia realized. She hoped it hadn't been too much, robbing her of her intended grand finale. She didn't want to be denied her moment: the vindication she had groped towards — fought blindly for and desperately for — until just a few hours earlier, never properly knowing what was being done to undermine her: to destroy her. Her and Sasha.

Natalia rose, regretting the dip of uncertainty because now there could be nothing to feel uncertain about. She attacked hard and at once. She reminded the inquiry of her original examination of Fyodor Tudin, to establish the responsibility she had given him to organize a service in the republics that he'd so miserably failed to fulfil. She denounced him as an internal, corrosive schemer, doing nothing to protect the newly constituted agency but everything to damage it. She called him a liar, turning to hurl the word at him. And insisted he'd twisted those lies to deceive the tribunal he himself had caused to be convened.

Korolov rose dutifully when asked, faintly smiling at the affectation of the proceedings. For the records, she went through the routine of establishing Korolov's name and authority. From her briefcase she extracted the first of her limited documentation.

She walked the few paces separating them and said: 'Do you recognize this?'

Korolov examined it before nodding. 'It is a memorandum I received from you.'

'It is dated? Timed?'

'It is dated the eighteenth. Timed at six-fifteen that evening.'

'What is the subject of the memorandum?'

'The arrest of your son, by the Organized Crime Bureau of the Militia.'

'*I* identified him as my son. Fully disclosed to you my relationship, at that time?'

'Yes.'

'Does that memorandum make any request for special or favoured treatment from your department towards my son?'

'On the contrary.'

'Would you explain that?'

Korolov went to the paper he still held. Quoting, he read: ' "I expect the full authority and punishment of the law to be exercised." '

There was movement from behind her, from where her son sat and then the hissed word: 'Bitch!' It was Eduard's voice. Natalia was glad it had been loud enough for everyone to hear.

'Is there, in that original memorandum, a request for a meeting between us?'

'Yes.' Korolov was relaxed, enjoying a cross-examination he imagined to be amateur but which came, in fact, from someone trained to be a more professional interrogator than any qualified lawyer in his department.

The faint condescension didn't upset Natalia. Charlie had always preached the benefit of being underestimated: it had perhaps been Fyodor Tudin's most serious failing.

'Is there a reason for the suggested meeting?'

'Yes.'

'What?'

Again Korolov went to the paper in his hand.

'A proposed discussion between prosecutors and investigators in my department with officers of the internal security agency to form a combined task force to combat the rise in organized crime in the Russian Federation.'

'Did I give any personal undertaking?'

'To make the same proposal to the chairman of your agency, for his approval, and to the appropriate officials of the agency's internal directorates, if that approval is granted.'

'Have you . . .' began Natalia, but Lestov cut her off.

'. . . Enough!' declared the agency chairman. 'This inquiry is over!'

So great was Natalia's disappointment that she practically blurted out a protest, stopping herself just in time. There was so much more she had wanted to get on the record: she felt robbed, cheated. She'd still won, she realized. She wished there was a greater feeling of satisfaction.

'Tudin wanted too much,' decided Lestov. 'If he'd put things before internal security, I would have probably had to find against you, without a hearing. That was his mistake: demanding an inquiry before which you could publicly destroy his case.'

'I had written to the Federal Prosecutor,' reminded Natalia. She had expected a personal meeting, but not for it to be so immediate, the same afternoon.

'Yes you had, hadn't you?' picked up the security chief. 'But not to me?' There was no positive suspicion in the man's voice, but Natalia thought there was a discernible reserve in his attitude.

'I wanted to get the opinion of the Federal Prosecutor, before raising it with you. If he had not been enthusiastic, there would have been no point,' said Natalia, easily.

'You had no suspicion what Tudin was doing?'

'None,' said Natalia, easily again.

'Some legal charges could be formulated against him.'

'Would it be wise, opening it all up to public debate in a court? I would have thought dismissal is sufficient.'

Lestov nodded. 'Perhaps you're right.' The chairman paused and then said: 'I'm going to liaise personally with Korolov about a task force. It is a good idea. Commendable, considering the personal circumstances.'

'I considered it my duty,' said Natalia, unembarrassed.

Lestov smiled, at last. It was still a brief expression. 'I really am most impressed at how you have reorganized your directorate. It's unfortunate this business had to arise.'

'It's resolved now. Very satisfactorily.'

'I would, in future, like copies of any communication *before* you send them to outside ministries.'

'Of course.'

'You have my sympathy, about your son.'

'We really have been apart for a very long time. There is nothing left between us.' *Adulterated drugs sometimes maim and kill*, she remembered.

Later, at the apartment in Leninskaya, Natalia rocked Sasha back and forth and said: 'We won, darling. We're safe.' She would have liked to have told somebody properly about it: been able to boast. To someone like Charlie, for instance.

With the pressure of Tudin finally removed she could think about Charlie again. She would have to take a holiday. She couldn't do what she intended from Moscow.

One of the most important strands of the safety net which Charlie Muffin always tried to have beneath him when he was working was the fullest knowledge possible before taking the first step forward, so he was glad of the delay on the visa application. He spent the entire day following his briefing from Patricia Elder studying the Beijing files, working from before Foster's appointment or even Snow's arrival through until the most recent folder. That folder contained duplicates of the incriminating photographs, as well as several of Li Dong Ming. Charlie thought the Chinese looked quite a pleasant-faced man. But then so had some photographs of Hitler and Stalin.

Charlie had finished his reading and was sitting in deep contemplation when Walter Foster entered, looking around in obvious and immediate disappointment. 'I was hoping this would be about a new assignment but it isn't, is it?'

'Afraid not,' said Charlie. 'But I know how you feel.'

'Have they got Snow yet?'

'I don't know.'

'They will. The man was an idiot.'

'Tell me about him. *Everything* about him.'

Foster frowned. 'There's not going to be *another* attempt to get him out?'

'I wouldn't have thought so,' avoided Charlie, smoothly. 'Far too dangerous. I've just got to write one of those reports: you know how bureaucratic everything is.'

'It's going to end in disaster,' insisted Foster.

'I hope not,' said Charlie, mildly. It really was time people thought of a different way to describe what the outcome was going to be.

Forty

It did not take Charlie long to form an opinion about Walter Foster and it confused him, as quite a lot in the files and records had confused him. Despite insisting that he wanted every detail — he actually used the word debriefing — Charlie had constantly to interrupt the former liaison man to clarify or bring out points Foster seemed to consider unimportant: it quickly became an account to justify himself. The priest, Charlie decided, had been handled very badly. Which added further to the confusion.

'You dictated the contact procedure?' queried Charlie.

'Not me,' said Foster, instantly defensive. 'London's orders. Standard stuff: the usual separation from the embassy.'

'Couldn't you have adjusted it?' Charlie wondered if that was what Gower had tried to do.

'Snow wanted too much: virtually meetings every week. That would have been dangerous.'

'Your decision?'

'Following orders.'

'How often *did* you meet?'

'Regularly enough, when there were things at the embassy that the British community came to. And then when we needed to, just the two of us.'

'How often were the embassy occasions?' persisted Charlie.

Foster shrugged. 'Once a month, I suppose. Sometimes a little longer. That was the benefit of how we worked: there wasn't a pattern that could be identified.'

'Why couldn't you meet Snow as often as the man wanted?'

'For *exactly* the objection I've just told you!' insisted Foster, indignantly. 'It would have created a pattern that could have been picked up.'

'Snow's not well?'

'He suffers from asthma,' qualified Foster.

'Badly?'

'Sometimes.'

'Wouldn't it have been the perfect way for Snow to have met you whenever he liked, coming to the embassy for medication or to see the resident doctor?'

From the surprise obvious on Foster's face, Charlie guessed the opportunity hadn't occurred to the other man.

'The instructions were always that there had to be no provable embassy link. That was always how I had to work.'

'How did you feel about him, personally?' Charlie was curious how Foster would explain the breakdown between himself and the priest.

The man coloured slightly, heightening the sandstorm of freckles. 'He was arrogant.'

'So you didn't get on?'

'That's not important.'

'I would have thought it was, in a place like Beijing.'

'We had a working relationship. It was satisfactory.'

It very definitely hadn't been, thought Charlie. It had been obvious that he should talk to the man who had been the priest's Control, but he wasn't learning at all what he'd expected. He wasn't sure, at that moment, exactly what he *was* learning. 'How were things between Snow and the other priest, Father Robertson?'

Foster shrugged again. 'Not particularly good, I don't think. Robertson was very worried about upsetting the Chinese and getting the mission closed down.'

Charlie frowned. 'Snow told you that?'

'Several times. He called Robertson an old woman.'

'What did you think of him?'

'I only met him a few times, at embassy things. He seemed nervous but I always thought that was understandable, after being jailed like he was.'

'Did he talk about that?'

'Not to me. It was something we all knew about, at the embassy. It made him kind of a celebrity.'

They didn't know yet how Gower had *been* arrested, Charlie remembered. 'Apart from the occasions when he could visit the embassy for some event, you always signalled Snow for a meeting? Or he signalled you?'

The other man nodded. 'Usually he signalled me. Like I said, he wanted too much contact.'

446

'You always met in public places? Never went to the mission?'

'Never!' Foster seemed appalled at the suggestion.

'You read about Gower's arrest?'

Foster nodded. 'I guessed he was ours.'

'I was wondering if he tried to do things differently from you. Tried to make a direct approach.'

'If he'd done that, they'd have picked up Snow as well, wouldn't they?'

Charlie nodded. 'I suppose you're right.'

'None of this would have happened if he'd done what I told him.'

'I thought there was some problem about leaving without his Order's authority.'

'An excuse, that's all,' insisted Foster. 'He wouldn't listen.'

'It can't have been easy.'

'Beijing isn't easy. People don't realize.'

'That's true,' sympathized Charlie. 'People never do.'

'I hope I've helped.'

'You have,' assured Charlie. 'A lot.'

'You're sure you haven't heard where my next posting is to be?'

'Sorry,' said Charlie.

'I didn't like Beijing very much.'

'I guessed,' said Charlie. 'It's all behind you now.'

'Thank God.'

Why was it, wondered Charlie, that things

dumped upon him so often didn't make any sense at all?

Julia had said she did not want to eat out, so she cooked at home, and Charlie quickly decided it was a mistake for him to have accepted. He tried very hard but she barely responded to anything he said. She pushed her plate away virtually untouched.

'This isn't exactly the last supper!' he protested, still trying.

'I don't think that's funny.' It had been Julia who'd returned his visaed passport and given him the plane tickets for the following day.

In view of the situation, Charlie had half expected a final briefing from Patricia Elder or even the Director-General himself, although he supposed there wasn't anything further for them to talk about. 'I'll be all right.' Julia's concern unsettled him.

'Gower's fiancée was on television before you got here. She looked dreadful.'

'Gower wanted me to meet her. I didn't.'

Julia nodded, not needing an explanation. 'The deputy Director has tried to get her treated properly, at the Foreign Office. That's why she was on television: going in to see one of the permanent secretaries.'

So Patricia Elder wasn't an ogress who used razorblades for tampons after all. 'That's considerate.'

'Won't do much to help, though, will it?'

'Still nothing on Snow? Or access to Gower?' He supposed he would have been told, but he'd known of worse oversights, in the past.

She shook her head. 'There was a request to the Foreign Office, to send a lawyer out to help. They refused.'

Drawbridges being raised, portcullises slammed down, recognized Charlie: he always had regarded that message about assistance and protection in the front of his passport as a load of bullshit. 'There's probably not a lot he could have done, in any practical sense.' Except hopefully put up a faint smoke-screen for him.

'For Christ's sake be careful, Charlie.'

'Always.'

'I mean it!'

'So do I.' The early flight the following morning gave him an excuse to leave: he was certainly anxious to get away from the awkwardness. 'I think I should be going.'

'If you want . . .' Julia started, then stopped.

'What?' asked Charlie, more unsettled than ever.

'Nothing.'

He was very glad she hadn't continued: Charlie didn't want anything to go beyond the stage of being platonic. He was comfortable at that level. Not at many others.

'Just don't take any chances,' she pleaded.

'I see them, I avoid them,' promised Charlie. Or sometimes turn them to my advantage, he thought, when he arrived in Beijing less than

449

twenty-four hours later, although not on the aircraft for which Julia had given him a ticket but on a Pakistani flight to which he'd changed at London airport.

He assimilated himself among the confusion of an organized tour group, staying close through the baggage collection and the straggling exit of overtired, overawed people as they crocodiled across the concourse to the waiting coach. Only then did he detach himself towards the taxis, but the tour guide, who wore an identifying armband and a lapel badge naming him as Peter, said: 'Visiting by yourself?'

'Yes,' said Charlie.

'We'll give you a lift in, if you like: there's plenty of room on the coach.'

'That's very kind of you,' accepted Charlie. He hoped his luck continued like this: it was long overdue.

Forty-one

The tactics changed, which was predictable, so Gower was able to hold the fear off and retain the disguised resistance to appear an innocent man. The possibility of Chen realizing that he *was* resisting them — and by so doing showing the professional training that would confirm their accusations — became a greater concern than anything they did in their efforts to break him.

Having announced their intention to set the trap at the Taoist shrine, they left him absolutely alone for what Gower estimated to be a full day and a night, broken only once by another delivery of foul and discreetly discarded food by the same bowed old man and his two army guards. And in contrast to his first day of imprisonment, there was absolute and echoing silence, so there was not the slightest distraction or interruption to his imagination conjuring the apprehension of what would happen to him if they did make another arrest. Gower refused himself any false assurances. If Snow was detained, simply by the suspicion of being a Caucasian near the Taoist temple, he *would* be lost. If it happened — if he was confronted by proof that the priest was arrested and had broken and had identified the shrine and the flower signal — then he was in a new and far more dangerous situation which he would have to handle when it arose. But not before. He refused to let his imagination do their job for them.

The silent treatment was actually counter-productive, and while recognizing its intention Gower was surprised by it, seizing the advantage properly to rest and push back as far as he could the effect of sleep deprivation. He did so now stretched full-length on the concrete ledge, for any observation through the Judas-hole, because that was how an innocent man, recovering slightly from the initial shock of detention, would try to sleep. It was still rigidly uncomfortable but he'd largely adjusted to the stink of the lavatory hole and the uniform he was forced to wear. There were occasions when he fully lost consciousness, and for the rest of the time he slept more deeply than when he had squatted, that first day, but there was practically always the vague subconscious awareness of everything around him. He came, for instance, quickly awake at the scratching.

One rat was already out of the toilet hole, easily climbing the table leg to forage along its top where any spilled or dropped food scraps would have been: the second was sniffing its way out, briefly disturbing the irritated flies. It followed the obviously familiar route, scuttling quickly up to join the first.

Gower remained lying as he was, making himself watch and accept, refusing the revulsion at the actual sight of what he'd already known to exist within the hole. The rats were brown and plump and their fur had a sheen of cleanliness he didn't expect from the imagined slime from which they had emerged. He wondered if these were the only two or whether there were more. Probably more. Probably a whole colony. He distantly remembered hearing or reading that rats always existed in colonies: he'd have to be particularly careful to keep his hands from coming into any contact with the tabletop over which they would have trailed their infections.

With his watch taken from him, denied any natural light and having slept for intermittent periods, Gower was unable to judge whether it was day or night when the peep-hole disturbance began again, which worried him, because losing track of time was a footstep on the way to disorientation. His concern was brief because Gower knew he could establish a rough schedule from the moment of his next interrogation.

The next meal was noodles, which were sour and which Gower guessed really did have maggots in them, from the shifting movement under the surface pasta strands that had nothing to do with the mucus-like soup in which they floated. The observation hole scraped open, so again Gower went through the eating and drinking pretence, his back to the person watching. He reset his mental clock to gauge the intervals between the apparently resumed inspections, to dispose of the entire contents of the bowl.

Not eating wasn't a risk to Gower's opposition:

wouldn't be for a very long time. He knew the human body could go for weeks without nourishment, before the hallucinations began. And so far he had not felt the slightest hunger.

Water was the problem. The effect of dehydration was far quicker, destabilizing in a matter of days. Already his mouth felt completely dry, very little saliva forming when he tried to generate it, and there was a scratchiness in his throat when he swallowed, which he tried to avoid as much as possible.

Gower supposed it would have been sometime during the third day — or maybe the third night — when he was finally forced to take the fetid water, unable to deprive himself any longer. He did not fully drink it. He took a minimal amount, four sips, flushing it around his mouth before spitting it disgustedly into the hole. The relief was very brief: his throat remained scratchy.

If he did develop diarrhoea he would quickly become even more dehydrated, Gower knew. And need to take even more of the water, which would worsen the infection and tighten the circle of demeaning, eroding illness.

Dear God let something, anything, happen soon! Horrified, Gower checked the thought. That was despair. And despair went with fear. He wasn't entirely successful in controlling it. Surely, he continued to think, somebody had to be doing something by now!

Snow felt he had exhausted all the prayers of

which he was capable, agonized by the immediate blasphemy of a priest ever exhausting the capacity to pray. Finally, as he'd always known he would, which wove thorns into the guilt, Snow went to the mission chief, appalled at his own hypocrisy.

'Father,' he said. 'Would you please hear my confession?'

Forty-two

The dust fell about him when Snow parted the curtains, filling his throat and mouth and banding his chest more tightly. The slide of the dividing grille jammed when Father Robertson initially tried to draw it back, never quite fully opening the space between them.

'Forgive me Father, for I have sinned. For these and all my other sins that I cannot remember I humbly ask forgiveness.' Even the rote of the beginning was difficult. The dust seemed to be blocking the way to his lungs and his chest positively ached, but Snow knew the agony had nothing to do with any of it, solely caused by the enormity of what he was doing.

'Go on,' urged Robertson, when Snow did not continue after several moments.

It was still some further time before Snow could speak and then, initially, the words were badly chosen and disjointed, sentences half finished, the worst parts of all delivered scarcely beyond a whisper.

But Snow told it all, in every detail. He fought against the wheezing breathlessness to force himself to talk and had a greater, choking struggle to keep Father Robertson listening in the linked cubicle. The older priest positively tried to stop the admission, of everything, protesting he would hear no more and scuffling to his feet, so that Snow had to break the ritual — as Father Robertson was breaking the ritual — and insist, over and over again, his mouth tight against the grille, that Father Robertson's vows made it impossible for the man to refuse to let him finish.

'Men have confessed to murder in a confessional and been heard!'

'Continue.' Father Robertson's voice was strained tight, as if he were having as much difficulty to speak as the younger priest.

Snow talked on, but Father Robertson heard the last few minutes in such utter silence that Snow thought at one stage that the man had slipped out anyway. Then, almost imperceptibly, he detected the faintest sound: short, sharp intakes of breath, a man gasping.

The continuing silence, when Snow finished, was absolute. Snow waited a very long time before speaking further. 'I seek absolution.'

'No! This is a travesty! Obscene!'

'I demand absolution.'

'Absolution is for the repentant. Are you repentant?'

He wasn't, not at all, Snow accepted: what he'd done was right. What he was doing now was a sin greater than any he had committed outside this dust-swirled box. For this he would be damned. 'I am repentant.'

'I will not give you absolution!'

It didn't matter, accepted Snow, sadly. The old

man had been right. What he had done that morning was a travesty and it *was* obscene, and the point had not been to seek forgiveness. This moment, Snow supposed, marked his failure as a priest. But what about as a Jesuit, a Soldier of Christ? He didn't think he had the intellect or the theological philosophy to answer that question. That was a question to be put to other priests and other judges far away from Beijing, before whom he accepted he would have to place himself.

He heard the swish of the curtain pulled back in the other stall and smelled the dust driven through the lattice. He followed more slowly, so that Father Robertson was already some way across the nave when Snow emerged. Snow followed, more slowly: only when he neared the end of the walkway connecting the church to their living quarters, coming close to the room in which Father Robertson normally worked, did Snow become concerned that the older man might have gone out into the city.

He hadn't.

Father Robertson was at his desk, bent slightly forward as he had when he was ill, and tremors were vibrating through him as they had then. Snow's renewed concern was that the mission chief was suffering another collapse. He remained uncertainly at the door. Finally Father Robertson straightened, looking up at him. The man's eyes were wet and red-rimmed, like the eyes of a person who had been crying.

'Do you know what you have done?'

'What is talked about in the confessional is sacrosanct.' Snow wanted Father Robertson to know and to think about it, but never to talk about it. Which he couldn't.

'You dare lecture me on ritual!'

'I did not wish — *do* not wish — to endanger the mission.'

'You have! You know you have! This Englishman who's been arrested! He's all part of it, isn't he?'

'I don't know. I think so.'

A shudder worse than the others went through the old man. 'Lost. Everything could be lost.'

'I was told to get out,' disclosed Snow.

The rheumy eyes came up to him. 'When?'

'Soon after Li began taking an interest.'

'Does he have something incriminating to put against you?'

'Possibly.'

'Does he?' Father Robertson's voice creaked, so it didn't come out as the intended shout of anger.

'Yes.'

'Terrible. This is absolutely terrible.'

'I could not have left without permission from the Curia, in Rome.'

Father Robertson looked directly at him again, one hand gripping the other, physically clutching himself for control. 'That is true,' he agreed, but doubtfully, more curiosity than anger in his voice.

Snow hesitated. 'In exceptional circumstances,

a head of mission in our Order could grant such dispensation.'

Father Robertson became suddenly and completely still, all the shaking gone, face suffused in livid outrage. 'You *bastard!* You absolute and utter *bastard!*'

Snow hadn't imagined such an outburst — he hadn't imagined anything — but he accepted at once that it was true, that he was a bastard. He was surprised Father Robertson was so quickly realizing, in its entirety, what he had done. 'I'm sorry.'

'You're not! There's no contrition: that's why I wouldn't grant you absolution . . .' The old man stopped, mouth slightly apart at a further awareness. 'You weren't even seeking absolution, were you?' He paused, momentarily beyond speech. 'I'll inform the Curia! See to it that you are dismissed the Order you are disgracing.'

'What is talked about in the confessional is sacrosanct,' repeated Snow, quietly.

Father Robertson's mouth gaped fully, in complete comprehension. 'You've actually *abused* it, to save yourself! Knowing I can't bring any complaint against you because of how I learned what you've done: what you are! You are beyond belief . . .' The priest twisted his own word. 'You can't believe, to behave like this!'

'I am prepared to face the judgement of our superiors. To explain myself, *my* way. Not have a case presented for me: against me.' Snow was hating the confrontation: hating himself. Despis-

460

ing what he'd done and how he'd done it, unable to find any vindication, any excuse. A man was suffering unspeakable horrors because of him: the Jesuit mission in Beijing was endangered because of him. And all he could think of doing was to run away, like a coward. But wasn't that the mitigating factor, the only thing he *could* do? Without him there would be no corroborated case against the arrested Englishman. Who would have to be released, eventually. And just as the man's safety depended upon his getting out of the country, so did the continuing existence of Father Robertson's precious mission. So he was not acting cowardly — he was not ceasing to be a Soldier of Christ — by running. It was an act to save others first, himself very much last.

'Get out!' rejected Father Robertson. 'Out of Beijing as soon as possible! Go to Rome. You need help: a great deal of help. You're surely going to strain God's compassion.'

'You will inform the Curia of my permission to travel?'

'Go!' repeated Father Robertson, exasperated.

'Li is demanding something: some photographs. I do not believe I will be allowed to leave until I pass them over.'

Father Robertson shook his head, a man pummelled with too much, too quickly. 'Give them to him!'

'I do not have them, not yet.'

The elderly man shook his head, wearily. 'I do not understand. Do not *want* to understand.

All I want is for you to go. Please go.'

'As soon as I find a way,' promised Snow. But who was there to show him?

'So he *is* a spy?' demanded Patrick Plowright.

'He came to clear up some sort of mess, after that bloody man Foster. I've no idea what,' confirmed Samuels. The feet of the diminutive embassy lawyer sitting opposite only touched the floor when the man stretched his toes, to make contact. Samuels tried to avoid obviously looking at them.

'Still nothing on access?'

The political officer shook his head. 'The ambassador has delivered three Notes, so far. The same number have been given to their ambassador in London.'

'What's the next step?'

Samuels looked uncomfortable. 'Someone else is coming in.'

'What!'

'I know. It's appalling, isn't it?'

'When's he arrive?'

Samuels shrugged, realizing he was looking at the tiptoe difficulty of the other man and hurriedly averting his eyes. 'He wasn't on the plane we'd been told to expect. We've asked London what's happened.'

'Surely there's something else we can do about Gower! Something practical?'

'As a gesture of protest, Sir Timothy could be recalled to London. But that would blow up badly in our faces if the Chinese *proved* espionage.'

'Which still has to be denied?'

'Emphatically.'

'It's ridiculous!'

'Of course it is. Sir Timothy is privately making the strongest protest imaginable to London.'

'I thought all this spying nonsense was a thing of the past.'

'I only wish it had been.'

'What's this new person going to do?'

'God only knows.'

Charlie believed he'd moved around like a blue-assed fly, although making less noise. And achieved some early, possibly useful impressions.

He was pleased with the Hsin Chiao, a hotel reserved for Western tourists among whom he could merge and become lost. The reception desk wouldn't let him have their only street map, so he had to memorize the position of the British embassy, which was marked, against the district containing the mission, which wasn't. He studied a separate map, listing in English the numbers and routes of the buses, which looked comparatively convenient but which he guessed wouldn't be. They weren't. It meant a lot of walking.

Charlie went close enough to the embassy on Guang Hua Lu to fix it in his mind but not close enough for him to become identified with it. He didn't try directly to approach the mission, either. Instead he circled where he knew it to be, always keeping a street distance away, until he found the logical main road leading away from it. There was a convenient park, where he remained for an hour, and a stall market in front of several shops, where he immersed himself for slightly longer. He identified two cars that made more than one journey up and down. One stopped within sight of Charlie, so he was able to see the two men who got out. And then he recognized Father Robertson from the photographs he'd studied in London. The priest strode from the direction of the mission remarkably quickly for a man of his age, and with purpose, as if he were keeping an appointment. Charlie was still in the final shop, supposedly looking at bolts of silk, when he saw Father Robertson returning. It was automatic for Charlie to check the timing: the mission chief had been away an hour. Seeing Father Robertson was a plus he hadn't expected: it was too much to hope that Father Snow might use the approach road. Charlie still lingered, but the younger priest didn't appear. Charlie wouldn't have approached him, if he had.

Charlie had to walk much further than he anticipated, to get to the bus-stop. And then had to stand for almost forty-five minutes, because the first bus was filled. By the time he got back to the hotel his feet were on fire. It was just his shitty luck, he thought, to be in the land of The Long March.

Forty-three

With convoluted but personally adjusted logic, Charlie decided early the next day that what he had to do was comparatively simple because it was so difficult. Impossible, in fact, without unacceptable risks. And Charlie Muffin never took unacceptable risks.

Had Gower? There could be a logic to that, too: an over-ambitious officer on his first foreign assignment, taking too few precautions in an eagerness to prove himself. Charlie wouldn't have thought Gower would do that. But the further, unarguable logic was that John Gower *had* done something wrong. And was now in jail because of it. Not just Gower's failure, Charlie corrected. He himself surely had to share in whatever had happened? He'd been the graduation teacher, the supposed expert: Mr Never-Been-Caught, according to Patricia Elder's well deserved sneer. So why had Gower — his apprentice, according to another sneer — been caught? Maybe easier here to come some way towards an understanding, by examining more inconsistencies. He'd certainly tried to teach Gower never to take unacceptable risks, and he'd preached about over-eagerness, but what else had there been that was applicable here? Bugger-all, decided Charlie, never to know how close his reflections were now to those of John Gower, so very recently. What benefit was learning about vehicle evasion in a city of bicycles? Bugger-all, he thought again. What could a Caucasian do to watch — or to avoid being watched — in a country of such different physiognomy? Once more, bugger-all.

Gower had come to him green and left him green, to come here. It didn't make operational sense. What did then?

The impossibility of working safely outside the embassy, he recognized, reluctantly conceding that the iron-drawered deputy Director-General had been right. That morning he'd gone back to the main approach road, near the silk shop, and seen the rare and therefore recognizable cars repeat their up-and-down journeys of the previous day. Once more the second vehicle had discharged two men, and one had carried the same brown briefcase and the tightly furled umbrella of yesterday.

If he couldn't approach Snow, then Snow had to approach him. But how? And where?

Charlie had the mission telephone number and could have dialled from an untraceable outside kiosk or stand, but the intercept would be on the mission line. And Snow anyway would have been followed to any outside rendezvous. So how . . . Charlie stopped, his mind snagging but unable to recognize upon what. Something else that didn't make sense. Why? he demanded of himself. Why, trying to work out how to make contact with a sealed off priest in a much watched Jesuit mission, had his train of thought suddenly been de-railed by something he couldn't identify? He ran the reflection he had been having back and forth but still nothing came. It had to remain another question without a proper answer.

So how and where? The second query was easy. It had to be in the unapproachable security of the embassy. But how to get the priest there?

They wouldn't like it, Charlie knew, when the idea came to him. The man would probably refuse and be quite entitled to do so, and if he did Charlie had no better suggestion at that time. But it was the best he could come up with at the moment and it was a relief to think of some-thing that had a chance of working. It was his partially simple way out of the initially difficult situation. But still with a long way to go. Like how to get a followed and watched suspect priest out of a watched British embassy and on to a plane away from the country, without detection or interception.

One problem at a time, decided Charlie: until he won friends and influenced people he hadn't solved the first one yet.

The receptionist at the embassy looked up en-quiringly when Charlie reached her desk in the vestibule.

'I think some people are expecting me,' he said, smiling to ingratiate himself. He usually tried at the beginning.

It wasn't dysentery but it was bad enough, and

instead of throwing most of the water away Gower used it to keep himself as clean as possible. He tried to cleanse his hands as best he could, too. He was still managing to restrict himself to the four sips of water at a time, hovering on the brink of dehydration, and his lips had begun to crack, widening into painful sores risking further infection through their being open. He hadn't eaten the food.

He hadn't been taken for any further interrogation, and without being able to count whether it was night or day, from seeing sunlight or darkness, he had completely lost track of time. He guessed he had been in custody for more than a week — it certainly couldn't have been any less — but it could have easily been longer, nearer two. He was expecting another questioning session soon: the constant noise had erupted again, as well as the perpetual rattle of peep-hole surveys to which he performed. Gower believed he had restored a lot of his sleep bank, and even though the noise had been resumed he still found it possible to close much of it out, suspending himself into something approaching rest.

It was night when he was taken from his cell again. Gower had tried to exercise, in between door-hole inspections, but out of the restricted cell he had great difficulty walking properly. It seemed impossible for him to retain a straight line, wavering from side to side and twice colliding with the escorting soldiers. It was hard for him to lift his feet, as well; he tried at first but then relapsed back to shuffling, hoping it would help maintain a better direction, but it didn't.

'It's all over!' announced Chen. He was smiling, triumphant.

Nothing to which he should respond, Gower told himself. Keep everything to the minimum.

'We've arrested him!'

'Him', isolated Gower: no longer the mistake of 'them'. So it could be Snow, picked up at the shrine. 'I don't know what you're talking about.' He lisped because of the cracks in his lips.

'Just a few hours ago. And already he's confessed. Admitted everything. Hardly worth protecting, was he? You've lost.'

Still no response. Worryingly, Gower was hearing the Chinese oddly, the words loud and then receding, although the man was remaining in the same position directly in front of him.

Chen nodded to the waiting note-takers at the side of the room. 'They're waiting.'

Something to which he could reply. 'What for?'

'Your denials are ridiculous!'

'Nothing to deny.'

'Exactly! It's all written down, elsewhere.'

'Not guilty of anything.'

'You'll be treated better when you confess: give up this nonsense. Be allowed to bathe. Eat better food.'

'I want contact with my embassy.'

'They've been told.'

Momentarily the reply off-balanced Gower.

'Why haven't I seen anybody?'

'You will see somebody when you've told us the truth.'

'I have told you the truth.'

'We can hold you for as long as we like,' threatened Chen. 'Weeks if we want to.'

Gower wished the voice did not keep ebbing and flowing. It was becoming difficult for him to remember everything that was being said. There'd been a lecture about that: always vital to recall every word. And then he did remember. *We've arrested him,* Chen had said. And then: *Just a few hours ago.* That wasn't possible! Despite the time loss, he had to have been in custody for more than a week: more than seven days. And the arrangement was for Snow to check the signal spot every *three* days. Any arrest would not have been just a few hours before. It would have been *days* before. So they still didn't have the priest: suspected him but still hadn't seized him. And all this was still a bluff, to get a confession. 'You are holding me illegally. With no justification.'

'You are subject to our laws,' said Chen. 'You will tell us what we want to know.'

Not yet, thought Gower: not for a very long time yet. If ever.

'Why the hell wasn't he on the plane he was supposed to be on?' demanded the enraged Miller.

'It's typical,' said Patricia. She hadn't anticipated Charlie's manoeuvre and it irritated her, although not as much as Miller. 'At least we know it's not sinister. Special Branch got a definitive photo identification from the Pakistan Airlines desk.'

'Why does the bloody man *do* things like this?'

'I don't think he knows himself a lot of the time.'

Forty-four

The embassy introductions were formal but not as immediately hostile as some Charlie had experienced. There seemed to be a slight surprise at Charlie's appearance, but then he was accustomed to that. On this occasion he returned the curiosity, head tilted upwards: the man had to be a long way over six foot tall. There was, of course, no open conversation until they got to Samuels' office. Once inside Samuels said: 'This is a hell of a mess.'

'So everyone keeps telling me.' Even seated, Samuels seemed as tall as he was when he was standing. Which gratefully he wasn't.

'Gower was accredited to this embassy, for God's sake! If they proceed with these espionage accusations, and prove them to their satisfaction, there could be diplomatic expulsions.'

'That's why I am here. To try to stop them being proved.'

'You weren't on the plane upon which we'd been advised you'd arrive. I waited for two hours.'

'Sorry about that,' said Charlie, emptily. 'Decided on a different flight.'

'London want an explanation: they're very annoyed.'

'I'll give it to them later,' said Charlie, casually.

'Are there any more details about Gower's arrest?'

'Only that it happened near a Taoist shrine, to the west of the city.'

London had already inferred that, merely from learning the district of Beijing. Just as they'd inferred Gower had been moving *to* place the signal, so that the seizure had been made before he had done anything incriminating. 'Nothing else?'

Samuels shook his head. 'And there's no movement on access.'

Time to see how things were really going to be here at the embassy. 'There should have been a request from London to give me every possible assistance.'

Samuel's face tightened. 'There was.'

'With Foreign Office endorsement?'

'Yes.' Samuels appeared reluctant to make the admission.

'I need to call upon it.'

Samuels raised his hands, in a stopping gesture. 'The ambassador has protested in the strongest terms, about what's already happened because of you people. And about this . . . your coming and possibly further involving the embassy.'

'I'm trying to avoid a problem, not worsen it.'

'Sir Timothy met Gower. Warned him . . .' The man snorted a laugh. 'For all the good that did! You can see the danger, can't you?'

'Help me,' suggested Charlie. To get the maximum cooperation he'd have to go along at the diplomat's pace.

'If Gower makes a confession, Sir Timothy could be named in it!' said Samuels, impatiently. 'Associated with an espionage situation! He could be one of the expulsions!'

He shouldn't have been such a silly sod to have got involved in the first place, thought Charlie. 'All the more reason for me to be given as much assistance as possible, so the whole thing can be contained.'

'He won't see you,' declared Samuels.

Charlie blinked in genuine surprise, which didn't occur often. 'I don't want to see him.'

Now Samuels appeared surprised. 'He thought you might. Because of the Foreign Office pressure.'

'Even without the benefit of the hindsight we now have, I think it was unwise of him to have met Gower.'

'Something else,' Samuels bustled on, raising a stopping hand again. 'We want to know as much as possible: we don't want to be caught out, not as we were with Gower. The ambassador demands . . .' The man hesitated, smiling in apology. '. . . is requesting, that you tell me as much as possible, of what's going on. And it's going to be me you'll deal with all the time. No one else. That clear, too?'

Charlie frowned, in a different sort of surprise. The suggestion was illogical, following so immediately after the regret at any personal connection with Gower. And an absurd expectation that he'd discuss intelligence matters in detail with them, anyway. Or was it either? In usual operational circumstances, perhaps. But this was anything but a usual operational situation.

Seeing the expression on Charlie's face, Samuels' smile became even more apologetic. 'This is Sir Timothy's first prestige posting: all his other positions have been relatively minor. He's still feeling his way.'

Charlie nodded, accepted the explanation. 'I'm going to ask for certain things which I would not normally think of doing.'

The smile on Samuels' face died. 'I want a full explanation of that!'

'I have to bring someone to the embassy,' announced Charlie, shortly.

'The person you want to get out of the country!' seized the political officer, at once.

He couldn't give the confirmation, Charlie knew. It was unthinkable, professionally, for him to offer or professionally for Samuels to ask: inconceivable, no matter how desperate they considered the circumstances, that the political officer or the ambassador or the Foreign Office would countenance the entry into the embassy of a man so close to exposure as Jeremy Snow. Lie and cheat time, Charlie recognized: it was like discovering an old friend, lurking in a dark corner. 'No. I would not put everyone to that sort of risk. The person I wish to see is a conduit, that's all.'

'Don't be ridiculous! There would still be a provable connection! I cannot agree to it. Neither will the ambassador.'

'Gower was clearly trying to do it *away* from the embassy. Now he's in jail. And we're facing a diplomatic fiasco . . . possible expulsions, as you say: maybe expulsion *of* the ambassador.'

'I don't consider that an argument.'

Charlie thought he detected a weakness in the rejection. 'The man is a Westerner. Someone who has visited the embassy on occasions. His coming here will arouse no suspicion.'

Samuels' head was to one side, an attitude of intent curiosity. 'Someone who's attended public events here, as part of the Western community?'

Charlie paused, not wanting to give a millimetre more than he felt necessary. 'Yes.'

The smile returned. 'No problem. We have an event here in a fortnight! You can attend as well: carry out your business without anyone being the wiser!'

Charlie sighed. 'John Gower is under interrogation. Denied contact with anyone who might give him the slightest indication what's happening, outside. You think he can last two more weeks, before collapsing? Possibly say something to bring the ambassador into the problem, by name? With our exposed person still here, in Beijing? I don't: I really don't. I think there is going to be a God-almighty explosion long before then.'

Samuels looked away, but having done so seemed uncertain where to direct his attention, his eyes darting all over the office for focus. 'A hell of a mess!'

'We've already agreed to that.' They hadn't even got to the bad part yet.

There was a silence each wanted the other to break. Charlie outlasted the diplomat.

'Just for someone to come here? Someone who's known: won't arouse suspicion?'

'That's all.' Charlie wondered why he didn't feel any guilt: long practice, he supposed.

'Then he goes away?'

'Yes.' A moment of truth.

'Then what?'

'So do I. And the problems with us. Leaving you to get Gower out. Which you will, if the Chinese can't bring their case.'

'You realize my whole career could stand or fall on this?'

Tough shit, thought Charlie: Gower could be hanging by his balls from a rusty nail. 'Of course I realize that: wouldn't do anything to jeopardize it. *My* career depends upon it.' The last bit was certainly true.

'I have your word?'

'Absolutely.'

'All right!' declared Samuels, in the voice of a headquarters general five miles behind the lines ordering soldiers to go over the top into enemy fire. 'I agree! You can bring him in! The important thing is to get the whole stupid nonsense over. Out of the way, once and for all.'

'I'm grateful we've been able to reach this degree of cooperation. I'll pass a memo on, when I get back to London.'

The light-bulb smile went on and off. 'Most kind.'

'We need to agree a little more,' ventured Charlie.

'What?'

'How to get him here.'

'But I thought . . .'

'. . . he has to know I'm here. To be told. I can't go, an obvious stranger, to where he is. That could be what Gower tried to do. I don't trust the telephone, either.'

'How then?' All the rejecting hostility was back.

'Someone who *isn't* a stranger: someone who's been there so many times recently that his going again probably wouldn't even be noticed.'

'Someone from this embassy!'

There were remarkable flashes of prescience in between the diplomatic pomposity, thought Charlie. 'Yes.'

'You need to tell me everything.'

He did, acknowledged Charlie: not everything, exactly, but far more than he would have liked. 'There were several references in Foreign Office reports, in your name, to a recent illness of Father Robertson . . .'

'. . . He's the man?' burst in Samuels, astonished.

'. . . which the embassy physician, Dr Pickering, treated,' completed Charlie. 'And those same reports said Dr Pickering was maintaining a medical check, after the apparent recovery.'

'That's true,' agreed Samuels, doubtfully.

'So there is every proper reason for Dr Pickering to go again to the mission. Tomorrow, for instance?'

'I asked you a question you haven't answered.'

Charlie wished to Christ there was a way to avoid the identification, but there wasn't. 'Not Father Robertson. Father Snow.'

'Snow!'

'Nothing more than a message-carrier: he's not even aware of what he's doing,' lied Charlie.

'No!' refused Samuels, indignantly. 'I've agreed to the man coming here. I accept it has to be this way: that there's no alternative. But this is inveigling an actual *member* of the embassy staff. Exposing him to God knows what! He could be swept up, like Gower. I can't possibly condone that. It's too much.'

It probably was, conceded Charlie: certainly if the person was aware beforehand what he was doing, so that he was denied the benefit of genuinely innocent denial. 'Exposing him to nothing,' argued Charlie. 'All I am asking is that Dr Pickering makes a routine house call at the Jesuit mission, which he has been doing irregularly for the past two or three weeks, to carry out one of the established checks upon Father Robertson. And while he is there tells Snow there is someone at the embassy who wishes to see him at once. Where's the danger? The exposure?'

'It's too much,' insisted the political officer.

'Compared to a diplomatic disaster? The expulsion of an ambassador?'

'That's . . .'

'. . . the choice.'

The unusually tall man came reflectively forward on his desk, a bend at a time, like a tower building collapsing from a controlled explosion. 'It's too . . . I can't . . .'

'Why don't we ask the doctor?' If he spread even the limited awareness much further he might as well take out newspaper advertisements and make radio announcements from the roof, thought Charlie. He loathed being this dependent on other people: loathed being anything but entirely self-contained, entirely self-dependent, having to trust and rely upon no one except himself. This really was a shitty job: the shittiest.

'You'll accept his refusal?'

'If you'll accept his agreement.'

Samuels hesitated, for several moments. 'Which of us will explain it?'

'You,' said Charlie. 'Or me, if you'd prefer.'

'Me,' decided the diplomat.

Charlie at once recognized the man introduced to him as George Pickering to be the sort of doctor who made patients feel guilty for being ill. The man's suit strained around his bulging body, and the moment Samuels began a limited explanation Pickering turned to fix Charlie with a disconcertingly unblinking stare through oddly large spectacles. Charlie thought the man looked like the grandfather to all the owls. He stayed with his eyes on Charlie after Samuels finished, initially not speaking. Then he said: 'This arrest business?'

'Yes,' admitted Charlie.

'Bugger off.'

'Where's the risk?'

'I'm a doctor. Nothing else.'

'Can you imagine the physical condition Gower's in by now?'

'A risk with your sort of job.'

'Whose medical philosophy is that?'

'Mine.'

'Don't you talk to Snow, when you go to the mission?'

'Of course I do!'

' "Someone at the embassy wants to see you." Eight words.'

'Do it yourself.'

'You've heard why I can't.'

'I said bugger off.'

But he hadn't left the room in offended indignation, realized Charlie. 'Eight words.'

'Why should I?'

'To prevent a diplomatic débâcle. And stop the suffering of a man in prison.'

'Neither is my concern.'

'I would have thought both were,' insisted Charlie.

'We want to get it over as quickly as possible, George,' intruded Samuels. 'And as best we can.'

'You asking me to do it?' demanded Pickering.

Samuels shook his head. 'It's got to be your decision.'

Sensing the weakening, Charlie reiterated: 'Eight words.'

Pickering was silent again for several moments. Then he said: 'Bloody lot of nonsense, all of it: kids' stuff.'

'You'll do it?' asked Charlie.

'Only pass on that exact message. Nothing else.'

Charlie guessed Pickering had been quite prepared to do it from the beginning but had put up the token rejection to see them plead. People played all sorts of games, he reflected. He had a lot of his own to play. He managed the airport conversations himself but needed Samuels' Chinese for the rail enquiries and reservations. It took two hours. As he thanked the political officer, Charlie said: 'From what I've read in his personal file, you and Snow must be about the same height. Coincidence, that, isn't it?'

'Whatever it is you're thinking of, don't even bother to ask,' said Samuels.

The request from the State-appointed defender for Natalia to appear as a character witness for Eduard was made through Agency channels, which surprised her: if it had come at all she would have expected it to have been sent direct to Leninskaya. She used the same Agency route to reply, refusing the request.

Forty-five

The problem of Jeremy Snow took on a whole new and deeper significance as soon as the priest entered the room at the embassy that Samuels had made available. After the meeting with the liaison man in London and from much of what he had read in the files, Charlie had expected a bombastic, self-opinionated man. But there was no arrogance at all. The asthmatic priest was wheezing with apprehension. Almost as soon as he came in he said: 'Thank God you're here: I've been terribly wrong,' and Charlie guessed Snow would collapse and make a full confession within minutes of being seized.

'It can still be sorted out,' said Charlie, seeing the priest's need for reassurance. Although he knew the personal statistics from the file, Snow's height still surprised him.

'What about the man who's been arrested? He came for me, didn't he?'

'Your safety is his safety.'

'Are you sure?'

He wasn't, realized Charlie. 'Positive,' he said. 'But there can't be the slightest mistake. We'll only get one chance. So I want to know everything from the beginning. And from the beginning I mean from the moment you were approached to work for London. In as much detail as you can recall.'

It took a very long time, because Charlie frequently interrupted, pressing constantly for every possible thing, refusing even to accept a generality he could have filled in for himself from the dossiers he had studied in London. Several times Snow had to stop completely, until his breathing improved, and when he finally finished he was slumped, drained, in his chair. Still Charlie wanted more.

'This problem of contact only began with Foster?'

Snow nodded. 'In the last six months. With Bowley and Street everything was fine. Foster said we had to be far more careful: that the times I could legitimately come here were sufficient and that we should keep the outside visits to the barest minimum.'

'How long was this man, Zhang Su Lin, a source?'

'Just under a year, I suppose. He started at the classes very soon after Tiananmen, but I had no idea he was a dissident at first, of course. He was *in* Tiananmen when the massacre happened.'

'How good was he? As a source, I mean?'

'He seemed very well in with people in Beijing. He told me once that he expected to get arrested after Tiananmen because all the others rounded up knew him and he thought they would name him during questioning. But he wasn't. He gave me some Shanghai leads, too.'

'Why did he cease coming to the classes?'

'I never knew. He just didn't turn up one day: there was no warning. I wondered if he had been arrested, after all: he was very much into writing and issuing the protest wall posters and bulletins. But he obviously wasn't. Not until last month.'

'Did he know you were passing the information on?'

'Not in the way you mean. As far as he was concerned, we were just talking, but of course he expected me to tell others, outside China. That's the whole point, getting the information out that there is protest, within the country.'

'So he'll name you?'

'He could say he attended my English classes, for a period. That was no secret anyway. But not that I knew him as anyone actively connected or particularly interested in the dissident movement.'

It wouldn't matter, thought Charlie. The connection between Zhang and Snow would emerge, during the questioning of the Chinese dissident: it probably already had. Which gave them more than enough for a completely genuine spy trial, according to Chinese law. And that was before they even got to Snow's trip and the material he had gathered in Shanghai, for which they were patiently waiting, believing Snow trapped and Gower at their mercy, for whatever they chose to do. Reminded, Charlie looked to the side of the room, where the small desk obviously utilized when it served as an office had been pushed against the wall in an unsuccessful effort to create more space. Nodding towards the package lying on it, he said: 'There's your photographs.'

'I've got what Li gave me,' announced Snow, in return, groping into the inside pocket of his jacket.

Charlie laid out on the table the Shanghai shots that had been doctored in London and then directly beneath each frame made the match from what the Chinese had provided. They weren't absolutely identical — the innocuous Chinese shots were not precisely from the same spot — but Charlie accepted that scarcely mattered, for the use the Chinese intended to make of them. The technicians in London had done the best job they could. Snow's prints appeared to have been very badly developed: in only one was there even a suggestion of a ship, and if he had not been looking specifically for it Charlie's first impression would have been that it was a low cloud base. The down side was that the Chinese would *be* looking specifically.

'They're very good!' said Snow, at his shoulder.

'Not good enough,' said Charlie.

'What are we going to do then?' demanded the priest, in instant alarm.

Charlie thought again how quickly the man would collapse, under pressure. 'There's a way round it,' he promised, in fresh reassurance. 'It's all going to be all right.'

'When?'

'Tomorrow.'

Snow's sigh of relief was audible, beyond his strained breathing. 'I've got Father Robertson's permission to leave.'

'You told me.' Charlie still wished the stupid clerical bureaucracy hadn't been necessary, despite the security of the confessional.

'I want to go to Rome, as soon as possible. I'm going to ask to go into a retreat. I need a lot of time.'

'Let's just think of getting out of Beijing at the moment,' urged Charlie.

'I won't do any more,' declared Snow.

Charlie frowned at the man, not understanding. 'Any more what?'

'Work for you. I thought it was important: still do. But it's brought too much suffering. To the man who's been arrested. And to Father Robertson. I have a lot of apologies to make, in prayer.'

'We wouldn't expect you to, not any more. We accept that this is the end.' The man wouldn't have any use, once he was out of Beijing, but Charlie decided it wasn't necessary to make the cynicism as clear as that.

'What must I do?' asked Snow, obediently.

'Everything exactly as I say,' insisted Charlie. 'And in precisely the sequence I set out. Don't deviate, in any way . . .' He picked up the London-supplied photographs, keeping them in his hands. 'It'll take the Chinese a while to prove these have been altered. Certainly more than a day . . .' He started to separate the prints into two sets, carefully putting to one side the particular print that more obviously than all the rest showed something that Snow should not have photographed. Charlie added one more Shanghai picture and three innocent prints to the held-back pile, offering the rest to Snow. 'For Li.'

'He'll know some are missing.'

'I know he will,' agreed Charlie, at once. 'You're going to tell him. Remember, everything in the order I dictate.'

'Tell me how.'

'You're not sure if Li is Foreign Ministry or definitely the Public Security Bureau?'

Snow shook his head. 'I'm fairly sure it's the Bureau. He refused to let me try to contact him, when I offered. Said he'd always come to me.'

'Good,' said Charlie. He hesitated, wanting his explanation to be as clear as possible, to avoid Snow misunderstanding. 'What we're trying to achieve is the maximum confusion among people who might be watching the mission or watching the embassy and trying to connect the two of us.'

'How much time do you think we've got?' demanded the priest, dispirited.

Don't collapse on us yet, thought Charlie: it was unsettling enough to consider the man collapsing at all. 'Enough,' he encouraged. 'It won't be easy and there are things that could go wrong, but if you do it like I say, there's a bloody good chance it'll all work out fine.' That was an exaggeration, conceded Charlie: he couldn't think of a better way and he'd known escapes far more tenuous than this — his own from Moscow, the first time he turned his back on Natalia, for instance — but this was pretty threadbare.

'Just tell me what to do.'

There was a dullness in the way Snow was talking, a resignation that Charlie didn't like. 'Tomorrow morning, early, telephone the Foreign Ministry. Try to reach Li. But don't try too hard. All we want to establish is that you *tried* to get in touch, and then get him and everyone else moving in the wrong directions when they get the message and you start to do what I'm going to tell you. Leave a message that you're sending something to him. Then go personally to the Foreign Ministry . . .'

'Go there?' exclaimed Snow, astonished.

'First,' expanded Charlie. 'Before you go to the Security Bureau offices.'

Snow was shaking his head, bewildered. 'This doesn't make sense . . .'

'Neither will it to anyone who is watching the mission, to see what you are going to do. Think about it! Where is the last place in the world they would expect you to go?'

The head movement now was a slow nod, but there was more doubt than agreement. 'Certainly not there.'

'So they'll be thrown off balance?'

'Possibly.'

'The Bureau is a large building? Like the Foreign Ministry?'

'Yes.'

'Leave the photographs I've given you at the Foreign Ministry, addressed to Li. With a letter apologizing that they are incomplete. Say you're trying to find out what has happened to the rest. Leave the Foreign Ministry by a different door than how you entered. At the Bureau, enquire the possibility of your taking another trip: go through the formalities of making an initial travel application . . .' Snow was looking at him but Charlie was unsure if the man was comprehending it all. 'Do you understand what I'm saying?'

'I understand what you're saying: not what it's going to achieve.'

'Confusion,' repeated Charlie. 'Leave the Bureau differently from the way you entered, too. This will be the most dangerous time: this is when you start to run.'

'To the airport?' guessed Snow, wanting to contribute.

'That's what they'll hopefully think. I shall make a reservation in your own name, on a plane leaving direct for England the day *after* tomorrow. I want them to think they've got time to get into position. I don't want confusion to become panic.'

'How then?'

'Time your visits to get you out of the Bureau by mid-afternoon. Walk, initially. So that any pursuit will be on foot, not by car that can more easily pick you up when you switch to public transport. Go direct to the main rail terminus, for the five o'clock express to Shanghai.'

'It takes . . .'

'. . . I know how long it takes,' cut off Charlie. 'And you're not supposedly going there anyway. Book yourself to Nanchang. There's an express leaving for there at four forty-five: I've already checked. Your ticket will get you on to the platforms: if you are followed it'll take longer than fifteen minutes for them to check *where* you've bought a ticket for, and when they find out it will be a long way away from where you're going. According to the schedules, they can't get on the Nanchang express en route for the first eight hours of the journey, at the first stop. And if they do — it'll be in the middle of the night and I doubt they could organize themselves that quickly — it'll take them at least until Nanchang to go right through the train to discover you are not on it. Actually board the Nanchang train, so that you'll be remembered. Just before it leaves, get off. I've checked the track numbers, too. You'll be two tracks away. Cross directly to the Shanghai train. I'll have a two-berth, soft sleeper cabin. And a ticket for you. Which *I'll* present around the door during any ticket inspection checks, so that once inside the cabin you'll be out of sight. The majority of the journey is through the night, when everybody will be asleep.'

'What happens in Shanghai?'

'Nothing, I hope. There's a plane out, four hours after we arrive, to Manila. Both tickets on it will again be in my name. We'll go direct to the airport from the railway station.'

'You've forgotten the need for travel permission.'

'That only applies to restricted areas. There is none, on the route between Beijing and Shanghai. I checked that, like everything else. And you won't be on the Nanchang train, where it *does* apply, anyway.'

Snow sat for several moments with his head bowed, deep in thought. 'All right,' he said.

Charlie was unsure to what the priest was agreeing. 'You think you can do it?'

'Yes.'

'All of it?'

There was another pause. 'I've got to, haven't I?'

Charlie matched the cynicism. 'Yes.'

'From the moment I get into your cabin on the train you'll be linked with me: as liable to arrest as I am? As that other man was?'

A fact that was paramount in Charlie's mind. 'Yes.'

'I don't want to cause any more problems, for anyone!' insisted the other man. 'Why can't I do it by myself?'

'Because it's not a one-man job!' rejected Charlie. 'You need help and concealment on the train and help at Shanghai airport, to collect a ticket to get you out . . .' Charlie hesitated. Then he said: 'This is the only way to get you out.' He wished to Christ there was a choice.

'I have to return to the mission tonight?'

Charlie was torn between wishing to see the man show either something beyond dull obedience or a spark of initiative which might have risked the danger of improvisation. 'Until tomorrow morning, when you call the Foreign Ministry, you've got to continue normally in every way at the mission.'

For the first time, Snow began to show some reaction. 'What can I take with me, when I leave?'

'Your passport,' said Charlie, regretting the irritation in his voice. 'That's all! You can't carry anything that will give the slightest indication that you're not going back to the mission!'

Snow frowned. 'I must have a rosary. And my bible.'

'Will the bible fit into your pocket?'

Snow was clearly uncertain whether to lie outright. In the end he said: 'Not really.'

'Then no.'

'I have always had it.'

'No!'

'I suppose I could ask Father Robertson to send it to Rome.'

'Father Robertson has to believe you're coming back to the mission, like everybody else.'

'But he's . . .' Snow started, but Charlie wouldn't allow the protest.

'. . . exposed,' he said, shortly. 'His *protection* is not knowing! If he gives any indication of being aware in advance, he could be accused of colluding with you!'

Snow shook his head again. 'I'm not sure . . .' he began and trailed away.

'No luggage. No goodbyes,' insisted Charlie. 'It's not a matter for you. Not just your safety. You're agonizing over the poor bastard they've already arrested. What happens to him depends upon their not getting you. My safety, too. Two people, utterly dependent on your doing everything right. OK?'

'OK.' It was very uncertain.

'No deviation! None whatsoever!'

'I said I understood!' Now Snow was showing irritation.

Charlie was abruptly very nervous. Apart from Edith, a long time ago, and Natalia, much more recently, there was only one person in the world upon whom Charlie had ever felt able completely to rely. Himself. He'd never really liked operating with other supposed professionals, because invariably something got cocked up somewhere. This time he wasn't even being forced together with a professional. He was being harnessed with someone he'd already decided was a collapsing liability. 'Repeat it!' he ordered. 'Repeat everything back to me!'

Snow had to make two attempts, to get it right. At the end he said: 'I've got it all clear in my head.'

'I hope to Christ you have!' said Charlie, unthinkingly.

'And I'll pray to Him,' promised Snow, quietly.

Miller had not referred to the left-behind perfume after that one confrontation and obviously Patricia hadn't. She hadn't asked, either, when or how long Ann might be at Regent's Park because it would have seemed she was anxious, which she was, but didn't want to show it. He'd have to ask her to go there again: Patricia was determined that was how it would be. In the beginning, she had made up her mind to refuse the first time, putting up some excuse, but as the days passed her resolve about that lessened and she knew she'd agree, as she always agreed. But he'd still have to ask her: she wouldn't suggest it.

'There wasn't a lot of point in Muffin making all that fuss about going in solo if he was going to approach the embassy as quickly as this, was there?' demanded the Director.

'At least we know he's there. And that there is definite surveillance on the mission.' Why wouldn't Peter ask her? She was *sure* Ann wasn't there.

'That's the most worrying part.'

'I would have thought the continued refusal over Gower might have been?'

'Then you're not thinking clearly enough,' said Miller, brusquely. 'It can only mean Gower's hanging on.'

Patricia's face burned at the curtness but she chose not to argue against it. 'What next?'

'The Chinese ambassador is being told we are considering withdrawing our ambassador, for consultations.'

'Isn't that dangerous?'

'Of course it is!' said Miller, brusque again. 'We're bluffing. We've just got to hope the bastards don't call it.'

Forty-six

The enmity between them had become absolute after the confession, which should have made it easier for Snow to leave the mission without any farewell, but he was reluctant to go like that. Despite no bond ever having grown between them, Snow felt the older priest deserved a warning at least. It was a deceit not to say something, just as it had been a deceit contriving the protective confession. The justification from the man who had come to get him out — *his protection is not knowing* — did not seem as acceptable in the echoing, dust-clogged church during early morning prayers as it had in the cramped embassy room less than twenty-four hours earlier.

Snow prayed for a long time. He prayed most fervently for forgiveness, for what he now accepted to be the mistakes and the wrongs he had committed. And then for courage, for what he had to do that day. And finally to be allowed to escape, apologizing as he did so for the weakness it showed.

He was aware, while he prayed, of Father Robertson entering and then leaving the church for his own worship. When Snow reached their living quarters there was no sign of the other priest. Snow felt positively sick, so he did not want anything to eat, but he brewed coffee, enough for both of them. Still Father Robertson did not appear. Finally Snow called for the man. There was no response. Snow looked into the empty office and finally knocked tentatively on Father Robertson's bedroom door, beginning to fear another collapse. When he pushed the door open, the room was empty, the bed tidily made.

Snow accepted, sighing, that the problem of leaving the mission had been resolved for him. Father Robertson wouldn't think any less of him, when he realized what had happened: it was probably impossible for the man *to* think any less than he already did. So it would have been a gesture entirely for his own benefit. Unimportant, then. Snow fervently hoped there was protection, in Father Robertson not knowing.

After just a few sips of the coffee the feeling of sickness worsened, so Snow threw the remainder away: the nausea was more discomforting than the tightness in his chest, which really wasn't too bad at all, not as bad as he'd expected it might be. There was certainly no need at this stage for an inhaler.

With the edited pictures set out on the table before him, Snow wrote to Li as he had been instructed, apologizing for the photographs being incomplete, pausing briefly when he'd finished that letter as the idea came of writing also to Father Robertson. Positively Snow laid the pen aside, rising from the desk. The decision had been made for him, he repeated to himself.

He failed to reach Li by telephone at the Foreign Ministry. The switchboard at once put him on the carousel of Chinese bureaucracy, plugging him through to one department who put him on hold to transfer him to another. On the second connection, Snow was careful to identify himself and leave the required message before the third attempt at a transfer. Before it succeeded, he disconnected.

Snow had looked nostalgically around the church before he'd left it. He did the same now around the mission, and finally in his room there. And then concentrated upon his desk. The passport slipped easily into the inside of his jacket. He put the rosary into an outside pocket, patting it needlessly to ensure it did not bulge. His bible, the well thumbed, much used book his parents had given him the proud day of his graduation, was the only object left in front of the tiny, private altar. It was too big, both in length and width, for any of his pockets. He replaced it on the table, flicking open the cover to read the inscription he knew by heart: the ink in which his mother had written his name was already fading, tinged with brown. He closed it again but did not move from the desk. He wanted to take it. Needed to take it, his most precious possession. Carrying it in his hand would not indicate he was leaving. He was a priest. Priests carried bibles, although not often in proscribed China. But Catholicism was not proscribed: officially it was permitted. Snow picked the bible up again, testing how it looked if he held it upright, in his cupped hand close to his body. He was sure it hardly protruded to be visible at all: didn't appear to be anything more than a wallet if it did show, and a wallet did not mean he was going anywhere.

He *would* take it, Snow determined.

He was at the door when he remembered the asthma medication. The two inhalers from the bathroom cabinet made a bigger bulge in his pocket than the rosary. Snow was at the door of the mission, about to step out into the street, when the abrupt fear gripped him, so that for a moment he was physically unable to move.

'Dear God, please help me!' he said aloud. 'Help me!' He forced himself to move, which he did with great difficulty, like someone suffering cramp or paralysis.

The overcast sky seemed to blanket the heat upon the street outside, which was, as usual, jostled with people and bicycles: he couldn't see the nightsoil-collectors but the stink of their cargo hung in the air. The last time I'll walk this way, among these people, among these smells, Snow thought: I'm leaving, running. I'll never see this place again.

Were there people watching him? The man at the embassy clearly thought so, and from Li's behaviour he supposed he had to accept it was so. But Li hadn't been to the mission for over a week now: nearer two, in fact. Perhaps the suspicion was lessening. Perhaps . . . Snow stifled the hope, annoyed at himself. He didn't know why Li hadn't been to the mission but he did know the district in which John Gower had been arrested, which meant there hadn't been any lessening of suspicion. It was a miracle he hadn't been seized already, so he had to get away and today was his chance. His *only* chance, according to the scruffy man at the embassy. Snow wished he knew how to spot people watching him. Would it be easy, confusing them and evading them, as the man had made it sound yesterday? It *had* sounded easy then. It didn't now. The instructions he'd been told to follow, to the letter, seemed totally inadequate now: impossible. He still felt sick and his chest was tightening. Should have remembered the mask: several people around him were wearing them and it might have helped. Too late to go back. No turning back. Just had to go on. Perspiration was making the cover of the bible wet and slippery in his hand. He didn't want to draw attention to it, switching it from one hand to the other. Have to take some relief for the asthma soon. Stupid to put it off, which he knew he couldn't: always had to be quick to prevent it becoming too severe. Couldn't risk a severe attack today.

Snow held out until he reached the bus-stop and its straggled queue. He used the inhaler there, grateful for the immediate relief and the awareness that he hadn't left it too long. He put the bible in his other hand, too.

Snow changed buses twice, which was necessary to reach the Foreign Ministry. The beginning of

501

the confusion, he thought, hopefully, as he approached the building. He would have liked to know if those watching him were more confused than he was. There was certainly a babble of confusion inside the building. It was packed with people moving against each other and from place to place upon the insistence of officials who saw their function as never to make a decision, always to defer or sidetrack it untraceably on to someone else. The priest tried to use the mêlée, going into two crowded offices with only the minimal contact with officials to account for his moving on to yet further divisions. Only at the fourth did he attempt proper, sensible contact, repeating the name of Li Dong Ming, becoming finally convinced from the blankness with which he was met that Li was definitely attached to the Public Security Bureau. He had to insist the clerk take his offered, apologetic package addressed to Li, only at the last moment remembering further to insist upon a receipt, which would establish on its counterfoil proof of the delivery of the photographs.

People were all too close, too cloying, all about him in the eddying corridors, and Snow felt the fresh distress, wanting to stop and rest and knowing there was no possibility of his doing so. He let himself be carried along by the human tide. Once he collided with an unmoving, rocklike knot of people and felt the bible begin to go from his grasp, snatching out to get a fresh grip only seconds before he lost it completely. His breathing worsened: trying to confuse he was becoming confused himself.

The side door was small, quite different from the elaborate main entrance through which he had entered. Snow let himself be washed aside, thrusting gratefully out into the street: despite the overcast oppression it was cooler than inside the building. He wanted to pause, to relieve his breathing, but knew he couldn't. He drove himself on, glad that this time he didn't have to wait for a bus: one was pulling in as he reached the stop and he was aboard and moving within minutes. Snow slumped, panting, into a seat. He was soaked in perspiration and people immediately around were looking at him because of the snorting intake of his breathing. Snow put the bible openly on his lap, to free both hands from its wetness and let everything dry. Gradually his breathing quietened. No one had boarded the bus after him: he was absolutely sure of that. So if he had been under surveillance, he'd evaded it. Suddenly — wonderfully — what he'd been told to do didn't seem inadequate or impossible any more. It was all going to work: make it possible for him to escape. His breathing became more even.

The offices of the Gong An Ju were very different. This was the headquarters of the omnipotent control of the People's Republic, the all-seeing eyes that saw, the all-hearing ears that heard. There were a lot of people in the outer corridors and vestibules, but none of the hither and thither turmoil of the other place. Snow was uncomfortable here, anxious to get away, but he obeyed the instructions, waiting for a vacant booth and talking generally of taking another country tour, to the north this time, leaving his mission address and his name. Feeling increasingly confident, he allowed himself to stray very slightly from the script, suggesting he return the following day to fill out a proper application form to establish his hopeful itinerary. Automatically responding to the possibility that he would not have to be the one to process the paper work the following day, the clerk instantly agreed.

Almost there, thought Snow, going out once more through a side door and once more being lucky with a bus, which was again in sight as he came to the stop. Two men did get on directly behind him this time but both got off, long before the rail terminus. It was still only twenty to four: more than enough time for everything else he had to do, even taking into account the customary delay at the ticket office.

There *was* a delay. In front of every window there was a meandering line of patient travellers, almost everyone burdened with enough belongings to start life anew in another part of the country. Snow started, actually emitting a cry of frightened surprise, at the sudden but insistent plucking at his elbow. The money-barterer was gap-toothed and moustached and wore a Western-style suit that didn't fit. Snow went through the ritual of offer and rejection, concerned how quickly his breath was snatched: it was five minutes before the tout gave up. Something else I'll never know again, thought Snow. Nor want to. He was getting away: leaving forever. And glad to be going. Whatever worth he'd had here was over.

What explanation was he going to give the Curia, in Rome? Not the complete story, he thought. Just enough. He could talk of having had Zhang Su Lin as a pupil. Which was true. And of his not knowing, for a long time, that the man was a political activist and therefore dangerous. Again true. Zhang's arrest was public knowledge. Which therefore made it essential he get out, with the emergency permission of Father Robertson, to avoid his becoming innocently involved and risking the very future of any Jesuit mission in Beijing. More than enough, Snow decided: Rome would accept the account and be grateful for his political acumen. And his conscience would be clear: there was no deceit, in anything he was going to say.

He didn't feel sick any more and his breathing had settled down after the fright of the money-changer. The bible felt solid and comforting in his hand, no longer wet. His confidence, just as solid and comforting, was returning, too. What would he read, when he was hidden away on the Shanghai-bound sleeper? There were several teachings about overcoming evil, in Philippians: one very apposite tract, about wrestling against the rulers of darkness, which he'd surely been doing for the past three years in Beijing. Snow at once curbed the arrogance. Perhaps the Book of Proverbs was more fitting: particularly the warning of pride going before destruction and haughty spirits before a fall. Except that he was not going to destruction. He was going to safety with a man whose planning was working out just as he had promised it would. By this time tomorrow they would be secure in the Philippines: maybe even have moved on. There was no real reason for his going to London: the man had already accepted the end of any relationship. He didn't know, but it was probably easy to get a flight from Manila to Rome: if not direct, then by changing somewhere en route. He would have to talk about it, on the way to Shanghai. He'd definitely go straight to Rome, if it was possible.

Snow finally reached the window. He hesitated, at whether he wanted a single or return to Nanchang, confronting a question they had not rehearsed. He asked for a return, guessing the clerk would remember him if any enquiry was made because he was a Westerner who had chosen hard-seat travel.

Snow patiently queued to pass through the barrier, unconcerned at the returning shortness of breath. It wasn't bad, hardly anything, and it was obvious there was going to be something because of the tension of these last few minutes. Literally minutes, he calculated: seven, before the Nanchang train pulled out, twenty-two before the departure of the train he'd really be on, to Shanghai. He filed through, without any interest from the inspectors, on to the common, linking concourse that joined all the tracks at their very top, where the expresses arrived and departed. Everything was exactly as it had been promised at the embassy, with two tracks, both empty, separating the trains. Maybe a hundred yards between them: a simple, unhurried walk. He was anxious now to get to the embassy man: to be hidden away and from then on be told by him what to do and how to do it. He'd done very well by himself though: gone through it all precisely as he'd been instructed, without any deviation. Apart from the bible. He was glad he'd brought it.

So close to departure, the Nanchang hard-seat carriages were overflowing with people, every available space already occupied. Snow didn't bother to move from just beyond the door. Four minutes. As a precaution he brought the inhaler to his mouth. Three minutes. The noise of departure grew from outside, on the platform: a public address announcement, difficult to hear, and shouts from railway guards, and steam hissing up from beneath the skirts of the carriage. The whole train jerked forward, as the brakes began to release.

Snow got off. He actually descended on to the platform into the billowing steam, glad of its concealment. No need to hurry: no need at all. Plenty of time. Beside him the train groaned into life, coughing more steam: asthmatic, like he was. Near the concourse now: ten yards, no more. Once he was on the concourse there were just the two intervening tracks to pass. Very close. Practically there. Snow turned on to the concourse.

Which was when Charlie saw him.

Charlie had been a long time at the window of their two-berth sleeper, straining for the first sight of the priest, wanting to be at the door when the man boarded, to hurry him inside as quickly as possible. Snow appeared to be moving well, just as he should, purposefully but without any hurry to attract attention. It was going fine, Charlie thought: absolutely fine.

There must have been a shout, a challenge, but enclosed and still some distance away in his tiny compartment Charlie never heard anything. It all unfolded before him in a silent, sickening tableau. Snow jerked to a halt, staring straight ahead at something concealed from Charlie by the curve of the carriages. Then twisted behind him. Charlie did see them then: men in khaki uniforms and plainclothes officers as well, fanning out from the barrier. There was a lot of arm-waving from the men in suits. Still Charlie could hear nothing. Snow turned back again and began to run towards the train he was trying to reach, but halted almost at once. Into Charlie's view came the squad Snow had first seen. The priest was looking frantically, hopelessly, in both directions: Charlie could make out the open, gasping mouth and the rolling eyes bulging in terror.

'They've got you,' said Charlie, to himself. Got us all, he thought.

Snow ran again. Not towards either group but jumped off the raised platform on to the track, stupidly and pointlessly, so stupidly pointless that neither squad made any attempt to chase him because there was nowhere for him to run.

Charlie realized what Snow was trying to do. The Nanchang train was starting forward but hardly moving, the brakes still not fully off, and Snow was stumbling across the empty lines to get to it.

It was blind, desperate, unthinking panic, with no possible chance of escape because he was level with the tracks, putting the closed doors far above him, tall as he was. Snow still tried. In those last few moments he didn't run properly at all. It became a lurch, arms clasped about his chest. Alongside the train he staggered parallel for a few moments, bringing himself to one last, supreme effort of leaping upwards for the door handle to pull himself aboard. The priest actually did get a hold on the handle and briefly, for just a few seconds, appeared to hang suspended. Then he let go and fell backwards, not on to the empty track but beneath the wheels of the Nanchang train. It continued on, carriage after carriage, no one ordering it to stop.

Charlie didn't wait to see it clear the station. He walked in the opposite direction from the platform from which the Nanchang train had just left, getting off the concourse by a far gate but turning back on himself when he was on the other side of the fenced barrier to see everything. There were a lot more soldiers, running from beyond the Shanghai express. And a lot more, with plain-clothes Security Bureau men all down on the tracks, formed into a solid circle around the body, which was hidden from view. There was a lot of shouting and gesticulating but mostly they just looked. Charlie recognized one of the plain-suited men in the very centre of the gathering as the bespectacled Li Dong Ming, whose photograph he had memorized in London.

As he passed, Charlie saw it was a bible that Snow had been carrying. He must have dropped it when he fled down on to the lines. It had fallen open on the concourse and the wind was blowing the thin leaves one way and then the other, like an unseen hand hurrying through for a lost passage.

'Oh my God!' Samuels swallowed, heavily, his throat going up and down. 'You sure he's dead?'

'A train ran over him. At least four carriages. Of course he's bloody dead!'

'What about you? Do they know about you?'

'No,' said Charlie, shortly. He was glad the sleeper reservations had not been made by name. The flight bookings, which had been in false identities, would have to be cancelled.

'You'll have to tell London. We both will, to our respective people,' said the political officer. 'What are you going to say?'

'That Snow's dead. And that the chain's been broken. Providing he doesn't confess, there's no accusation that can be brought against John Gower now.'

Samuels regarded Charlie with his lip curled. 'Just that!' he said, disgustedly.

'That's all they wanted,' said Charlie. 'All any of them wanted. They'll think it worked out well.' He didn't. He thought he was going to have to watch his ass more closely than he ever had before. And a few others, too.

Forty-seven

A lot of things happened in a very short time. Some good. Some bad. Some Charlie couldn't decide one way or the other.

The official notification of Snow's death came to the embassy from Father Robertson, who was officially informed by the Chinese. There was no public denunciation of the younger priest as a spy, which had been the immediate concern in messages to Samuels from the Foreign Office and to Charlie from Patricia Elder. In that same first cable to Charlie, the deputy Director-General ordered him to rebase to London as soon as possible. He didn't acknowledge it.

Father Robertson made two visits to the embassy to arrange for the shipment of the body back to England for burial in the family vault in Sussex. Samuels met him on both occasions, and on the third accompanied the elderly man from the mission to the Foreign Ministry, to complete the final formalities for the release of the body. Charlie asked to sit in unobtrusively on the embassy meetings. Samuels refused. Charlie, who thought Samuels was a pompous shit, did however time his own visits to be at the embassy when Father Robertson came. He saw a slightly bent, careworn man making an obvious effort to cope with circumstances threatening to over-whelm him. Dr Pickering was necessarily part of the group that met the priest on every occasion. In addition to Samuels and Pickering, both Plowright and Nicholson were at the meetings and also went to the Foreign Ministry interview, in the event of a legal question arising. None did.

Samuels agreed with visible reluctance to see Charlie after that Chinese Foreign Office encounter.

'I really can't understand why you're hanging around any longer!' protested the political officer. 'You've been ordered home. Why not go?'

'I want to make sure something doesn't come up that we didn't expect: that's important, don't you think?'

'Nothing will,' said Samuels. 'They've released the body. Signed all the forms. It's over, thank God.'

'How's Father Robertson? He looks wrecked.'

'Hanging on by a thread.'

'He didn't say anything that I should know about? That my department needs to hear?' Charlie disliked getting things at second hand.

'Of course not!' said Samuels, impatiently. 'He doesn't know I'm aware of what Snow was doing. And Snow's admission to him was covered by the secrecy of the confessional, wasn't it?'

'I thought he might have told you if Li had come to the mission again.'

'I can hardly ask, can I? Again, I'm not sup-posed to know.'

'What's coming from Rome?'

Samuels shrugged. 'Shock and mourning. As far as they are concerned, Snow was the victim of a tragic accident.'

'It's not all over is it?' reminded Charlie. 'It won't all be cleared up until John Gower is released. Which won't happen if he admits who he really is.'

Samuels shifted, uncomfortably. 'The ambassador expects to be recalled. It's a hell of a risk, if Gower does break: confirmation of direct British government involvement. Another reason we want you out. We need to be able to account for every person at the embassy: you've been coming too much.'

'I can't be connected with anything,' said Charlie, irritably.

'You got Snow here, to the embassy. Which makes the connection. You were at the railway terminus when he got killed.'

'But I was never identified,' rejected Charlie. He'd been bloody lucky as well as professionally very smart.

'This is China, for God's sake! It would be enough if they wanted to move against you: certainly if Gower cracks and they want someone else to make a show trial!'

Charlie nodded, solely for Samuels' benefit. 'Certainly no reason to stay: I can't officially become involved in helping John Gower.'

'I can tell the ambassador you're going? The Foreign Office, as well?'

'Very soon,' assured Charlie. In your dreams, he thought.

'I know what you're hoping for!' declared Samuels, suddenly. 'You're hoping Gower's going to be released, for you to escort him home. Like looking after like. Which is stupid, bloody madness.'

Something was, conceded Charlie: he wished he could work out what it was. 'It would be stupid, bloody madness. That's why I'm not even thinking about it.'

'Get out!' insisted Samuels. 'Your being here is endangering the embassy.'

Not really, Charlie decided. He acknowledged that the frequency with which he visited the legation *had* probably identified him for what he was to several members of the embassy, although they would have linked him to the publicly accused Gower, not to Snow. And he had connected himself to Snow with the message-passing request to Pickering. But that was all internal. Safe. There wasn't anything *external*. So Samuels was panicking, talking through the hole in his ass.

Charlie made a point of seeking out the doctor the same afternoon as his encounter with Samuels. Pickering greeted him with expected brusqueness but not with positive hostility, not even as dismissive as the political officer.

Pickering agreed with Charlie's easy opening that Father Robertson was showing signs of understandable strain. 'Which I don't like, coming so soon after the other business.'

'Snow told me you'd diagnosed nervous exhaustion.'

Pickering nodded. 'We reached an understanding then — Snow and I — that if I thought Robertson was medically incapable of remaining here I should tell their Curia, in Rome.'

'*Is* he medically incapable in your opinion?'

'Close,' judged Pickering. 'I've got to make allowances for the shock of how Snow died, of course. He could pick up when he's properly realized what has happened.'

At once calling to mind Snow's admission at their first meeting, Charlie decided the old man would probably have more difficulty accepting, and living with, what he'd been told in the confessional. 'What if he doesn't?'

Pickering humped his shoulders. 'I don't know who to tell in Rome. The assumption was always that Snow would handle it. Certainly from the outburst from Robertson, when it arose before, he wouldn't admit any incapacity to Rome himself. He'd do the reverse.'

'How many British patients do you have in Beijing?' asked Charlie.

There was another uncertain shoulder movement. 'No idea. Quite a few, as a regular panel. And it's obvious that in emergencies I'm here for any Brit that gets ill. It's regulation Foreign Office advice.'

'Like Father Robertson was an emergency?'

'Snow thought so.'

'Father Snow was ill: a chronic asthma sufferer.

He told me, although he didn't really have to.'

'Yes?' Pickering was shifting, irritably, a busy man whose time was being too much imposed upon.

'Why didn't you prescribe his medication? He needed inhalers all the time but told me he didn't come to the embassy to collect them: to collect anything. It all had to come from Rome. I don't understand that.' It would, thought Charlie again, have given Snow a perfectly acceptable reason — and contact opportunity — to come to the embassy as frequently as he'd wanted.

Up and down went the shoulders. 'Never arose,' said Pickering. 'Everything for the mission was simply channelled through here for convenience. I inherited the system when I arrived. Told Snow early on, of course, that if there was ever a problem he should call me. He never did: never had any reason. He was young, after all. Asthma is a condition its sufferers live with.'

Charlie had the briefest of mental images of the tall, ungainly priest clutching himself against the agony as he stumbled beside the moving train beneath which he'd fallen. 'Maybe that was a mistake.'

Pickering frowned. 'What you mean by that?'

The doctor wouldn't have understood, conceded Charlie, breaking away from the reflection fully to concentrate. 'Nothing,' he said.

'I'm worried about this man Gower,' said Pickering.

'So am I.'

'I can't guess how he'll have been treated, but I don't expect it to have been very good.'

'They've got to grant access soon.'

'One would have thought so. After living in China, I'm not so sure. There's no logic here: no Western sort of logic, that is.'

'I wish there were: it would be easier.'

'What *are* you going to do?'

'Leave, I suppose.'

'When?'

'I've already had the lecture from Peter Samuels.'

Surprisingly Pickering smiled. 'It's pretty easy to become paranoid in a society like this.'

'I'm coming to realize that.'

'We're all very nervous. None of us have known anything like all this recent pressure and accusation. It's pretty frightening if you've got to live here all the time.'

'I guess it must be,' allowed Charlie.

Back at his hotel, Charlie conceded there was little purpose in his remaining any longer in the Chinese capital. He had never imagined escorting Gower home. And Snow, his reason for being there in the first place, was dead. But still Charlie was reluctant to leave. It was instinctive in a situation which still troubled him for Charlie to pick and probe and turn stones over even when he didn't know what he was looking for beneath them. And Charlie always followed instinct.

He stayed away from the embassy for several days. Experimentally he embarked, almost immediately sore-footed, on a strictly limited tourist trail, ending the painful test reasonably sure he was not under surveillance and therefore in no immediate danger, although yet again acknowledging the difficulty of being as convinced as he would have been in a Western environment, and yet again thinking how inadequately Gower had been prepared for the situation into which he had been pitched.

Eventually, inevitably, Charlie was drawn to the district in which the mission was located. He went without any positive intention of meeting Father Robertson, which might have been dangerous. He was glad he chose the time to match that of his first visit and followed the same, most obvious route, although Charlie was unhappy having to use the same silk shop for concealment because it was repetitive and therefore not good tradecraft. It was a passing uncertainty, instantly replaced by another far greater curiosity at something immediately obvious to Charlie's trained eye and which, like so much else, didn't make sense.

He confirmed his impression, to be quite sure, from the more open park in which there was sufficient protective, personal cover. It was from there that Charlie saw Father Robertson, thinking at once that he could confront the man now. He didn't attempt to. The priest was still careworn but slightly less stooped than when Charlie had unobtrusively watched his arrival and departure from the embassy. That day there seemed more spring in his step, too: Dr Pickering would be pleased at the advancing recovery. It was even better the following day. And the third, when Father Robertson positively bustled up the road, exactly on schedule. A man of regular pattern, Charlie recognized, glad of the park concealment and deciding that he wouldn't try to talk to the mission chief after all. Charlie liked patterns that fitted, although always with others, never himself. Sometimes it was really surprising what lurked under overturned stones.

Samuels greeted Charlie furiously when he reappeared at the embassy. 'Where the hell have you been?'

'Staying away, like you wanted.'

'God knows what's going on in London. They're frantic about you . . .' He offered a sheaf of cables. 'A lot have been duplicated, to me. They want to know why you didn't rebase days ago, as you were ordered.'

'Didn't feel it was right, not then.' Another question to be resolved, he thought, remembering an earlier conversation. 'Why didn't you call the hotel? You knew where I was.'

'I didn't want it to appear the embassy were chasing you,' said Samuels. 'I wouldn't like to be you, when you get back!'

'I'm not looking forward to it myself,' admitted Charlie, sincerely. He still had to *get* back.

They sat facing each other in Samuels' office for several moments, with no conversation. Then Samuels said: 'I am authorized by the ambassador — and empowered by the Foreign Office — positively to *order* you out of this embassy and out of the country. On the next plane to London. Which leaves tomorrow morning, at ten. *I'll* make the reservation.'

'That would be good of you,' smiled Charlie. 'Actually, I'd already decided to leave. So we're both going to be happy, aren't we?'

'I don't think you're going to survive this.'

'I was supposed to teach Gower that,' said Charlie. 'How to survive.'

'You didn't do very well, did you?'

'That's what other people have said.'

'We're being given access, at last. No definite day, yet. But there's been a formal agreement. And without the ambassador having to be recalled, in protest.'

Charlie came forward in his chair. 'No charge or accusation?'

'No.'

'So he held out?'

'It looks like it. That's why there was so much panic about you in London. You were the last loose end.'

It really was time to go home, Charlie decided. He supposed it probably was an accurate enough description of him, a worrying loose end. 'It's good, about Gower. A relief.' How long would a proper recovery take?

'Don't forget,' cautioned Samuels. 'Tomorrow morning: ten o'clock.'

'I won't,' promised Charlie.

He did leave the following morning, although

521

not on the London plane. Charlie took an earlier, internal flight to Canton and from there caught a train further south. As he crossed by road into Hong Kong Charlie thought that Samuels would get an awful bollocking for not personally ensuring he was on the London flight.

At Chung Hom Kok, in the very centre of Hong Kong island, there is an installation known as the Composite Signals Station. It is an electronic intelligence-gathering facility run by Britain in conjunction with its other world-spanning eavesdropping centre, the Government Communication Headquarters at Cheltenham, in the English county of Gloucestershire. Although the Composite Signals Station is much smaller than the facility in England — and is in the process of being dismantled prior to the return of Hong Kong to the Chinese in 1997 — there is still at Chung Hom Kok equipment sufficiently powerful to listen to radio and telephone communications as far north as Beijing and to both the Russian naval headquarters at Vladivostok and their rocket complex on Sakhalin Island.

Charlie's security clearance was high enough for him to be given all the cooperation he sought: his requests were quite specific and therefore easily traced. He only needed to spend four hours there, so he was able to catch the night flight back to England, via Italy.

He boarded the plane a depressed and coldly furious man, believing he knew enough to be able to guess other things. Charlie didn't sleep and he didn't drink: booze never helped at the deep-thinking, final working out stage. Halfway through the second leg of the flight, from Rome, he decided he might not have reached that final stage after all, so did not return to Westminster Bridge Road immediately after reaching London.

Instead, he took a train north to the national registration centre for births, deaths and marriages at Southport, near Liverpool. Again he knew exactly what he was looking for, even though he had to go between two different departments, so he wasn't able, more depressed than ever, to catch the afternoon train back to London.

There, the following day, he went to the Records Office at Kew for back editions of the Diplomatic Lists, which led him to the directory of the General Medical Council. He was lucky. The men he was looking for had both retired, but to Sussex, so he only had an hour to travel. It wasn't necessary to spend a lot of time with either.

Charlie expected his internal telephone to be ringing when he entered his office at Westminster Bridge Road, because it had been obvious from ground-floor security that his arrival was flagged for instant notification.

It was ringing, stridently. Julia said: 'For Christ's sake, Charlie, where the hell have you been?'

'Here and there.'

'They want you!'

'I thought they might,' said Charlie.

John Gower was never to know how close he was to giving up. Didn't want to know. Ever. But later — much later — he openly admitted during his debriefing that he wasn't far off. A day maybe. He was badly dehydrated by then, constantly hallucinating, and the dysentery had become so bad he wasn't able to keep himself clean any more. He was too far gone to be personally disgusted.

So far gone, in fact, that he failed to realize the awakening sounds, even the spy-hole scraping, had ceased. It was the chance to get clean that told him he had won.

He shuffled dutifully to his feet when the escorts entered the cell, needing their support either side initially to move. He'd started to turn automatically to the left down the corridor, towards the interview room and the persistent Mr Chen, but they steered him in the opposite direction. He did not realize it was a shower stall until he was standing before it and they were helping him out of his stinking, encrusted uniform.

The awareness came as he stood under the needle-stinging spray, drawing up the last reserve of adrenalin. Won! he thought: beaten them! I've beaten them! He risked letting the water from the shower into his parched, cracked mouth, although he held on to the presence of mind not to gulp too much, further to upset his stomach.

There was a razor and soap with which to shave when he stepped out, and the clean uniform waiting for him wasn't stiff as the other had been, from previous unwashed use. He wasn't taken back to the cell but to a ground-floor room where the toilet closet was partitioned off from a proper bed, with a mattress and a pillow and clean sheets.

A doctor came in what he gauged to be the afternoon to examine the lip sores, producing a salve which he had to administer himself, every three hours, over the course of two days. The food that was delivered wasn't bad any more. The water came in a covered tin mug.

On the fourth day of his release from the cell, he was taken to meet a Chinese who gave no name. 'You are seeing people from your embassy tomorrow,' announced the man.

'Where's Mr Chen?'

The man ignored the question.

When the moment came, Natalia couldn't bring herself to do what she had so carefully planned. For several days she kept the necessary files in her personal office safe, taking them out and re-placing them, telling herself that so many things might have changed. Charlie could have married. Found somebody else at least. So for her to do what she intended had no point or purpose. There had been, after all, two opportunities for Charlie to be with her and he'd turned his back on both. Going beyond any professional reasoning, it had to mean he didn't love her enough: if he'd loved her enough, he would have found a way. Any way. And if he didn't love her enough what interest would he have in Sasha? How, sensibly and logically, could they do anything about it in any case, even if he *were* interested? They were separated — and always would be — by far more than miles.

Then she told herself that he deserved to know: had the right. What might — or might not — have existed between her and Charlie shouldn't come into her thinking. The only consideration was Sasha. So Sasha's father had to know.

Know more, in fact. Not just that she herself had survived the London episode but that she had maintained a position — risen in rank, even — and that therefore Sasha would always be cared for and protected.

She didn't want to write. Not more than she had already decided to do. Apart from the obvious danger, minimal though it might be after the destruction of Fyodor Tudin, for her to write might make it seem that she was asking for something, and she wasn't. All she was doing was telling Charlie what he should know. Nothing else.

Gazing down at the London file she had ordered assembled, Natalia suddenly smiled when the way occurred to her, carefully extracting one photograph. She took another, from her handbag this time. It was on this one that she wrote, very briefly.

That night, packing in the bedroom of the Leninskaya apartment, the baby awake in the cot beside her, Natalia said: 'We're going on holiday, darling. Germany is a beautiful country.'

It was a further and obvious precaution for Natalia to go outside of Russia, which it was now very easy to do under the new freedoms. She supposed she could have even gone to England. She wouldn't, though: determined as she was — having tried as hard as she had — she could only go so far. But no further. Not to England.

Forty-eight

Julia Robb pointed with an outstretched finger to the open intercom, shaking her head but mouthing the word 'later', and Charlie nodded his agreement. He started to move towards Patricia Elder's room but Julia stopped him, gesturing towards the Director-General's suite as she announced his arrival. Charlie winked at her as he changed direction. He thought she looked very pretty.

Peter Miller was rigidly upright at his desk. The woman was seated alongside it but with her chair turned outwards, also to confront him. There was no chair for Charlie. Bloody fools, he thought. The stupidity of having him before them like an errant schoolboy didn't upset him. Schoolboy, schoolmaster, it was all the same. Bloody daft. Standing upset him, though. His feet were playing up: he guessed he must have travelled about fifteen thousand miles and at the moment it felt as if he'd walked every one of them.

'I want an explanation! A proper one. And it had better be good,' declared Miller. His usually bland voice was tight with anger.

It was unfortunate he couldn't give it to them outright, reflected Charlie. 'It all seems to have worked out pretty straightforwardly,' he suggested. 'Samuels told me before I left Beijing we were finally going to get Gower.'

'He's to be released, without charge,' disclosed Patricia. She seemed to be having difficulty with the tone of her voice, too.

'So there's been no public embarrassment, apart from the initial business with Gower,' assessed Charlie. 'We can surely smother that with a public relations blitz, about false arrest and imprisonment? Everyone must be very happy.'

'You were supposed to have left Beijing five days ago! On a flight the embassy booked for you. Where the hell have you been, for five days?'

They really weren't very good, either of them, reflected Charlie: certainly Miller shouldn't have been showing this degree of anger. 'Being careful,' said Charlie, easily. 'Snow's death was a tragedy. Didn't want any more, did we?'

'You're arrogant!' declared Miller. 'Arrogant and supercilious! I told you I wanted an explanation!'

'I don't understand how I've upset you,' said Charlie, open-faced.

'You disappeared off the face of the earth!' shouted Miller. 'We thought the Chinese might have swept you up, like Gower. We were about to approach the Chinese authorities for information, as we did with him.'

'We want to know!' insisted the woman.

'A lot's happened that hasn't made sense — still doesn't make sense — so I avoided the obvious risks,' smiled Charlie, hopefully.

'Don't patronize us!' warned the Director-General.

'I'm not!' asserted Charlie. 'But you've got to admit some odd things happened. Things that just didn't add up.'

'Like what?' demanded Miller.

Charlie levered his shoulders up and down. His feet really did hurt like a bugger. 'You'll think I'm rude.'

'We think that already,' said the woman.

'Gower, for instance,' continued Charlie, unruffled. 'This *could* have been one God-almighty problem, if Snow *had* been roped in with Zhang Su Lin and all the other political protesters. So it was vitally important to prevent. Too important, I would have thought, for a first-time operation for someone untried and untested, as Gower was. And not just untried and untested. Hardly prepared at all, for the special circumstances of working in China.'

There was a shift of discomfort, Miller looking briefly to the woman. 'That *was* a mistake. I'll concede that.'

'Which might have been mitigated if you had properly fulfilled the job you were appointed to do,' said the woman, defensively.

'My fault?' asked Charlie, ingenuously.

'An admitted mistake not alleviated by any instruction or advice you gave,' she said.

You won't annoy me, my lovely, thought Charlie: I wonder how much I am going to disconcert you. 'Then there's that business of keeping Snow away from the embassy. Never quite understood the reason for that.'

'Our operation decision: I think the reason was obvious.'

'Then there was the quickness of things. And their sequence,' continued Charlie. 'If the Chinese were seeking to identify a cell, why did they jump Gower when they did? Why didn't they let him set his signal and wait until Snow came to pick it up? That would have been the obvious thing to do.'

'That was their mistake, moving too early,' said Miller. 'What other reason can there be?'

'Don't know. They were certainly quick at the railway terminus, when they *did* try to pick Snow up. That really puzzles me, how that happened.'

'Why?' asked Patricia.

'How they knew he was there,' said Charlie.

Miller sighed, impatiently. 'For God's sake man, that's obvious, surely! They followed him!'

Charlie shook his head, doubtfully. 'It wasn't easy, evolving a way to get Snow out: nor accepting, as I had to accept, that there would be a watch for him at airports. That's why I made the phoney plane booking out of Beijing. And rehearsed him through the visits to the Foreign Ministry and the Security Bureau . . .'

'Which failed as badly as everything else you tried to teach him and Gower!' sneered Miller.

'But that's the problem,' persisted Charlie. 'It was the best I could think of — the only thing

I could think of — but I wasn't happy Snow could carry it off. He hadn't had any proper training, after all. So I didn't trust him to do it by himself. I set the routing: knew where he was going and how he was going to try to do things. So I picked him up when he left the Bureau. Not that he could see me, of course. Stayed a long way off. To see if he *was* still followed. If he had been I was going to feign some encounter at the terminus: lost Westerner approaching another obvious Westerner for help, to abort the whole thing and try to think of something else. But he wasn't followed. I was sure he wasn't. He *had* confused them. I covered him all the way to the ticket queue. And became even surer there. That's why I got on the Shanghai train, to wait for him . . .'

Miller sighed again. 'This sounds to me like a weak defence to a miserable failure that's going to mark the end of any future for you in this department.'

Charlie frowned at the threat, refusing to be stopped by it. 'Think more about it!' he urged. 'There were at least twenty people there. Soldiers and civilians. And Li, in control of it all. To keep the hypothesis going, let's concede that they *did* follow him, even though I know they didn't. It would have been two or three men. Four at the most. From the time he arrived at the station and queued to buy his ticket to the time he disembarked from the Nanchang train to cross to where I was waiting was precisely seventeen minutes. I know. I counted every one of them.'

'What is this laborious point?' demanded Miller, a man close to exasperation.

A point for my benefit, not yours, thought Charlie. 'There wasn't enough time, even if they had followed him, to get more than twenty people, soldiers as well as civilians, into position. With Li in charge. You'd agree with me about that, wouldn't you?'

'You were clearly mistaken, about his not being followed,' insisted Miller.

Wrong! thought Charlie. 'Still not enough time.' How much more could he say, at this stage? How much more could he say at all? Not much. It was a pity: more than a pity.

'The fact is they *did* get into position!' rejected Miller. 'Where's all this getting us?'

'I was trying to explain why I took a long time to get home,' offered Charlie. 'I thought it best to use my own airline reservation as a decoy and come out another way.'

'Which way?'

'Through Hong Kong, on the first leg,' disclosed Charlie. 'It was a hell of a trip. I had chronic jetlag.'

'You took a holiday, at our expense!' challenged Patricia.

'There were some other things in Beijing that didn't make sense to me,' continued Charlie. 'Like the obvious observation on the mission. There *was* observation, you see. It was easy to locate, when I approached the mission the first time

533

'. . .' Charlie paused, coughing. 'But then there was a funny thing. I made another check, the day after Snow died. And do you know what? All the surveillance had been lifted. No one was watching the mission any more.'

'What's so surprising about that?' demanded Patricia. 'Snow, their suspect, was dead!'

'One priest out of two,' reminded Charlie.

'What?' asked Miller.

'Snow was the younger priest, the man better able physically — despite the asthma — to move about on fact-finding trips. But if you had been carrying out the investigation, from your long previous career in counter-intelligence, wouldn't you have suspected that Father Robertson and Snow might have been operating together? And that it might be useful to maintain the watch on the mission to see what Father Robertson might do? Particularly when Father Robertson was somebody who had been arrested and jailed, in the past? Was someone they'd already accused of crimes against the State?'

Miller remained clearly disdainful. 'My interpretation is that the Chinese *aren't* interested in him.'

'Oh but they are,' said Charlie. 'I wanted to be very sure the surveillance had been lifted from the mission. I was thinking of going there, to talk to Father Robertson. But I was glad I didn't. On the last two days I watched the place I saw Father Robertson with Li Dong Ming, the man who escorted Snow on his trip and then pursued him, right to the time he went under the train and was killed . . .'

'*What?*' It was Miller who asked the question, voice scarcely above a whisper.

'Li and Father Robertson,' Charlie said again. 'Very friendly with each other. Laughing, in fact. Once they walked quite a long way up the road leading from the mission and Robertson even held Li's arm, for support, although he didn't look like the frail old man I had seen at the embassy.'

They were both looking at Charlie. Patricia's mouth was slightly parted. All the attitudes had gone from both of them.

Charlie was regarding them just as intently in return. 'I could never quite understand why, having arrested and jailed Robertson like they did, the Chinese let him stay on to run the mission. But what if he broke, in jail? Agreed to work for them? It all makes sense then, doesn't it? They'd have someone who is part of the Western community in Beijing, with access to the British embassy, perfectly in place to spy. The perfect asset . . .'

'. . . No!' said Miller, shaking his head, his voice still distant. 'No!'

'Wouldn't that also explain why Robertson is *still* there: why the mission is still open? They lost their chance to stage a trial with Gower and Snow, but they'd have closed the mission down. Thrown Robertson out. But they haven't, have they? Because he's too useful to them, remaining in place.'

'There's no proof of any of this!' said Patricia. 'It's all surmise, based solely upon your seeing Li and Robertson together. And we've only got your word for that. It might not even have been Li.'

'It was,' insisted Charlie. 'Definitely. I think for a long time the Jesuit mission in Beijing had one priest working for Britain and one for the Chinese. With neither supposedly knowing about the other. We'd better warn the embassy, hadn't we?'

'Yes,' agreed Miller. He sounded distracted.

'So it wasn't a miserable failure, was it?' pressed Charlie.

'No . . . maybe not . . .' faltered Miller. 'We need to analyse everything.'

'Yes,' agreed Charlie. 'It all needs to be analysed.' But not any more by me, he thought: I'm sure I've got it all right.

Natalia based herself in Cologne and on the third day took a river trip on the Rhine. The ferry made several stops, the longest in Koblenz.

Forty-nine

It was Charlie's suggestion they go to Kenny's, in Hampstead's Heath Street, where they'd eaten the first time they'd gone out together. Julia agreed without apparent thought and didn't remark upon it when they got there, so Charlie didn't bother either. He hadn't chosen it for any special significance anyway. Charlie was careful with the choice of table, getting them into a far corner, close to the speaker relaying the background music which would overlay whatever they talked about. They had a lot to talk about. He ordered Chablis and told the waitress not to worry about the food for a while, they weren't in a hurry.

'Let me guess,' he said. 'There was chaos after I left.'

'I've never seen either of them like it before,' agreed the girl.

Charlie smiled, happily. 'Miller said he was going to dump me. But that was before I told him about Robertson.'

'It's been a bloody awful business. All of it,' she said.

'You don't know the half of it,' said Charlie. 'Enough.'

'I don't think so.'

Julia frowned up from her wineglass. 'I'm personal assistant to both, remember.'

'So who do you think Robertson's working for?'

The frown remained. 'Maybe I don't know everything.'

'It was a set-up,' announced Charlie. 'All of it. Right from the very beginning. From Snow getting permission to make the trip south with Li and me being put under the control of Patricia Elder and told I only had a menial future, to make me resentful and distracted, and then Gower, the man who could resist interrogation, being selected for me to train and afterwards sent to China, where he *hadn't* been trained to operate.'

Julia shook her head. 'Charlie, I'm not getting any of this!'

'I didn't, not for a very long time. It was sacrifice time: me, Snow, Gower. We should have all been in the dock together, all part of the dissident trials the Chinese are putting on. *Would* have been in court, if Snow hadn't been killed. That really did break the chain. Ruined it all, for any public display at least. It was still good enough for Robertson: would have been, that is, if I hadn't realized the mission surveillance was lifted and then seen him with Li . . .'

'Please, Charlie!' begged the girl.

'Robertson isn't supposed to be theirs!' said Charlie. 'He's supposed to be *our* source, the man we thought we had deeply in place and would need even more when we lost all our facilities in Hong Kong after 1997: need him enough to sacrifice all of us.'

'How do you know this?'

'You tell me!' Charlie came back. 'You're in a position to know. Isn't Robertson supposed to be ours?'

'There are things I'm not allowed to know,' insisted Julia.

'I'd hoped you would know: and that you'd tell me.'

'I'm sorry.'

'I would have been, if I had been swept up. Very sorry.'

'I can't believe it! Won't believe it! You must be wrong!'

Charlie topped up their glasses. 'I suppose they imagined a lot would be concealed in a Chinese prosecution that could be manipulated to cover anything, but they were still very clumsy. Samuels should be withdrawn. Pickering, too. They're no bloody good, either of them. And according to what Snow told me, from their visit to the mission when Robertson was ill, they're not getting on. Rowing all the time.'

Julia was looking at him unblinkingly, only her throat moving, wine forgotten in front of her.

'And you don't have to say anything,' smiled Charlie. Like she hadn't had to enunciate, confirming word for confirming word, the situation with Miller and his deputy.

'I said from the beginning . . .'

'. . . I know,' said Charlie, indifferent to the

protest. 'I'm really not asking you to tell me any-thing . . .' He seemed surprised to find the bottle empty, holding it aloft for the waitress to see and bring another. 'I came out through Hong Kong. Did you hear about that?'

She shook her head. 'No.'

'But you know about the Composite Signals Station at Chung Hom Kok, from which all the electronic traffic in Beijing is listened into?'

'Yes.'

'It was all picked up there, of course,' said Charlie. 'Not a risk, as far as Miller or the woman were concerned, because they were controlling it all and could dismiss it as unimportant. Its only significance was if someone else saw it. Some-one like me, for instance.'

She had gone very white. 'You're not sug-gesting . . . !'

'Not suggesting,' agreed Charlie. 'Definitely *saying*. Snow's cable name was "Hunter". He actually told me so. Chose it himself, from Gen-esis. *Esau was a cunning hunter, a man of the field.* That's what Jeremy Snow thought he was: cun-ning. Poor bugger. London cabled Foster while Snow was travelling, asking on an open wire when "Hunter" would be getting to Beijing. And Fos-ter, who was a frightened idiot and chosen because of it, replied, again on an open link because it's the system, providing the actual day. Which gave the Chinese, who maintain their own electronic surveillance on all the embassies, a date from which Snow could be positively identified, at any subsequent trial. There was another reference to "Hunter" in an emergency cable that Foster sent, after Li's visit to the mission to ask for the photographs.'

'This is all circumstantial,' suggested Julia, uncertainly. 'You've no proof the Chinese monitor.'

'*Every* country monitors embassy traffic!' insisted Charlie. 'There was a lot for Beijing to listen to. The day before Gower went out, there was another cable from London, to the embassy. It said *Second Hunter arriving*. All Gower needed, from the moment of his arrival, was a sign around his neck.' Charlie paused. Why, he wondered, hadn't Gower done what he'd been told, always to travel under his own, personal arrangements? Too inexperienced, Charlie guessed. He smiled again, this time in his acceptance of the second bottle. Julia's glass was still full, untouched, so he only bothered with his own. 'It didn't stop there. I made a specific request, to Patricia Elder, that everything about my going to Beijing should be by diplomatic pouch, so there couldn't *be* any electronic interception. Yet the day *before* I got there, there was an open cable message about *Hunter Three*. It was lucky I wasn't on the plane they expected me to be.' Luck, reflected Charlie, had nothing at all to do with it.

Julia drank at last. Soft-voiced, she said: 'I typed the cables . . . I didn't realize . . . Christ, Charlie, I did it and I didn't even realize what I was being told to do . . . !'

'It's not your fault: not important.'

'Not important! Snow's dead. We don't know yet what Gower went through. You could have gone through the same. Worse even!'

Time to move on, Charlie decided. 'I might not have thought about looking in Hong Kong if it hadn't been for something Samuels said. Silly really. It's just that I listen to everything. He talked about Snow being "swept up". That's a trade expression: departmental. Not the way a diplomatic officer talks. And then, later, he referred to the fact that Snow had used the *confessional* to tell Father Robertson what he had done, to get permission to run. Snow told *me* he'd done it. Only me. And I didn't tell anybody. So the only other person from whom Samuels could have learned about it was Robertson himself. There were a lot of other things, as well. Like a political officer baby-sitting a sick missionary, which a person of his rank and pomposity would never have done, unless of course he was the man's Control and worried that Robertson, sick with remorse at what he was doing, might have hallucinated and talked about it. No message ever got to or from Rome, about Robertson's illness, incidentally. Or about the Chinese targeting Snow. I know because I stopped off in Rome on the way back: the Jesuit Curia didn't know what I was talking about. That was the advantage of mailing through the British embassy: Samuels could filter everything. Run a very tight ship.'

Julia moved her head, aimlessly, stunned.

'Samuels *is* the Resident, isn't he?'

The head movement was more positive, a refusal to confirm the question.

'Snow's death told me,' said Charlie. 'English was OK to set up the airport decoy, making plane reservations I never intended to take up. But I needed Samuels' ability to speak Mandarin to go through the train departures. That's how the Chinese were able to have so many men in place, at the station: Samuels told Robertson how we were planning to get away. And Robertson alerted the people to whom he is really answering these days.'

'No!' disputed Julia, at once. 'If they knew Snow was on the Nanchang train — moved against him when he left, to get to you — how come they didn't get you, as well?'

'They tried,' said Charlie, smiling across at her. 'The Shanghai express wasn't the only train leaving at five that afternoon. There was one to Changsha, four tracks further along the concourse. That's the train I told Samuels I was catching: the train I saw surrounded by troops as I left.'

'Jesus!' said Julia, aghast.

'Which was another very good reason why I didn't want to catch the plane out of Beijing that Samuels ordered me to catch: considerately booked for me.'

'You think they'd still have tried to put you and Gower on trial, if they'd got you?'

'If they'd caught me.'

'You sure Pickering was part of it?'

543

'It all goes back to the nonsense of how Snow was treated. Not in the beginning. Then Snow was properly handled by his Control. There was a man called Bowley. Another named George Street. Their liaison procedures were impeccable. Snow could make his meetings through the public event visits through the embassy but more regularly by using the trips for his asthma medication from the resident doctor. I checked with two who have retired to Sussex. But then Pickering arrived. The same Pickering who sent a cable on a security reserved line to London — but monitored in Hong Kong, where I found it — informing Miller directly of a meeting I had with him. The same Pickering who from the moment of his arrival in Beijing closed down the asthma drug facility and told Snow he had in future to get his stuff from Rome, separating him from the embassy. Like Foster kept the poor bastard at arm's length, although Foster didn't know how he was being used in the scheme, constantly to expose Snow and force him into that ridiculous message-signalling crap, which really did become obsolete with the ending of the Cold War that everyone keeps on about. Foster — another first-time appointee, according to the files — was too stupid to have realized or suspected, of course.'

'Why *was* Foster withdrawn, for Gower and you to go in?'

'Foster's withdrawal indicated panic, for the Chinese to pick up on: don't forget, we were doing it to fool them and keep Robertson safe:

we didn't know we were fooling ourselves. Gower going in — and me after him — showed more panic. It was all part of Miller and Patricia Elder's perfect package. With the Chinese laughing their balls off at all the effort we were going to for their benefit.'

'It's inconceivable that Snow and Gower and you were considered expendable, to protect one man!' refused the girl.

Charlie slowly moved his head from side to side. 'Not to keep someone like Robertson in place. I don't know, but Robertson must have proved himself over and over again to London. The Chinese would have guaranteed that. They must have passed over an enormous amount of genuine stuff to have built up Robertson's credibility. You any idea what a completely trusted agent can do, feeding disinformation back to people who never query it because he's so reliable?'

Julia visibly shuddered, pushing her glass forward for more wine. 'Why?' she demanded sharply. 'Why any of this? Why did Snow and Gower and you have to be entrapped? I can't accept what you're telling me!'

'Robertson was an asset, always to be protected,' insisted Charlie. 'That's why Snow was approached, as permanent, in-place insurance against Robertson being suspected by the Chinese: approached by our idiots who didn't know Robertson was with the Chinese ever since his brainwashing imprisonment. Snow told me at the embassy our people came to him within days of his appointment to Beijing being decided by his Curia, before any public announcements. Again, that could only have come from Robertson, who would have been consulted beforehand. Any mistake Robertson made could have been switched on to Snow. Who was *always* expendable, as far as London was concerned. But it wasn't London who became concerned. It was Beijing. Because Snow was *too* good. Look what he got on that trip, *despite* being chaperoned by Li. Snow was bloody marvellous! So he had to be got rid of. And then there was the Chinese decision to move against their dissidents again. But not like before, in Tiananmen. The international outcry was too much then: they couldn't risk arbitrary round-ups and imprisonment. It had to be internationally acceptable. Robertson would have marked Zhang Su Lin the moment he came into the mission. What better way of staging a countrywide swoop and a huge and genuine show trial than by being able to prove a connection between Zhang and Snow — both of whom would have confessed — with Gower and me thrown in for good measure? It was perfect.'

Julia was slumped wearily over the table. 'It's still difficult to follow: I'm not even sure I want to follow it!'

'No one was supposed to follow it,' said Charlie. 'Not the way Miller and Patricia Elder set it up, believing Robertson at risk of exposure because of the past connection of the mission with Zhang

546

Su Lin. And certainly not how the Chinese twisted it back against us, to rid themselves of a troublesome priest.'

Julia straightened, seemingly too overwhelmed to argue against him any more. 'So what are you going to do?'

'I've done all I can,' said Charlie. 'I've warned them against Robertson, which is the most important thing. It means we haven't got an asset left in Beijing, but at least we're not going to be misled with phoney information, for as long as the old bastard goes on living . . .' He shrugged, resigned. 'I could challenge them, about Samuels and Pickering and all the intercepted messages, but you know and I know that I'd achieve bugger-all. There'd be denials. Within an hour, there would be no evidence left in the Hong Kong files.'

'I suppose you're right,' agreed Julia, sadly.

'I'm screwed,' said Charlie. 'Not as badly or as much as they intended me to be. But I'm still screwed.'

'I wish there was something — anything — that I could do!'

Now Charlie straightened. 'You've done a lot already.'

'It just doesn't seem fair!'

'Life isn't.' Charlie looked enquiringly around the room, for their waitress. 'We haven't even ordered yet.'

'I'm not hungry.'

'I am!' said Charlie, enthusiastically. 'A lot of

that Chinese food was shit!' He ordered cajun blackened chicken. It was good.

It was an easier run down from London than he'd expected, so Charlie had time to stop at the Stockbridge hotel that allowed the exclusive fishing club their special privileges. They had Islay malt, which he recognized as his privilege. He savoured two whiskies, still trying to plan his moves to survive in the department, which he was determined to do. The snare he'd already laid seemed very inadequate: he still wasn't sure whether — or how — to play his trump card.

Charlie was still at the nursing home when visiting began, hesitating at the matron's office to apologize for his recent absence.

'I'm glad you're here at last,' said the woman. 'We've got something for you.' Seeing Charlie's reaction when he opened the package, she said worriedly: 'Whatever is it? I thought for a moment you were going to faint.'

'Nothing,' said Charlie, thick-throated. He'd thought he was going to collapse, as well. And he'd never done that before, no matter how great the shock.

The package contained two photographs.

One was of the Director-General and Patricia Elder which he guessed he had actually seen being taken that morning outside the Regent's Park penthouse.

The other was of a baby. Written on the back,

in handwriting he recognized because they'd often left notes for each other in Moscow, was: 'Her name is Sasha' and a date.

Fifty

Charlie cut the visit as short as he could, but it still took a supreme effort of will to sit by his mother's bedside and maintain even a minimal conversation. It didn't help that she was more alert than she had been for months, talking incessantly and clearly expecting him to stay much longer, as did the nursing home staff. He left promising to extend his next visit.

He stopped again at the Stockbridge hotel, the first available convenient place, still feeling shaky. He couldn't believe how close he'd been to collapsing when he'd recognized Natalia's writing! He was getting far too bloody old for shocks like that. Shock wasn't the right word, although it described how it had affected him. He couldn't think how he wanted to express it, but revelation was one word that occurred to him. Escape — inexplicably — was another. Then he asked himself why it was important to categorize it at all, so he stopped bothering, because there was so much else he had to think about. He bought another Islay malt, a large one, and settled in a corner far away from any possible interruption. He drank, settling himself further. He laid the package on the table in front of him, but did not immediately take out the contents — stupidly reluctant to touch it in case it wasn't true, stupid because it *was* true — staring down at it instead like a fortune-teller consulting a crystal ball.

This had to tell him much more than a crystal ball had ever told any fortune-teller, he determined. And he had to read and understand every sign.

His first and most important realization wasn't that he was the father of a child named Alexandra, wonderful and incredible though that was: so wonderfully incredible that he knew he would need much more time to fully comprehend it.

His initial and most important awareness was that Natalia had survived his abandonment in London, thus answering the persistent and recurring uncertainty that had nagged at him ever since he watched her keep the rendezvous from which he'd held back. Very quickly came the only possible progression. He hadn't lost her! Natalia had traced him, so she didn't hate him, as she had every right to hate him. As he'd expected her to.

What else? Read the signs, read the signs! Too much nostalgia risked obscuring the reasoning she expected him to follow. Which he *had* to follow, not to lose her again. Only consider the important facts that the nostalgia had provided, then. Two essential points: that she had survived and that she'd found him. More to learn from the second than the first. Not just found him. Found Miller and Patricia Elder and the significance of Regent's Park. Careful here! Nothing to do with the sort of bluff, double-bluff, agent, double-agent bullshit he'd so recently been involved with in Beijing. What Natalia was offering was personal, not business. Her dilemma, when she'd agonized about staying in London with him, had always been about an absolute refusal to become an informing defector against her own country, and because he knew her so well Charlie was sure that loyalty hadn't changed.

So why had she included the photograph that he'd actually — by astonishing coincidence — witnessed being taken? Not just taken, he qualified, moving towards a hopeful conclusion: *officially* taken. As part of an operation. Abruptly Charlie remembered the grey Ford in his rear-view mirror as he travelled back to London from the nursing home, briefly allowing himself the satisfaction of knowing that he had been right that day. The same operation?

It all had to be guesswork, the most obvious and logical surmises he could reach, but Charlie thought he saw it. Natalia was telling him she hadn't just survived but was now powerful enough to use the resources of the Russian agency virtually how she liked. To do which she had to be very powerful indeed.

And the package at which he was still staring confirmed it! Powerful enough to travel to Koblenz, from where she'd posted it. But why to the nursing home? Because they'd talked about it! For all those months he'd been in Moscow he'd worried about not being able to make his usual visits and he'd talked about it to Natalia, although he couldn't recall what he'd said that had remained with her after all this time to lead her to the location from which they followed him. But then lost him. Or rather he'd lost them! So the nursing home was *all* she had: the only way of reaching him again, if she chose to do so.

Charlie pulled the contents from their folder at last, smiling down at the Moscow photograph. It *was* a Moscow photograph and a place he recognized. Alexandra — Sasha as Natalia obviously preferred to call her — was in an adjustable buggy, tilted back, seeming to smile up at the camera although she was obviously too young, not yet a year old, to know how to smile for a camera. But it was the background in which Charlie was interested. There appeared to be a monument of some sort but it was incomplete, only half a sphere. He was sure he knew it but couldn't bring it to mind, no matter how fixedly he stared at it.

Gradually, inevitably, his concentration slipped sideways to the second print, and then he fully appreciated what he was looking at — and how he could use it — and Charlie sniggered aloud, quickly stifling the reaction.

For the moment Natalia and a baby he had never seen and never expected to have would have to wait. There was his own survival to guarantee. Charlie considered just one more drink, believing he deserved a celebration, but didn't have it, anxious to get back to London to complete everything.

The paper upon which the photograph was printed could be forensically proven to be Russian, and photographic paper anyway provides one of the best possible surfaces for fingerprints, so it had to be changed. Natalia's fingerprints could be upon it and his own certainly were and Charlie wasn't satisfied with just wiping either side with a cloth. He did that anyway, of course, as thoroughly as he could, before taking the print of Miller and Patricia Elder into a department store photocopying section. The assistant wore gloves, the way they all do. Charlie was extremely careful handling the copies that were returned to him, cupping his fingers only at the edges, where no print could register. When he got back to the Primrose Hill flat he actually used tweezers.

He cut newsprint letters from that night's *Evening Standard* to address the first envelope to the security division at Westminster Bridge Road, enclosing one duplicate photograph of Peter Miller and Patricia Elder arm-in-arm on the ring road around Regent's Park.

He addressed with the same cut-out letters the second duplicate print, again by itself without any attempted explanation, in a second envelope to Lady Ann Miller at the Berkshire stud listed in *Who's Who*. Knowing that the franking was relevant, Charlie travelled back to Kensington to post them. He didn't touch either envelope at any time with his bare hands.

He'd fucked them, Charlie decided: either way he'd fucked them, which they'd deserved for what they'd done to Jeremy Snow and John Gower and tried to do to him. They really should have read and understood how vindictive he could be.

He had, of course, got printouts of the transmissions that Hong Kong had intercepted, going to and from the Beijing embassy, and the whole point of telling Julia Robb was to panic them into trying to sanitise the records. But they would have still had enough power to overwhelm him if it had got to an official inquiry when they'd tried to dump him. Now he didn't have to bother with any of it.

As she had predicted herself, Julia would probably go when Miller and Patricia Elder were discreetly retired and yet another Director-General and deputy were appointed. But then it was simple justice that she should.

In a way, she had been shittier than either of the other two. They at least hadn't pretended the friendship, like she had, even hinting at the end it could go deeper than being platonic. Although he supposed it had been they who'd persuaded her to see him as often as she eventually had, to pass back whatever he'd said in off-guard moments of any suspicions he might have had before going to Beijing. She hadn't been very good, Charlie reflected: she'd given away far more than she'd learned, particularly about the relationship between Miller and Patricia Elder.

He supposed protecting himself at all times,

in whatever circumstances, came down to never trusting anyone, although he'd trusted Julia until the idea had occurred to him on the flight back from China. He was glad it had. It really hadn't taken very long at the national registration unit at Southport to discover that Julia Robb had never been married but had always been a spinster. And that she didn't have a sister, either, with whom the non-existent husband could have run away. Julia really shouldn't have tried to make her sob-story so wet-eyed.

With the one photograph so protectively utilized, Charlie concentrated again when he got back to his flat upon the print of the daughter he had never seen and hadn't ever believed he was going to have.

She *was* beautiful, he decided. Wonderfully, innocently, diminutively beautiful. He wanted to know what she felt like, smelled like, sounded like, *was* like. Just wanted. But how? How? How?

And then he recognized the background. It *was* half a sphere, a replica of the capsule in which Yuri Gagarin had been blasted up to become Russia's — and the world's — first man in space: the replica which rested at the foot of the ugly tower monument to the achievement in Moscow's Leninskaya Prospekt. But what did it mean? Did it mean anything? It had to. Natalia wouldn't have done all this, without *everything* having some significance. Charlie turned the photograph back and front, from Natalia's inscription back to the print, and then revolved it again.

And then stopped. She hadn't simply written *Her name is Sasha.* There was the date, obviously of Sasha's birth. By which Natalia was telling him she had been pregnant when he'd abandoned her to go back alone to Russia. And that he was the father. An anniversary recurring in two months' time.

He had a date, Charlie realized. And a place.

We hope you have enjoyed this Large Print book. Other G.K. Hall & Co. or Chivers Press Large Print books are available at your library or directly from the publishers. For more information about current and upcoming titles, please call or write, without obligation, to:

G.K. Hall & Co.
P.O. Box 159
Thorndike, Maine 04986
USA
Tel. (800) 223-6121
(207) 948-2962
(in Maine and Canada, call collect)

OR

Chivers Press Limited
Windsor Bridge Road
Bath BA2 3AX
England
Tel. (0225) 335336

All our Large Print titles are designed for easy reading, and all our books are made to last.